Routledge Revivals

Community, Gender, and Individual Identity

David Aers explores the treatment of community, gender, and individual identity in English writing between 1360 and 1430, focusing on Margery Kempe, Langland, Chaucer, and the poet of Sir Gawain. He shows how these texts deal with questions about gender, the making of individual identity, and competing versions of community in ways which still speak powerfully in contemporary analysis of gender formation, sexuality, and love. Making wide use of recent research on the English economy and communities, and informed by current debates in the theory of culture and gender, the book will be of interest to those concerned with Medieval studies, Renaissance studies, and Women's studies.

Community, Gender, and Individual Identity

English Writing 1360-1430

David Aers

Routledge
Taylor & Francis Group
Routledge Revivals

First published in 1988
by Routledge

This edition first published in 2018 by Routledge
2 Park Square, Milton Park, Abingdon, Oxon, OX14 4RN
and by Routledge
711 Third Avenue, New York, NY 10017

Routledge is an imprint of the Taylor & Francis Group, an informa business

Publisher's Note

The publisher has gone to great lengths to ensure the quality of this reprint but points out that some imperfections in the original copies may be apparent.

Disclaimer

The publisher has made every effort to trace copyright holders and welcomes correspondence from those they have been unable to contact.

A Library of Congress record exists under ISBN: 88009704

ISBN 13: 978-1-138-30567-0 (hbk)
ISBN 13: 978-1-315-14199-2 (ebk)
ISBN 13: 978-1-138-30672-1 (pbk)

COMMUNITY, GENDER, AND INDIVIDUAL IDENTITY

English writing 1360–1430

DAVID AERS

ROUTLEDGE
London and New York

First published in 1988 by
Routledge
11 New Fetter Lane, London EC4P 4EE
29 West 35th Street, New York NY 10001

British Library Cataloguing in Publication Data

Aers, David
Community, gender, and individual identity: English writing 1360–1430.
1. Poetry in English, 1066–1558
Critical studies
I. Title
821'.1'09

ISBN 0-415-01378-X
ISBN 0-415-01379-8 Pbk

Library of Congress Cataloging in Publication Data

Aers, David.
Community, gender, and individual identity: English writing, 1360–1430/David Aers.
p. cm.
Bibliography: p.
Includes index.
ISBN 0-415-01378-X. ISBN 0-415-01379-8 (pbk.)
1. English literature—Middle English, 1100–1500—History and criticism. 2. Identity (Psychology) in literature.
3. Individuality in literature. 4. Community in literature.
5. Sex role in literature. I. Title.
PR275.I34A35 1988
820'.9'001—dc19 88–9704
CIP

Thus the original doubt as to which was more real, the common sense world or the transfigured one, could now be answered: the transfigured world was the real one, potentially, because the mystery was there in the developing living facts evolving under one's own nose, not in some far away fairy-land.

(Marion Milner, *On Not Being Able To Paint*, 1957)

CONTENTS

ACKNOWLEDGEMENTS

There are many people I would like to thank in connection with making this book. Those whose admirable labours in the field of medieval studies I am most conscious of leaning on, and to whom I am immensely grateful, I have sought to acknowledge in the notes. Rodney Hilton kindly read and commented on an early version of the first chapter with his habitual depth of knowledge and clarity of perception. Barrie Dobson also commented on that version and an outline of the book. For helpful discussion of some of the concerns informing chapters 2 and 3 I would like to thank Linda Macfarlane, Sarah Beckwith, and Paul Gilbert. I am very grateful to Derek Pearsall for an exceptionally scrupulous, helpful, and generous reading of the typescript. Many of those who have influenced my writing most profoundly may well not appear in the book or the notes at all – either because the assimilation has been so thorough that the influence is pervasive or because the influence is on a way of looking at things rather than any specific point that could appear in a note. But I would at least like to thank Sita Narasimhan, Tony Spearing, Derek Pearsall, the late Elizabeth Salter (in whose memorial volume *Leeds Studies in English* an early version of the first chapter appeared), Bob Hodge, and Gunther Kress. Perhaps I should also note that some very diverse and deeply contradictory writings within some of the various psychoanalytic traditions, feminist traditions, and Marxist traditions have constantly engaged my attention and stimulated my reflections.

I have enjoyed working out much of the material in the book in seminars with students in the School of English and American Studies at the University of East Anglia. That institution has constantly enabled the kind of courses from which this book emerged. I hope it may long survive the current government's attack on the humanities in Britain.

My thanks are due to the British Academy and the School of English and American Studies for grants towards the preparation of my manuscript, and to Ann Cook for typing it. Acknowledgements are also due to Oxford University Press for permission to quote from *The Works of Geoffrey Chaucer*, ed. F. N. Robinson, 2nd edn (1957); Athlone Press for *Piers Plowman. The B Version*, ed. E. T. Donaldson and G. Kane (1975); Malcolm Andrew and Ronald Waldron for permission to quote from the edition of *The Poems of the Pearl Manuscript* (Arnold, 1978).

University of East Anglia, Norwich
December 1987

INTRODUCTION

Pleas held, on Thursday 16 July 1381, before Hugh la Zouche and his fellows, assigned to hear, punish and chastise the rebels and disturbers of the peace in the said county (of Cambridge).

John Shirle of the county of Nottingham was taken because it was found that he had been a vagabond [*vagabundus*] in various counties during the whole time of the disturbance, insurrection and tumult, carrying lies as well as silly and worthless talk from district to district, whereby the peace of the lord the king could rapidly be broken and the people be disquieted and disturbed. Among other damaging words, namely after the proclamation of the peace of the lord the king made on the aforesaid day and year, when the justices assigned by the lord the king were holding sessions in the town, he said in a tavern in Briggestrete [Bridge Street] in Cambridge, where many were assembled to listen to his news and worthless talk, that the stewards of the lord the king as well as the justices and many other officers and ministers of the king were more deserving to be drawn and hanged and to suffer other lawful pains and torments than John Balle, chaplain, a traitor and felon lawfully convicted. For John Shirle said that he [Ball] had been condemned to death falsely, unjustly and for envy by the said ministers with the king's assent, because he was a true and worthy man, prophesying things useful to the commons of the kingdom and telling of wrongs and oppressions done to the people by the king and the aforesaid ministers; and Ball's death would not go unpunished but within a short space of time he would well reward both the king and his said ministers and officers. These sayings and threats redound to the prejudice of

> the crown of the lord the king and to the contempt and manifest disturbance of the people. And thereupon the said John Shirle was immediately brought by the sheriff before the said justices sitting in Cambridge castle; and he was charged about these matters and was diligently examined as regards his conversation, his presence [in Cambridge] and his estate; and when these things had been acknowledged by him before the said justices, his evil behaviour and condition were made plainly manifest and clear. And thereupon trustworthy witnesses in his presence at the time when the above-mentioned lies, evil words, threats and worthless talk had been spoken by him, were requested; and they, being sworn to speak the truth about these matters, testified that all the aforeside words imputed to him had indeed been spoken by him; and he, examined once again, did not deny the charges laid against him. Therefore by the discretion of the said justices he was hanged; and an order was made to the escheator to enquire diligently about his lands and tenements and his goods and chattels, and to make due execution thereof for the lord the king.[1]

This book explores some versions of community and individual identity in a few especially resonant works written between about 1360 and 1430. The continuation of the human species, let alone the practice of what may count as vices and virtues, is inextricably bound up with the existence of particular communities, a fact as axiomatic to Aristotle as to Thomas Aquinas and much pre-enlightenment moral thought – no Robinsonades here.[2] Human beings are necessarily born into communities they did not choose and they grow into given social identities with which they encounter their specific circumstances. The terms 'individual identity' and 'community' are interdependent, the story of a human life, as Alasdair MacIntyre has argued, always embedded in the story of those communities from which that life derives its identity. Even if, as in some of the late medieval material studied in this book, the given 'communal roles' become deeply problematic, they will be an inescapable part of self-identity, however perplexing.[3]

In exploring the representations of community and individual identity in four very different works I have also sought to understand their relations to the historical communities in which they were made, some of whose concerns they articulated and whom they addressed. These historical communities, their economies and their social relations, their discourses and practices, are not a 'background' to the individual texts we read, a remote reference point comprising a domain one may or may not consider according to taste. Nor are they unknowable and Kantian 'things-in-themselves', nor the merely 'indeterminate' effects of free-wheeling textuality, the self-referential play of 'undecidable' signifiers outside of which nothing exists. On the contrary, they provide the collective practices, including language, out of which texts are made: they permeate the minute particulars of the writings we study. No static dualism of 'literature' and 'background' or of 'individual' and 'society' can help us understand this situation, nor can any variety of the idealist epistemologies currently propagated in poststructuralist teaching. Here, it seems to me, Bakhtin/Volosinov offers extremely helpful reflections in a book published in 1929 and available in English since 1973:

> Each person's inner world and thought has its stabilized *social audience* that comprises the environment in which reasons, motives, values and so on are fashioned . . . specific class and specific era are limits that the ideal of addressee cannot go beyond. In point of fact, *word is a two-sided act.* It is determined equally by *whose* word it is and *for whom* it is meant. As word, it is precisely *the product of the reciprocal relationship between speaker and listener, addresser and addressee.* Each and every word expresses the 'one' in relation to the 'other'. I give myself verbal shape from another's point of view ultimately from the point of view of the community to which I belong.[4]

If linguistic, social, and subjective processes are isolated at moments in the analysis of cultural practices, this model demands that they are ultimately understood as bound together in the structure and history of particular communities. Even when we consider utterances that are not referential messages we find that they are 'socially oriented', determined by the 'immediate social situation and the broader social milieu':

> Even if we were to take an utterance still in process of generation 'in the soul,' it would not change the essence of the matter, since the structure of experience is just as social as is

> the structure of its outward objectification. The degree to which an experience is perceptible, distinct, and formulated is directly proportional to the degree to which it is socially oriented. In fact, not even the simplest, dimmest apprehension of a feeling . . . can dispense with some kind of ideological form.[5]

The generation of meaning and individual experience cannot be understood apart from the social relations of a specific community, its organizations of power manifest in the prevailing arrangements of class, gender, political rule, religion, armed force, and, not infrequently, race. So any reading that hopes to have relevance to a particular text must include an attempt to relocate it in the web of discourses and social practices within which it was made and which determined its horizons. At the same time, every text discloses aspects of this web, potentially revealing something about contemporary projects, ideologies, and anxieties. Some texts may manifest disturbing contradictions or tensions in prevailing theory and practice while others, probably rather few, may even dramatize and explore them critically. Such dynamic and reciprocal relations between 'word', 'inner world', and 'the community' are ones that Bakhtin, in *The Dialogic Imagination*, urges us to pursue in the quest for what he calls the 'socio-ideological meaning' of the texts we study. This, he argues, can only be discovered in terms of a 'knowledge of the social distribution and ordering of all the other ideological voices of the era'.[6] Such a task conjures up an ever-receding goal, but as a model for a basic task of literary and cultural criticism it is admirable.

The reciprocal relations described by Bakhtin involve a dialogue between received cultural categories and the demands posed by present practical realities. The demands may or may not prove compatible with the categories through which members of the community perceive them and seek to answer them. The dialogue is acted out in historical circumstances which may put even the most revered categories and interpretations at risk, a process we will meet on more than one occasion in the following pages. It has been exceptionally well illustrated by Marshal Sahlins in his study of the encounter between Hawaiians and Captain Cook, a study of the interactions between cultural categories whereby a contingent happening (the accident to the *Resolution*'s mast which led Cook back to Hawaii for repairs) was made into a momentously significant event, fatal to the Captain.[7] Reflecting on the dialogue in this history, Sahlins makes 'two elementary observations':

> Human social experience is the appropriation of specific percepts by general concepts: an ordering of men and the objects of their existence according to a scheme of cultural categories which is never the only one possible, but in that sense is arbitrary and historical. The second proposition is that the use of conventional concepts in empirical contexts subjects the cultural meanings to practical revaluations. Brought to bear on a world which has its own reasons, a world in-itself and potentially refractory, the traditional categories are transformed. For even as the world can easily escape the interpretive schemes of some given group of mankind, nothing guarantees either that intelligent and intentional subjects, with their several social interests and biographies, will use the existing categories in prescribed ways. I call this double contingency the risk of the categories in action.[8]

In social practice people necessarily 'put their concepts and categories into ostensive relations to the world. Such referent uses bring into play other determinants of the signs, besides their received sense, namely the actual world and the people concerned. *Praxis* is, then, a risk to the sense of signs in the culture-as-constituted.' It is also an intrinsic part of human knowledge in a world that always 'may prove intractable', defying the concepts 'indexed' to it.[9] Acknowledging the inescapability of culturally contingent interpretation in the production of knowledge, Sahlins's approach avoids the errors of vulgar empiricism and positivism. But by attending to the role of 'praxis' and the potentially 'intractable' other we strive to know, it also avoids the fashionable idealism of poststructuralism. The latter habitually results in what Perry Anderson describes as a 'free-wheeling nescience' where the 'megalomania of the signifier' ensures that there is 'no determinable relation to any extra-linguistic referents' and no 'possibility of truth as a correspondence of propositions to reality'.[10] Once more it is worth quoting from Sahlins:

> All *praxis* is theoretical. It begins always in concepts of the actors and of the objects of their existence, the cultural segmentations and values of an *a priori* system. Therefore, there

is no true materialism that is not also historical. Marx said as much, but a certain current and trendy Marxism, bemused by the opposition of theory and practice would deny it.

Against the rather confused idealism of Hindess and Hirst, with their denial that any historical analysis of the current situation is even possible in principle, and with Hirst's poststructuralizing assertions that 'the products of signifying practices do not "represent" anything outside them', Sahlins's book shows how 'culture is precisely the organization of the current situation in the terms of a past' with all the inescapable difficulties that entails.[11] The 'praxis' of medieval people, like that of the Hawaiians, Captain Cook, and ourselves, involves practical reference which put their cultural systems at risk in changing historical circumstances. This world seemed profoundly intransigent and baffling to some, while to others it seemed full of welcome opportunities worth struggling to realize – even if this meant challenging some dominant cultural systems and risking one's life in struggles like those embodied in June 1381 or engaging in the very different ones we shall explore in Margery Kempe's book.

Despite the recollection of 1381, some readers will ask what talk about a world proving intransigent in the face of received cultural categories could have to do with the later Middle Ages and its writings. This book seeks to offer some answers to such questions, but it seems worth considering where the questions are likely to come from. Such readers probably have received or are receiving their version of this period from specialists in medieval language and literature occupying a virtually autonomous sector of traditional departments of English Literature, a sector which very rarely has anything at all to do with social history, economic history, sociology, and cultural and communications studies. These literary specialists have tended to present the period as one unified by Christian faith and a common moral theory, the antithesis to a 'modern' world riven by competing ideologies, conflicts, and tensions. Medieval society is imagined as three estates organically related in consensus and mutual support, the estate of those who pray, the estate of those who fight to defend the totality, and the estate of those who labour to maintain the harmonious ensemble on its unambiguous path to the heavenly Jerusalem. Even if 'sins' flourished amongst the fallen pilgrims as abundantly as sermons, penitential manuals, and satires liked to claim, they were merely deviations from norms that were unanimously agreed in medieval communities. Such teaching received one of its classic formulations in D. W. Robertson's *Preface to Chaucer*, first published in 1962 but many times reprinted:

> the medieval world was innocent of our profound concern for tension. . . . We project dynamic polarities on history as class struggles, balances of power, or as conflicts between economic realities and traditional ideals. . . . But the medieval world with its quiet hierarchies knew nothing of these things.[12]

These assumptions are still widespread and held quite independently of Robertson's allegorical methods of interpretation. They seem to guarantee a world free from anything remotely like the individual subject found in the 'modern' west, one organized in stable communities cemented by a universally accepted monologism. The version of 'the medieval world' found in such scholarship and the teaching it sponsors does have the seemingly historical authentication of being congruent with social models propagated by the medieval clerisy. Only *seemingly*, however. For these models were thoroughly partial. They were the projections of particular dominant groups seeking to control reality and shape the views of people on whose labour-power, forced services, and tithes their own privileged status depended. About this dependence they had no illusions:

> Riȝt so in þe chirche beeþ nedeful þes þre offices: presthod, knyȝthod, and laboreris. To prestis it falliþ to kutte awey þe voide braunchis of synnis wiþ þe swerd of here tonges. To knyȝtis it falliþ to lette wrongis and þeftis to be do and to mayntene Goddis Lawe and hem þat ben techeris þerof, and also to kepe þe lond fro enemyes of oþer londes. And to laboreris it falleþ to trauayle bodily and wiþ here sore swet geten out of þe erþe bodily liflode for hem and for oþer parties. And þese statis beþ also nedeful to þe chirche þat non may wel ben wiþouten oþer. For ȝif presthod lackede þe puple for defaute of knowyng of Goddis Lawe shulde wexe wilde on vices and deie gostly. And ȝif knyȝthod lackid and men to reule þe puple by lawe and hardnesse, þeueves and enemies sholden so encresse þat no man sholde lyuen in pes. And ȝif laboreris weren not, boþe prestis and knyȝtis mosten bicome acremen

> and heerdis, and ellis þey sholde for defaute of bodily sustenaunce deie.[13]

A terrible fate indeed! Worse still, as we shall see in chapter 1, certain people in the preacher's England not only were able to imagine this terrible fate but to propose it, not in scholastic disputation but, perish the thought, in 'praxis'. Such preaching and social theory tells us much about the projects and anxieties of its makers. But it is rather silly to confuse these projects with popular belief, customs, and 'the medieval world'. As Simone Weil notes in *The Need for Roots*, most surviving 'documents originate among the powerful ones, the conquerors', something Jack Goodie expresses in his study of the family and marriage in Europe:

> written norms can have a reference group whose members take them seriously, but there may be other elements in the population, who may be defined by class, ethnicity, sex or literacy, who work by very different sets of norms. . . . These alternative beliefs and practices cannot simply be regarded as variations on a common written theme, for they may represent different interests, different ideologies, and may thus stand in marked opposition to the other mode. . . . In Europe the ideology of the Church and the practice of the people frequently diverged.[14]

The economic historian J. L. Bolton shows us how 'the research of the past three-quarters of a century has destroyed the idea of a uniform medieval society', yet not all literary scholars are willing to take note of this work, preferring to reiterate claims about a homogeneous medieval culture and a society innocent of 'tensions' in its 'quiet hierarchies'.[15] While there is no substitute for paying attention to such research, it may be worth recalling a banality that is curiously overlooked by scholars homogenizing the Middle Ages, as it often seems to be by Foucaultian 'new historicists'. Namely this: were the practices, doctrines, and apparatuses of the ruling groups actually able to constitute subjects and to achieve anything like the assumed hegemony, they would hardly need such continual and elaborate legitimation. Social practices, after all, 'only need legitimating if there is some chance that they may be rejected'.[16] And plenty of evidence has survived from late medieval England showing that legitimation was much needed, in theory and coercive practice.

Instead of inventing 'quiet hierarchies' to bring correction or 'confort', as the Newbolt Report quaintly describes it, to a 'modern' world divided by social antagonisms, we should try to familiarize ourselves with the fact that late medieval England was a heterogeneous society confronting greatly changed circumstances in the post-plague period.[17] It was composed of communities and classes whose economic, political, and religious interactions did not dissolve distinctive social experiences, interests, languages, and norms. We cannot assert that texts, symbols, and rituals, whether *Piers Plowman* or the eucharist, must have been received in similar ways in a community of trained clerics or 'moral' Gowers as in a community of John of Gaunts and 'honour' pursuing gentry or in a community of peasants, labourers, and artisans whose members were converging on London on Corpus Christi day in 1381 and executing Archbishop Sudbury the day after. Indeed we have every good reason to argue quite the contrary.[18] The communities and classes of England were hardly bound together in the organic unities of 'quiet' consent and harmony. Local and central records have made it clear that the rising of 1381 'did not erupt in an otherwise tranquil society. The social harmony which ecclesiastical, political and social theorists constantly idealised in their writing and sermons, never in fact existed.'[19] As Mervyn James showed in his study of Corpus Christi ritual and drama in English towns:

> these attitudes, which conceived of society as a body in which differentiation was taken up into social wholeness, were in historical fact projected by societies which were deeply divided – riven by intense competitiveness: by the struggle for honour and worship, status and precedence, power and wealth.[20]

R. B. Dobson, a medieval historian free from any marks of marxism, corroborates such accounts:

> much of the recent spate of research devoted to late-fourteenth century English history has strengthened the old suspicion that many of the traditional institutions and even principles of church and state were undergoing what would now be termed a profound crisis of credibility . . . it seems increasingly hard to deny that the revolt of 1381 occurred at a time of exceptional disaffection on the part of many different English social groups.[21]

The social discontents which led to violence in, for example, York, Beverley, Scarborough, Lynn, Norwich, Southampton, Bury St Edmunds, and London did not come out of 'quiet hierarchies' free from 'tension'.[22] Dobson's comment on 1381 and 'the recent spate of research devoted to late-fourteenth century England' should help us recall that the transfer of massive resources from peasant communities to landlords (lay and ecclesiastic) was guaranteed in the last resort by coercive powers. How could this not be when the exactions of lordship amounted to about 50 per cent of villein produce?[23] As J. L. Bolton writes in his indispensable survey of the English economy between 1150 and 1500, the lords of the land composed 'a distinct class' which depended on exploiting the capital resources of the peasantry and profiting from their labour, rents, taxes, and fines: 'Their object was simple, to maximise revenues for an increased cash income' adapting modes of exploitation to the changed circumstances after the Black Death.[24]

While literary scholarship tends to ignore the material foundations of medieval culture, another form of amnesia habitually affects its version of the later Middle Ages. It often seems to forget that peasant communities resisted the dominant classes, lay and ecclesiastical, in a variety of ways, ranging from communal and individual non-performance of services, to grazing beasts on lords' pastures, to poaching, to seeking freedom from compulsory services by litigation in the *Curia Regis*, to what was the last resort in some especially bitter conflicts, 'open rebellion'.[25] As one would expect from the socio-economic contexts, such struggles are a marked feature of England in the second half of the fourteenth century. The processes involved are well documented in Z. Razi's study of Halesowen. Despite the 1323 commutation of Labour Services there, the ecclesiastical lord responded to the labour shortage, to which I shall return when discussing *Piers Plowman*, by requiring his tenants to do boon-works in peak periods. The records show increasing acts of assault and abuse directed against manorial officials, plundering of abbey property in daytime and by night, and unprecedented mass trespassing on the lord's crops, pastures, fish ponds, and warrens. In 1380 the whole tenancy was fined. In late 1385 all the abbey doves were released and the bondman Thomas Harbury found guilty of being 'Malicious with an intent of causing the lord a damage'. Early in 1386 the bondmen of the largest village in the lordship, Romsley, rebelled against the abbot, refusing the services he demanded and refusing fealty. With the named leaders including a woman, Agnes Sadler, the tenants apparently won this round of the struggle: the lord relaxed the new pressures. Still, Razi shows how he later imposed higher rents. There too the tenants resisted, and 'the struggle against the lord of Halesowen was carried well into the fifteenth century both by individuals and by the community'.[26]

In fact the wonderful section *de rebellione villanorum* in Walsingham's *Gesta Abbatum Monasterii Sancti Albani* is only one of the most accessible, rich, and moving accounts of the diverse traditions of resistance developed in village communities.[27] The struggles it represents can apparently be endlessly exemplified in the fourteenth century. So Rosamond Faith shows how the Coleshill (Berkshire) court rolls of the 1370s and 1380s typically contain 'many cases of refusal of labour services, sometimes by a dozen tenants at a time', as when the court roll for 24 October 1377 records that 'all the tenants who should work at harvest did not work'.[28] Similarly down in Hampshire the register-books of Tichfield Abbey, compiled between 1379 and 1405 from the Abbey accounts, court rolls, and other documents, recount a long history of conflict between lord and tenants on the various manors. In this D. G. Watts finds a 'vigorous and continuous resistance of the customary tenants', employing many strategies. *Custom*, such histories remind us, is a highly and explicitly *contested* category, a dynamic register of the balance of forces between lord and tenants, a thoroughly characteristic feature of pre-industrial agrarian social relations.[29] Michael Bennett's study of Cheshire and Lancashire mentions in passing a tradition of 'peasant resistance' including both 'legal' and armed wings of struggle, and when a Norwich adult education group decided to study the rising in Norfolk using a range of documents (court rolls, tax assessments, indictments after the rising) it found ample witness to Rodney Hilton's observation in 1973: 'as new evidence turns up, it seems to justify rather than contradict the view . . . that rural relationships in the middle ages were characterised by conflict rather than harmony of lord and peasant interests.' To recognize this, as Hilton emphasized, 'does not mean that one interprets the life of the medieval village as a constant and open battle. . . . Conflict could assume many forms, non-violent as well as violent.'[30] Such struggles were exacerbated by another dimension of 'the medieval world' that literary scholars tend to forget. Ruling-class wars and chivalry cost money, and in the period preceding the great rising costs reached sums 'that were astronomical in medieval terms', costs that were passed on through new and increased taxation to the lesser commons, 'on top of rent and other compulsory outgoings'.[31] M. M. Postan describes the transitions in late medieval taxation as suggesting 'that lords were able to pass much, perhaps even the whole, of their liabilities on to tenants of every kind including their villeins, and that it was the common folk who became the main payers of the new taxes.'[32] This, after all, was the specific catalyst of the 1381 rising, and we should not forget its contexts. It is not an insignificant dimension of social relations in the period or of the cultural productions we classify as 'chivalry'.

Another major factor contributing to social struggles in Langland's age was the demographic catastrophe of 1349. This collapse created new economic opportunities for the more substantial peasantry and for labourers prepared to seek out and bargain for improved wages. But these opportunities were bad news for the gentry who tried to stifle them with a series of legal, ideological, and coercive moves that we shall address in chapter 1. Suffice it to note here that only the most nostalgic scholarly faith could turn such social struggles into 'quiet hierarchies' and harmonies free from any 'class struggles' and free from all 'conflicts between economic realities and traditional ideals'. Still, this kind of faith is something literary scholars of the Middle Ages seem exceptionally well endowed with, as both A. C. Spearing and D. A. Pearsall have recently noted.[33]

Mentioning the struggles over wages and the mobility of labourers in the post-plague period brings me to the market, a vital aspect of late medieval communities that will emerge strongly in the first chapter, become especially prominent in the second but be occluded by materials considered in the second half of the book. To put my own view as concisely as possible, Langland, Chaucer, Margery Kempe, and many of their English contemporaries lived in pre-capitalist market communities where small-scale commodity production for exchange, rather than for use-value or subsistence, was an essential activity. This is not a question of small 'pockets' of proto-capitalist production in a feudal world, nor of scattered 'anticipations' of later forms, nor of merely 'transitional' ones. It involves a distinct form of production and exchange found widely in late medieval England and, indeed, in Western Europe to whose economic networks England belonged. The market and production for the market is itself a *social organization*, not some external and abstract mechanism. As such, it will inevitably affect people's practices, theories, and structures of feeling. Literary critics, whether specialists in the Middle Ages or the Renaissance, cannot ignore it without disabling consequences in their own account of late medieval culture, its writings, and the 'transition' to early modern Britain.[34] I shall now summarize some of the decisive factors in leading me to the view just expressed.

There has been a long tradition of research into the market in the commodities of international trade, their financing, their production and exchange. This has led to a concentration on the history of larger towns, merchant élites, the commodities they dealt in, and what some still call 'the commercial revolution'. We now have an impressively detailed literature describing how by the thirteenth century urban markets dominated by merchant entrepreneurs were vital to the economy which the sharply increased population both depended on and serviced. We also have detailed histories of specific towns, of their merchant oligarchies and commodities (there are studies, for example, of production and trade in fur, wine, wool, coal, iron, tin, and building).[35] This material shows conclusively that by the end of the thirteenth century, 'Communities of merchants, artisans, urban property owners and workers had become a powerful element in English society', communities with their own political order, social rules, economic regulations, and ethos.[36] Here was a social network stimulating a self-interested, competitive, and prudential outlook, one in which the propertied sought as great a monopoly of trade and political power as possible while enjoying the self-advertising display of these acquisitions. This social formation and the forms of life it favoured hardly fitted official social theory or its modern scholarly regurgitation.[37]

But commodity production and the development of a pre-capitalist market economy was not confined to the few large medieval towns and the international trade in wool, wine, timber, grain, and in luxuries consumed by the more affluent. The thirteenth century witnessed what Edward Miller and John Hatcher describe as 'the growth of a market economy' involving a great 'intensification' of simple commodity production and exchange in rural England and a proliferation of those organized markets we know as small towns and villages, ones increasingly integrated in a national economy and the economic system of Western Europe.[38] In the economic and demographic expansion of the thirteenth century English landlords produced agricultural commodities for both local and international markets, especially grain and wool, exploiting 'the expansion of market opportunities, buoyant prices, and plentiful supplies of cheap labour' while developing 'rational' estate management with an increasingly professional staff.[39] In this network peasant communities inevitably participated; as suppliers of labour, certainly, but also as producers of commodities for the market. A powerful force here was the demand of landlords and the growing state for rents, fines, dues, and taxes in *cash*, a demand to meet the expanding needs of the ruling class for military and luxury goods. Miller and Hatcher show how 'a very high percentage of the peasantry' were compelled to sell some of their produce if only to meet the rents and other charges:

> Thus development of commercial facilities (towns, fairs, markets) directly concerned a large part of the population, the activities of merchants influenced the fortunes of very many people, and the situation of landlord and peasant alike was governed by markets as well as by lordship and soil and weather. The development of markets in the twelfth and thirteenth century was a consequence of the intensification of economic activity during that period, but it was also one of the conditions which made possible the economic expansion of these generations.[40]

The chronology of this 'development of markets' and 'intensification of economic activity' should not be overlooked by those studying fourteenth- and fifteenth-century writing and culture, any more than should its substance. Furthermore, while a large part of the peasantry was forced to produce for the market, by the fourteenth century richer peasants 'were producing for the market on a scale which indicated the operation of the profit motive'.[41] There is no reason for literary criticism to ignore the evidence that by the era of Langland and Chaucer the peasant economy was what Postan described as 'market-oriented'.[42] The empirical evidence for this view has been gathered by historians of very different ideological conviction, the outstanding marxist historian of the English peasantry apparently in accord with equally distinguished non-marxist historians like Postan, Miller, and Hatcher. Even after the demographic collapse of 1349, Hilton emphasizes:

> there were some five hundred small boroughs with populations between, say, 500 and 2,000, and probably more market towns without any burghal status. In addition there were many village markets held weekly in settlements where arable cultivation and stock raising predominated, but which by their existence indicated a significant degree of commercialization of the economy.[43]

The Wife of Bath, like the rich vintner's son who made her, knew a great deal about the place of commodity production and markets in late medieval communities. It is out of this knowledge she assures readers, 'Wynne whoso may, for al is for to selle'.[44]

As both Langland and Chaucer knew, such a 'market-orientation' in social practice was not without consequences for values, self-identities, and structures of feeling. These emerge with great clarity in Marjorie McIntosh's study of the manor of Havering in Essex. By the late fourteenth century there was 'a strong market orientation, focusing upon production of animals and wood for the London populace'. The orientation was found at 'nearly all levels' and also in non-agricultural production where the largest group of craft-people was engaged in the making and selling of food and drink to outsiders as well as to locals, but other groups included ones involved in leather working, cloth making, building, and wood working. The crucial market here was Romford and by 1350 'Havering was highly commercialised', and wage-labour an intrinsic part of an economy which 'relied upon money', cash being the medium of exchange 'for nearly all transactions'.[45] Although Havering's status as a royal manor (ancient royal demesne land) gave it an unusual degree of economic freedom and its proximity to London gave it an exceptional market, the features McIntosh describes, in a detail my brisk summary cannot represent, are precisely those on which the last few pages concerning pre-capitalist market economy and society have focused. But her book also attends to certain consequences of this system, ones with which the present study is much preoccupied:

> Individualism flourished. The wealthier tenants were accustomed to complete freedom in pursuing profit for themselves and their families, and they expected to wield power in economic terms. In consequence they were ready to resist outside demands which might limit their autonomy and hence

their prosperity. Self-interest also dictated that they devote time and money to the manor court.[46]

At Havering the unusual absence of feudal appropriations did not lead to the lessening of productive enterprise: instead, the 'opportunities for profit' actually stimulated an individualistic quest for profit in which 'Havering people treated their property in an essentially instrumental fashion, as they did their employees'. This orientation and its 'fundamentally self-interested behaviour' was not at all incompatible with 'political and legal cooperation in face of the outside world when its rulers sought, for instance, to tax the people of Havering'.[47] Neither feudal nor capitalist, nor a merely transitional hybrid, this community was undoubtedly part of a market economy and society fostering particular forms of individualism and mobility that were deeply uncongenial to traditional moralists like Langland. Not for nothing did the contemporary of Margery Kempe who wrote *Dives and Pauper* complain that nowadays (around 1405):

> euery man wil ben his owyn man & folwyn his owyn fantasyys & despysyn her souereynys, her doom & her gouernance ne ȝeuyn no tale of Goddis lawe ne of londys lawe ne of holy chirche ne han men of vertue ne of dignete in worchepe but for pride han hem in dispyt and ben besy to worchepyn hemself in hyndryng of oþere.[48]

This is what Langland projects into Haukyn, a figure we will meet in chapter 1, 'so singuler by hymself' he considers himself 'an ordre by hymselue'.[49] The competition, the mobility, the reorganizations of opportunities, disadvantages, and social divisions sponsored by a market economy, all these are likely to undermine public roles prescribed by traditional moral and social theory. In these circumstances the relations between individual identity and community are likely to become problematic. This may well open out sharp splits between a 'private' and a 'public' domain making self-identity a necessary topic for difficult, perhaps painful reflections, difficulty we encounter at various points in the writings studied in this book. Haukyn's singularity is presented as part of a competitive drive for success in the market and the public domain but it also fosters feelings of isolation and separateness from the community, feelings we meet in various forms at some point in all the works studied in the following pages. Perhaps what Raymond Williams calls 'singularity' or 'individualism' was not quite as 'new' in 1611 as he and the conventional chronology of cultural history maintains.[50] Perhaps, too, it is thus time to put a self-denying ordinance on claims about the new 'construction of the subject' and its causes in allegedly new features of the sixteenth century,[51] at least until we have tried to learn more about the economic and social realities encountered and made by the peoples of late medieval England, and a lot more about their diverse experiences of community and individual identity. To this attempt the present book is a contribution.

The diversity of perspectives, concerns, and imagined communities in the works studied here gives at least some indication of cultural heterogeneity in late medieval England. The writings also represent relations of individual identities with historical communities and imagined alternatives as thoroughly problematic. In these texts individual identity often becomes an anxious topic for reflections, often intractable ones. Whether one is considering dominant or subordinate social classes, past or present, in the making of individual identity and experience the role of gender can hardly be overemphasized, with the massive political, legal, economic, social, and ideological downgrading of women. The role of gender emerges with especial force in two of the chapters (the second and third), and my analysis affirms that gender arrangements and ideologies, with the subjectivity, affective relations, and difficulties they foster, have important continuities with those in industrialized Western societies. Organized around exclusive male dominion in the public sphere and around the patriarchal nuclear family, cemented by cultural traditions 'whose ideas about women were, at worst, misogynistic and, at best, ambivalent', such continuities seem perfectly intelligible.[52] As the introduction has suggested, this book explores questions which demand transgressions of disciplinary boundaries operating so powerfully in our universities, though less so in the one where I have been fortunate enough to have worked for the last sixteen years. The only real difference, however, between the kinds of risky transgression demanded by a study such as my own and more conventional medieval literary history or criticism is that in the former one's understanding of late medieval economies, society, and culture can never be left as a determining set of assumptions which are not articulated and tested against the current work of colleagues in the relevant disciplines. In the latter they can be and habitually are. Not that the present work harbours illusions about transcending its own paradigms and arriving at an unmediated knowledge. We cannot dissolve our own contexts, horizons, feelings, and passions, although we can remain ignorant of their role in shaping our work, blindly denying their force. Frank Lentricchia describes the position very well:

> The historical consciousness, the will to knowledge itself, though it can never be neutralized, is itself open to historical exploration and at least partial definition. If we can admit to this, we will implicitly grant two points: (1) a perfectly objective interpretation is possible only if the interpreter is a transcendental being – that is, if he is not human; and (2) the unavoidable given of all cognitive processes – that knowledge, however we may define it, is received through a situated human consciousness that has spatio-temporal location, idiosyncratic colorations, and philosophical and sociopolitical prejudices – this is in itself no excuse to give up the labors of research or the rigors of historical self-examination.[53]

While I have not tried to conceal my own feelings and values, I have sought not to 'give up the labors of research', either mine or those of numerous writers concerned with medieval culture, economy, and society to whom I am indebted. The aim of my own labours is to reconstruct at least some of the social practices, discourses, and struggles which comprised the text's moment, together with those pressures which help us understand what its maker found intractable, perhaps even sought to evade. Without such reconstruction we are likely to project our own most unexamined assumptions onto very different forms of life and experience. I have also sought not to abandon attention to my own moment and what I take to be the current questions it puts to the diverse traditions within which I choose to write and teach. If, as Adorno, Horkheimer, and Marcuse maintained, 'All reification is a forgetting', these traditions demand a remembering, a resistance to that amnesia which is organized around the dominant ideology in both past and present.[54] They also involve a making in the present for the present, one which might help shape our perceptions, our activities, and what we leave to those who live after us. Tradition, like custom, is thus an inevitably contested activity, political in the deepest and most personal sense that word has been given in the feminist movements of the last fifteen years. So, inevitably, are cultural studies and those aspects of it we know as 'literary criticism' and 'literary history'.

Chapter One

PIERS PLOWMAN: POVERTY, WORK, AND COMMUNITY

To whom schal Y don myn elmesse?

(*Dives and Pauper*, IX xiii)

I

Piers Plowman involves a passionate attempt to address the contemporary condition of England. Its version of Christ, its moral theology, and its spirituality continually return to the poet's present, to English communities after the Black Death. The poem engages with a social world in circumstances thoroughly changed from those enjoyed, or rather, for most people, endured by preceding generations.[1] This chapter focuses on the poem's preoccupation with various kinds of people dependent on wage-labour and alms, its conceptualization of poverty, and its representation of the poor together with their communities.[2] *Piers Plowman* generates great difficulties in those spheres and the chapter aims to describe these, their sources, and some of their consequences. In doing so it seeks to contribute to the work of historians who have shown how changing attitudes to the poor and changing ideas about poverty provide major insights into prevalent mentalities and the processes of cultural transformation. It also seeks to contribute to our understanding of *Piers Plowman*, preoccupied as it was with a quite specific moment in English cultural history.

Before looking at aspects of England after the Black Death which Langland found most disturbing, I will offer an inevitably schematized account of the contrasting attitudes to poverty and the poor available in Langland's culture. The twelfth- and thirteenth-century expansion of urban and rural economies with the related demographic increase created a substantial population of people perceived as poor by their own contemporaries, ones who even when in work and when harvests were not disastrous lived at the margins of survival.[3] This development stimulated clerical reflection on poverty and charity.[4] However shameful and undesirable the state of poverty was to the laity, Jesus's teachings gave wealthier Christians cause for anxiety – 'It is easier for a camel to pass through the eye of a needle than for a rich man to enter into the kingdom of God.'[5] So the Church evolved a theory in which poverty was very far from being a mark of God's special disfavour. If the poor accept their poverty and suffering without complaint, they are in a holy state: this not only guarantees their own salvation but makes them vital instruments in the rich man's bid for salvation through the penance of alms-giving. It was a commonplace assumption that the 'pauper would seem to have been created and placed in the world for the sake of the rich man's salvation', the rich being reminded that 'whan þey schul stondyn at þe barre aforn þe souereyn iuge, Christ Ihesus, þan elmesse dede schal ben þe beste frend þat þey schul han, for þat schal spekyn for hem & preyyn for hem and sauyn hem'.[6]

Such a sanctification of the passive poor was not an inconvenient set of ideas for the ruling classes to embrace, one that fused their own salvation with the preservation of the status quo. But developments in Christian piety included a more evangelical position than this utilitarian one. St Francis was its culmination and exemplar. For him, as Mollat notes, 'the poor and the afflicted were valued for their intrinsic human and spiritual worth and not as mere instruments for the salvation of the wealthy', itself an unusual attitude.[7] To St Francis any poor person, even an idle beggar, bears the special merits of the poor and stands for Christ, his sacred image. Hence he approached the poor not as condescending or self-interested donor but to know them in a shared way of life: 'Let them [the friars] be happy to associate with humble and insignificant people, the poor and the weak, the sick, the lepers, and the beggars on the roads.'[8]

As for work in these Christian traditions, it was commanded to fallen sinners by God (Genesis 3.19) and its ends were to avoid idleness, to provide self-discipline, and to procure the necessities by which each social group could sustain life according to its status. Prayer, liturgical activities, and spiritual works in general were habitually seen as achieving the ends of work in a higher mode than direct activity in the basic processes of material production and exchange. Framing this tradition were the eschatological demands of Jesus to which we shall find Langland turning at a decisive moment in *Piers Plowman*:

> be not solicitous for your life, what you shall eat, nor for your body, what you shall put on. Is not the life more than the meat and the body more than the raiment? Behold the birds of the air, for they neither sow, nor do they reap nor gather into barns: and your heavenly Father feedeth them. Are not you of much more value than they?
>
> (Matthew 6.25–6)

This dominical teaching is part of the traditions Langland inherited, but its attitude to work had to compete with a very different evaluation that had emerged in European culture accommodating itself to the demographic, social, and economic changes of the fourteenth century.[9]

But before turning to this, it seems worth exemplifying what may be called the 'traditional' position on beggars and the able-bodied poor who were allegedly reluctant to work, an issue that was to become so important from the mid-fourteenth century to the 1834 Poor Law, and beyond. It was already proving highly perplexing to Langland. The position I call 'traditional' had been lucidly formulated by Clement of Alexandria (who died before 215) in a work devoted to 'The Rich Man's Salvation'. Writing in an urban milieu beset by large-scale poverty and indigence, he gives his view on whether Christians with possessions should evolve a discriminatory charity designed to exclude shirkers and the undeserving:

> Do not yourself decide who is worthy and who unworthy, for you may happen to be quite mistaken in your opinion; so that when in doubt it is better to do good even to the unworthy for the sake of the worthy than by being on your guard against the less good not to light upon the virtuous at all. For by being niggardly and by pretending to test who will deserve the benefit and who will not, you may possibly neglect some who are beloved of God, the penalty for which is eternal punishment by fire.[10]

This accords well with the commands of Jesus: 'Give to every one that asketh thee: and of him that taketh away thy goods, ask them not again' (Luke 6.30). The attitude combines unconditional generosity with great detachment from possessions. Nor was it unavailable in Langland's culture. It was invoked, for example, in contemporary disputes over poverty, begging, and alms-giving. So it is not surprising to find it in Richard of Maidstone's *Protectorium Pauperis* (1380), the response of a Carmelite friar to a newer Christian ethos I shall outline in a moment. Richard notes the relevance of Jesus's command in Luke 6 and argues that it is even a sin to complain about beggars. Explicitly he warns against scrupulous inquiry into the exact position of beggars, insisting that such prying is diabolic arrogance. So unacceptable is it that it lessens the merit of giving and imposes a trial on the recipient. While this was one of the deliberate aims of discriminatory alms-giving, Christ did not, Richard points out, suggest that sinful people should be excluded from alms.[11] Richard, however, was primarily concerned to defend his own vocation of voluntary poverty and religious mendicancy, conscious that 'traditional' and Franciscan positions here were likely to meet intense hostility in Langland's England. For Clement of Alexandria, faithful here to Jesus, the difficulty had been 'the salvation of the rich': was it now the support and salvation of the poor that had become the difficulty, the cause that might need sustained defence? Certainly there are arguments in *Dives and Pauper*, written some twenty-five years after *Protectorium Pauperis*, which follow similar paths to Richard's in response to similar pressures. The author acknowledges that there are inevitably priorities in alms-giving, an 'ordre'. Nevertheless he maintains that Christ will reward people for the alms they give 'to al maner pore men, boþin perfyt and vnperfyt'. He goes on to invoke St John Chrysostom in support of his position:

> he seith þat God schal nout ȝeldyn þe þin mede for þe gode lyf of hem whyche þu receyuyst but for þin goode wil and for þe worchip þat þu dost to hem for Goddis sake, for þin mercy & for þin goodnesse. And þerfor þe lawe seith þat men owyn ȝeuyn her elmesse to cursyd folc & to synful folc, ben þey euere so wyckyd.[12]

This ringing attack against discriminatory and judgemental charity, as we shall see, was going very much against the grain of prevailing movements in late medieval culture.

Not that these movements were without anticipation – what movement is? They found prefigurations in canon law and in the fierce mid-thirteenth-century conflicts over religious mendicancy and poverty between the Parisian secular masters and the friars. In his influential attack on the latter, William of St Amour opposed indiscriminate charity and argued that 'the right of the prospective recipient to alms should be carefully scrutinized, and he should be advised to find work to support himself'.[13] Changing attitudes to wealth, work, and poverty are voiced in these controversies and they seem to inform assumptions behind Pope John XXII's attack on the Franciscan ideas about poverty. In the Bulls *Ad conditorem canonum* (1323), *Cum internonnullos* (1323), *Quia quorumdam mentes* (1324) and the longer, confirmatory *Quia vir reprobus* (1329), John made the renunciation of possessions irrelevant to the highest form of Christian life. Despite the concentration on legal arguments John clearly upgrades the valuation of possessions, property, and dominion ('non commune') in paradise, before the fall. God himself thus instituted private property before any human legislator. With this John denied the traditional claim that 'abdicatio proprietatis et dominii sollicitudinem excludit [renunciation of possession and lordship excludes anxiety]', pointing with some justice at the state of the Franciscan order. Furthermore, he argued that the incarnate Christ held legal rights, dominion over temporal goods, and possessions (Judas's bag, for instance).[14] Gordon Leff's summary is very much to the point:

> The virtues of material poverty were brushed aside as irrelevant to evangelical perfection. . . . With *Quia vir reprobus* the Pope's *volte face* from his predecessors' sanctification of poverty to his own glorification of property was complete. . . . Lordship not renunciation was the badge of the apostolic life.[15]

So is Richard Tuck's commentary on John XXII in his book on the origins and developments of natural rights theories:

> property was thus natural to man, sustained by divine law, and could not be avoided. For John all relationships between men and their natural world were examples of *dominium*: for some lonely individual to consume the products of his countryside was for him to exercize property rights in them. Property had begun an expansion towards all corners of man's moral world.[16]

It is important to see that these developments in theory were not taking place in some transcendental realm peopled by disembodied thinkers. They were not only part of conflicts over authority, power, and resources within the Church. Significantly, they coincided with the historical changes in European societies, economies, and populations which had altered the composition and numbers of poor, stimulating increasingly fearful and hostile attitudes to the poor as potential 'agents of change and disruption', attitudes which were bound to affect people's feelings about religious poverty and mendicancy.[17] Miri Rubin's book on *Charity and Community in Medieval Cambridge* makes the connections most pertinent to the present chapter, ones we shall now pursue:

> As hostile attitudes towards labourers, and subsequently towards those deemed to be shirkers – the able-bodied beggars – hardened, the polemic on religious poverty was increasingly couched in terms current in labour legislation. Thus, poverty was divorced from its association with voluntary renunciation of goods . . . it came to be seen as a form of begging, of living off the hard-won earnings of others.[18]

It is certainly striking that in the mid-fourteenth-century crisis Richard FitzRalph should draw on arguments of William of St Amour and John XXII, attaining a wide and sympathetic readership. In his *Defensio curatorum*, translated by Trevisa, he treats material need as a main temptation to sin, claims that Christ himself never had the need to beg, and identifies perfection with possessions, emphasizing that 'prestes þat schulde be most parfite of life, schulde haue possessiouns'. In the state of Paradise FitzRalph finds evidence that God favours possessions and wealth, 'plente of good, & catel, meble and vnmeble'. Poverty, not property or dominion, is the product of the fall and sin: 'pouert is þe effect of synne'. 'Riches', however, 'is good hauyng & worþi to be loved of God, for he is richest of alle, & pouert is contrarie & ys priuacioun of riches'. He concludes, 'þanne pouert is euel'.[19]

FitzRalph also shows at least some signs of what looks like a new work ethic in which the production of material goods and material work seems glorified as an end in itself. His version of Eden involves an attitude to work more conventionally associated with Protestantism than with medieval Catholicism and its prelates:

> in þe first ordynaunce of man God ordeyned hym so þat anoon as man was made, God put hym in Paradys for he schuld worche & kepe Paradys; so hit is writen in þe begynnyng of

> Hooly Writ. Hit semeþ me þat þere God tauȝt þat bodilich werk, possessioun and plente of riches & vnmebles, & warde & keping þereof for mannes vse, schuld be sette to-fore beggerie; for god sett man in Paradys for he schuld worche. For man schuld kepe paradys as his owne & haue þere plente of good, & catel, meble & vnmeble.[20]

Disciplined work for the accumulation of 'worldli goodes' is so pleasing to God that it will even be rewarded among the reprobate. While systematic study of the precise contexts and incidence of the emergence of this ethos in the later Middle Ages is still needed, its presence has been indisputably demonstrated by the recent work of historians such as M. Mollat and J.-C. Schmitt.[21]

FitzRalph takes us into the contexts in which *Piers Plowman* was written, for he preached sermons in London during 1357 and 1358, denying Christ's mendicancy and denying that mendicant poverty possessed any scriptural basis.[22] We will now turn to the specific social circumstances in which he and Langland wrote, examining the bearing these had on current attitudes to the poor, poverty, work, and alms-giving in Langland's England.

The Black Death and the plagues of the 1360s and 1370s probably reduced England's population by between 40 and 50 per cent, and although vacant holdings were swiftly filled on English manors the consequent dislocations included sharp changes in the relations between employers of labour and labourers, between lords and peasants.[23] These changes offered opportunities for landless labourers, craftsmen, and many peasants, opportunities to improve the extremely vulnerable existence on the margins of survival led by their ancestors in the previous 150 years.[24] These opportunities were bad news to the gentry. This bad news included a fall in the value of their rents, a relative fall in the price of agricultural commodities (but not in the cost of luxury manufactures and imported commodities), and a sharp rise in the price of labour-power, the effect of demographic collapse following the Black Death. Indeed, increases in labour-costs of over 60 per cent were not uncommon in England.[25] These factors benefited the drives of larger peasants to accumulate holdings, but they also strengthened the bargaining position of those who sold their labour-power. This certainly helped the mass of poorer families who *depended* on such employment, and it increased the discontent of those forced to serve their lords rather than sell their labour-power on the market. (Note that here market represented freedom.) The knightly class or, as historians already find it appropriate to call the landed class below the level of magnates, the gentry (lay and ecclesiastical) responded in Parliament as well as on their estates.[26] They passed and repeatedly affirmed a statute which as Skeat observed 100 years ago is mentioned more than once in the sixth passus of *Piers Plowman*: namely, the Statute of Labourers (1351). It recalls the 1349 labour ordinances: 'Against the malice of servants who were idle [*preciouses*] and unwilling to serve after the pestilence without taking outrageous wages.'[27] But now, the Statute complains:

> such servants completely disregard the said ordinances in the interests of their own ease and greed [*couetises*] and . . . withold their service to great men and others unless they have liveries and wages [*liueresons et lowers*] twice or three times as great as those they used to take . . . to the serious damage of the great men [*grantz*] and impoverishment of all members of the said commons [*commune*].
>
> (Dobson 1970: 64)

How familiar such stuff has become! Across the centuries we recognize the high moral language, the outrage, the complaints of 'impoverishment', so many classic marks of ruling-class ideology. For that is what it is – the specific material interests of a small social group (about 2 per cent of the population) are claimed to be in the interests of 'all', to be the 'common profit', universal material and moral interests.

The Statute itself goes on to the enforcement of class law:

> [those labourers who refuse to accept the Statute] shall be put in the stocks for three days or more by the said lords, stewards, bailiffs and constables of the vills or sent to the nearest gaol, there to remain until they are willing to submit to justice. For this purpose stocks are to be constructed in every vill.
>
> (Dobson 1970: 65)

Indeed, in its attempt to impose 'harmony', the Statute discloses some of the reasons for the special singling out of justices, jurors, and lawyers for attacks in 1381:

> the said stewards, bailiffs and constables of the vills shall be sworn before the same justices to inquire diligently, by all the

> good ways they can, concerning all who infringe this ordinance. They are to certify the names of all these offenders to the justices. . . . And so the justices . . . shall have them arrested . . . the offenders shall pay fine and ransom. . . . Moreover, the offenders shall be ordered to prison.
>
> (Dobson 1970: 66)

Bertha Putnam pointed out in the major study of the enforcement of the Statute of Labourers that the justices of the peace were 'employers of labour in the very district in which they were acting, perhaps even of the very offenders summoned before them for trial'. They were, as Dobson too observes, 'usually county gentlemen with a strong personal interest in the policy of wage-restraint' and its punitive enforcement. And they were consistently resisted.[28]

Certainly the dominant class does record *anxiety* as well as aggression. The 1376 Commons' petition against mobile workers, or 'vagrants', complains that, 'although various ordinances and statutes have been made in several parliaments to punish labourers, artificers and other servants, yet they have continued subtly and by great malice aforethought, to escape the penalty of said ordinances and statutes'. The employers complain that when labourers are accused, 'they take flight and suddenly leave their employment and district, going from county to county, hundred to hundred, and vill to vill, in places strange and unknown to their masters. So the said masters do not know where to find them' (Dobson 1970: 73). Proceedings before the Justices of the Peace for the period present masses of examples of these struggles at the local and individual level. Typical are entries such as the following from Suffolk in 1361–2:[29]

> William son of Katerine Person was a labourer and now is wandering and refuses to labour. . .
>
> John Fisher will not serve for less than 1½d
> with food . . . William, once a carter of Edward
> Bertelman will not serve for less than 1½d
> a day with food. . .
>
> Robert le Goos, labourer, goes to other workers, warns and advises them that none of them should accept less than 3d a day and food because he himself will not accept less.

> Margaret the Reeve takes from Stephen the Cooper of Ipswich 10s and her meal . . . and withdraws herself from elsewhere to take higher and excessive wages.

In Lincolnshire, similarly, a ploughman refuses to work 'except by the day and unless he has fresh meat instead of salt', and in 1363 the master fullers of London asked that those workers who were combining to get wages raised should be imprisoned for a year.[30] Priests too come into conflict with the Statutes. A case removed from the Hertfordshire sessions to the King's bench involves a vicar and a hermit 'preaching that the statutes of labourers are wicked and that there is nothing to prevent labourers from taking what wages they please'.[31] Perhaps this was a stand made from a position like John Ball's; but perhaps it was from a far more pragmatic solidarity in the same struggle, one in which Commons and senior ecclesiastics attempted to apply the Statutes to their poor clergy and met sustained resistance, as legislation of the 1360s and 1370s complains, and as the increase in allowed rates over the period shows. Just as the following incident on 4 September 1364 does: a commission of oyer and terminer was set up 'to investigate the assault made by chaplains on the parsons who had been deputed to act as the bishop [of Lincoln's] commissaries in enforcing the second *Effrenata*. The chaplains, bound together by oaths, had broken up the parsons' sessions by horrible words, almost killing them and even lying in wait for the bishop himself.'[32]

So we find a context in which workers' mobility and the market on which they sold their labour-power could be a threat to employers who nevertheless were part of it and depended on it. The gentry even complain that they are losing the battle of social and economic control, hence this petition five years before the English rising: 'the workers go from master to master as soon as they are displeased about any matter. For fear of such flights the commons [i.e., the gentry!] now dare not challenge or offend their servants, but give them whatever they wish to ask, in spite of the statutes and ordinances' (Dobson 1970: 73). That is, the great God Economy overrules political ideology and new laws: with delightful irony it apparently forces the lords to break their own rules. Besides calling again for stocks and prisons, as well as bemoaning the imminent ruin and pauperization of the gentry, this petition nicely exemplifies the way language developed in the secular clergy's attacks on the friars in earlier European disputes was adapted.[33] Their terms, as Rubin observed, are now applied to mobile labourers who use market relations in ways which are not in the interests of the seigneurial class, ecclesiastic or lay:

> many of the said wandering labourers have become mendicant beggars in order to lead an idle life; and they usually go away from their own districts into cities, boroughs and other good towns to beg, although they are able-bodied and might well ease the commons [once again, the gentry] by living on their labour and services. . . . Many of them become 'staff strikers' and lead an idle life. . . . The majority of the said servants generally become strong thieves.
>
> (Dobson 1970: 74)

Classifying mobile workers, 'wandering labourers' as vagrants, as idle 'mendicants and beggars' is an important part of a social and political struggle – as rhetorical classifications always are. The classifications impose a grid which legitimizes coercion and violence against independent labourers (an 'independence' which in different economic circumstances was a cause of labourers' extreme vulnerability). As 'able-bodied' vagrants, 'strong thieves', they must be forced to work in the interests of what the lords' petition calls 'the common profit' (Dobson 1970: 74). But the issue had become, already, just what 'the common profit' actually was and who should define it. It is thoroughly fitting that in the next year, 1377, the Commons' petition against rebellious villeins links complaints about the force of peasant resistance, the violence and refusal of labour services, with complaints about their 'malicious interpretation' (*mavoise interpretacion*) of custom, history, and texts (Dobson 1970: 76). Knowing, however, that such hermeneutic conflicts do not flow undecidably and endlessly around gamesome chains of linguistic signifiers, the petition warns of civil war. In this, 'the villeins and tenants will, to avenge themselves on their lords, adhere to foreign enemies'. The gentry acknowledge that tradition, custom, is a *contested* category in a field riven by struggles between social groups. To the gentry the chain from conflicts over interpretation, over ideology, to power relations between conflicting classes of English people, to economic power, seemed all too clear. That this may also seem all too familiar 'modern' terrain will not commend it to critics who turn to the Middle Ages for lost harmonies and unities, nor to those who solemnly assure their students that to understand late fourteenth-century culture and literature one must realize that 'all things were theological' and that 'the layman's philosopher was . . . Boethius'.[34] Nor, perhaps, will these events, texts, and readings prove any more congenial to literary poststructuralists with their habitual setting aside of past and present social reality.[35]

Viewing the gentry's fear of civil war we should recall that both the legislation and resistance to it were found across Europe. Labour legislation, in more or less draconian forms, is also found in France, Spain, Poland, Upper Bavaria, the Tyrol, Hainault, and Portugal. The attempt was 'to crush the hopes of the poor for better living conditions and to remove the sole benefit bequeathed by the millions of cottars, servants, and day labourers mowed down by epidemics'.[36] As we have noted this attempt was strongly resisted and whatever success the employers had at first, by the 1370s wages had started to rise sharply and it became clear the legislation had only had a temporary effect.[37] As M.M. Postan laconically observes: 'In the end . . . the lords and employers found that the most effective way of retaining labour was to pay higher wages, just as the most effective way of retaining tenants was to lower rents and release servile obligations', heralding a period which compared to the thirteenth century is described by most historians 'as a time of economic decline' but simultaneously 'as the golden age of English peasantry'.[38]

We have seen how the gentry reacted to these improved living conditions, and to deepen our sense of the contexts of *Piers Plowman* it is worth illustrating how John Gower, a contemporary poet whose 'civilized' qualities have been admired by distinguished literary historians, responded to these circumstances.[39] In the fifth book of his Latin poem *Vox Clamantis*, Gower observes that the peasants are the people who get our 'food for us by the sweat of their heavy toil, as God Himself has decreed'. Nowadays, he complains, an 'evil disposition is widespread among the common people', and he holds ploughmen especially guilty:

> For they are sluggish, they are scarce, and they are grasping.
> For the very little they do they demand the highest pay. . . .
> Yet a short time ago one performed more service than three do
> now. . . . They desire the leisure of great men, but they have
> nothing to feed themselves with, nor will they be servants. . . .

> Everyone owning land complains in his turn about these people; each stands in need of them and none has control over them.

The ploughmen are only too representative, he complains, and he charmingly insists that just as 'the teasel harmfully thins out the standing crops if it is not thinned out itself', so 'let the law accordingly cut down the harmful teasels of rabble'. The violent rhetoric is a conventional enough marker of social conflicts and antagonisms deeply rooted in late medieval Europe: 'Unless it is struck down first, the peasant race strikes against freemen, no matter what nobility or worth they possess.' Even when the peasantry are carrying out the 'servile dues' on which the gentry directly or indirectly depends, the villeins 'have no respect for the law', their minds turning towards 'utter wickedness'. As for wage-labourers, their mobility and current relative independence of traditional controls is another cause for Gower's anger. He is outraged at their heightened expectations, their reluctance to live on the margins of subsistence their ancestors had been compelled to endure:

> Born of poor man's stock and a poor man himself, he demands things for his belly like a lord. The established law is of no help to one, for there is no ruling such men, nor does anyone make provision against their misdeeds. This is a race without power of reason, like beasts, for it does not esteem mankind nor does it think God exists.[40]

Like the rhetoric of the vagrancy petition, like all rhetoric indeed, this is a persuasion to perceive the world in a certain way, to classify large numbers of fellow human beings in a particular way which in turn legitimates particular ways of treating them, of seeking to control and punish them. In the light of this outlook, the poet's response to the great rising of 1381 is predictable. The peasants, that is, the majority of English people, are 'swine', 'monsters', 'slaves of perdition', 'the enemy', representatives of 'Satan's power'. Even though the rising has been defeated, 'overwhelmed by divine might', Gower is uneasy:

> For the peasant always lay in wait to see whether he by chance could bring the noble class to destruction. For his rough, boorish nature was not tempered by any affection, but he

> always had bitterness in his hateful heart. In his subjection the lowly plowman did not love, but rather feared and reviled, the very man who provided for him.[41]

Probably few people would have believed the inversion of real dependency relations in the final sentence here. Even in social groups with which Gower identifies it was rather well known that 'ȝif laboreris weren not, boþe prestis and knyȝtis mosten bicome acremen and heerdis, and ellis þey sholde for defaute of bodily sustenaunce deie'.[42] That was the problem. But there is nothing eccentric or surprising in Gower's representation of labouring people who sought to turn economic and demographic changes to their own advantage: representation, like rhetoric, is, after all, bound up in social struggles and identities.

Yet if historians write about the unfolding 'golden age of the peasantry' (relative to the previous century), and Gower laments it, we should not be tempted to underestimate the significance of the labour legislation, the vagrancy petition and the rhetorical constitution of labourers we have been glimpsing. For their cultural significance is far greater than their short-term role in the struggle between employers and labourers, as recent historians of poverty and the poor have understood so well. Lis and Soly summarize the conclusions of such work with admirable clarity:

> a sharp and explicit distinction was made between paupers, who had a right to assistance because of their physical weakness, and sturdy beggars, to whom alms might in no circumstances be given. This discrimination implied a break with earlier attitudes; collective glorification of poverty as such belonged *de facto* to the past. The duty to work was the harbinger of a new ethic: the exaltation of self-employment directed towards the production of material goods. Moreover, for the first time secular authorities were concerned about begging. Thus the basis was laid for the appearance of a coordinated system of social control directed by public authorities in place of private persons.[43]

In such circumstances forms of Christian charity, alms-giving, concepts of poverty, and general perceptions of the poor by the more affluent groups would inevitably shift. In such shifts we are engaging with deep changes in people's sense of community, changes in the prevailing mentality of a culture. In her illuminating study, *Charity and Community in Medieval Cambridge*, Miri Rubin traces how the burgesses' version and objects of charity changed over the later Middle Ages. By the fifteenth century they were:

> Those deemed worthy of help by the consent of gild members of society experiencing a temporary period of distress, but who were basically respectable, and not radically divergent from the giver's own self-image. With the general rise in the standard of living of labourers in the later Middle Ages, those who owned landed property and urban tenements, rentiers and employers, were witnessing a decline in their own fortunes. When an attempt to indoctrinate labourers with a work ethic which would curtail their freedom and welfare failed to produce change, the perception of the poor developed into a general denunciation of those members of society who were not fully productive, and who were seen to be the reason for economic hardship. Labourers and the poor were judged for what was seen as wilful withdrawal from the economy and slothful reliance on others. As the test of productivity came to rule in determining social acceptance and moral approbation, the poor, be they journeymen, servants, widows or friars, came to acquire a label, to be seen as shirkers or 'wastrels'. In the minds of employers and entrepreneurs struggling with an economy afflicted by acute shortage of labour, poverty came to be seen more as a choice than an affliction. Those hospitals founded and maintained in this period which did not become chantries were usually secular foundations with a pronounced punitive and corrective side, providing a regulated and controlled relief of parish poverty.[44]

No student of late medieval or early modern texts and culture can ignore these contexts or their chronology. Within them it does indeed seem that, however unintentionally, FitzRalph was assuming the newer ethos when he claimed, in his *Defensio Curatorum*: 'Holy Writ seiþ þat þe pore schal be hated of his neiȝbore. Prouerbiorum 14 [verse 20]; miche more a begger schal be hated of his neiȝbore.' With stunning confidence FitzRalph supports this view by asserting that correct Christian ethics tells us 'skilfullich euereche man schal raþer help hym-silf þan anoþer'.[45] This would have surprised St Francis and most traditional Christian moralists, but FitzRalph (like his translator) is unembarrassed. He even turns Christ's demand that those with possessions should feast the poor rather than the well-to-do (Luke 14.12–14), into a lesson on the need to draw a clear distinction between deserving and undeserving poor: 'pore men þat beþ stalworþe and stronge schulde nouȝt be cleped to þe feeste of beggers, for þei mowe quyte hit wiþ her travail.'[46] Later he recalls Christ's advice to the rich man who asked him what more he could do to receive everlasting life (Mark 10.17–27; Luke 18.18–27). Both gospel accounts agree that the advice was all too simple: 'Go, sell whatsoever thou hast and give to the poor: and thou shalt have treasure in heaven. And come, follow me' (Mark 10.21; Luke 18.22). Both agree that the rich man went away sorrowful, for he had great possessions, and that Jesus then commented on how hard it is for the rich to enter the kingdom of God: 'It is easier for a camel to pass through the eye of a needle than for a rich man to enter the kingdom of God' (Mark 10.24–5; Luke 18.24–5). So preoccupied is FitzRalph with contemporary battles against religious and lay 'vagrants', so natural is the newer ethos becoming, that he effortlessly turns this disturbing text into a reassuring polemic against begging: 'Crist tauȝt þe ȝong man to sewe hym & be parfit wiþ out wilful begging; & so he tauȝte specialiche þat parfit men schulde nouȝt begge wilfullich.'[47] A reading of the New Testament congenial to the new ethos is being forged, and a suitable Christ constructed at the same time. It is in this context and those outlined above, one which included both Richard of Maidstone and Richard FitzRalph, both mobile, active labourers resisting the gentry's new legislation and the gentry's justices and apologists, both John Ball and John Gower, that Langland encountered what had become the *problem* of the poor and the *problem* of mobile lower-class people, 'vagrants', 'able-bodied mendicants'.

II

Langland's opening vision of the human world, planted between heaven and hell, is organized around the concept of work and assumes the dominant traditional social model. This familiar theory envisaged three estates defined according to function and organically interrelated in a mutually beneficial, harmonious totality.[48] *Piers Plowman*, as I have sought to show elsewhere, is a poem which displays the severe difficulties traditional social models encountered in its world, shows how refractory that world proved to conventional categories, forcing their transformation or frustrated abandonment.[49] Here I will attend to a group that for Langland represents the grave risks now faced by his favoured categories. He calls its members 'wasters' and 'beggars'.[50] Introduced at the beginning of the poem, these people are defined as the antithesis to the gentry's ideal peasant, the ideal found in the hard-working ploughman of the *General Prologue* to *The Canterbury Tales*. Like Chaucer's, Langland's good peasant works 'ful harde', plays 'ful selde', accepts the version of community propagated in the dominant social model and unquestioningly yields up his labour-power and what he 'wins', his produce (Prologue, 20–1, 112–22). Not so the group branded as wasters and beggars. These people, the poet maintains, are able-bodied, gluttonous idlers (Prologue, 22). Such 'wastours' apparently include the following: mobile pub-frequenting, turbulent, lower-class people with full bellies and full bags, people classified as 'beggeres'; mobile fiction-making people who are 'pilgrymes' and 'palmeres'; mobile pseudo-hermits, strikingly like the figure of the poet gradually disclosed in the poem, men travelling with 'hire wenches' and driven by a hatred of work (Prologue, 40–57). These members of the third estate have their analogues in the clerical estate: equally mobile people, totally bound into the market and the quest for self-interest, they are religious mendicants, friars bound to a life of evangelical poverty (Prologue, 58–65).

The passage seems to share certain elements with the vagrancy petition discussed earlier in this chapter, but it raises some puzzling questions which need stating if we are to unpack the specific identity and function of 'wastours' in *Piers Plowman*. Who actually contributes with such unconditional generosity to fill the bags, bowls, and bellies of such hedonistic vagrants, ones merrily touring post-plague England to waste all that the hard-working winners have produced? Certainly not, by the poem's own eloquent account, the dominant classes, those who depend on controlling the manual working winners, for they are apparently marked by a self-indulgence 'moost vnkynde to þe commune' and most ungenerous (X 13–29, 57–66, 86–7). As for the kindly 'meene men' contrasted with the wealthier people (X 65–6), the poem does not present such producers as in any position to support a predatory class of wanderers as well as the dominant lay and ecclesiastical groups displayed in Passus X and elsewhere. The wasters' extravagant livelihood is more of a mystery than it might at first have seemed.

Once this is noticed, other simple questions become worth asking. Why do the 'good' winners tolerate this state of affairs in their own communities? After all, peasant communities in daily practice were self-governing: economic organization and enforcement of their own traditions, law, and order, was a reality quite independent of the miscalled 'protection' of the landlord, the extractor of rents, services, fines, and taxes.[51] Why does the armed ruling class tolerate this unarmed rival for the surplus on whose appropriation its own continuity and privilege depends? As exemplified by Bishop Despenser, Thomas of Woodstock, and Sir Henry Percy in June 1381, this class was perfectly able and willing to use armed force to kill and defeat peasant opponents.[52] Understandably, for the only *potentially* revolutionary class even in theory, indeed the only class that could offer *any* challenge to the late medieval ruling classes, in rural, urban, or national spheres, was the peasantry in alliance with 'their friends and relatives, the village craftsmen'.[53] Nothing, on the face of it, could be more absurd than to imagine vagrant 'wastours' having the power to appropriate the 'communes' that the working population produces for itself and for 'kyng and knyȝthod and clergie' (Prologue, 112–22). And yet this is the fantasy the poem now entertains. Why?

The mobile, able-bodied beggar could be figured as someone who chooses not to work, the perfect antithesis to the newer work ethos discussed above and the perfect way of demonizing all who opposed the rules of the current ethos drawn up by the gentry (lay or ecclesiastic). We are actually encountering the emergence of a stereotype with a long future before it, one that dispensed with any need for conceptual distinctions which might encourage discomfortingly complex analysis of the diverse causes pushing people out of their villages and onto the roads. It was to prove as usable in the possessing classes' violence against the dispossessed and unemployed poor during the later sixteenth and early seventeenth century as in facilitating the much later adaptation of perceptions of the poor and poverty in the transition to industrial capitalism.[54] However, the social, economic, and demographic situation of late fourteenth-century England was not that of later periods and we must try to grasp the particular meanings of the stereotype in specific, distinct circumstances. In the era of the first national labour legislation, we have observed, the gentry confronted a shortage of labour, higher wages, and considerable labour mobility as women and men took to the roads in search of the highest wages they could find. As Rodney Hilton has pointed out, 'this mobile population probably did beg *en route* from one job to another, but they were far from doing so professionally, though to punish them for begging was one way of getting at them for not keeping in their proper place and station'.[55] To Langland this mobility threatened community solidarities and the traditional social model he cherished almost as much as the market which he represents as transforming all relationships and sweeping away venerable human bonds.[56] But at this stage of the poem he seems only able to oppose such threats from within the framework of the gentry's perceptions and rhetoric as he tries to imagine a congenial reformation of this world (IV 171 – VI 320). Preaching with a cross, the agent of reformation, 'Reason', raises the issue of 'wasters'. He assumes that work is constantly available in forms that are congruent with the poet's favoured social model, that it will be morally enhancing and that those who do not work in the approved manner should be beaten (V 24–34).

Such assumptions are elaborated during the famous passage on the deadly sin of Gluttony (V 296–377). Langland now figures forth 'wasters' *exclusively* through labourers and artisans: breweress, cobblers (of both sexes), warrener and wife, tinker and servants, hackneyman, needle-maker, digger, rat-catcher, raker (binman), ropemaker, female dish-seller, garlic-seller, second-hand-cloth-seller, butcher (female?), hostler, with the clerk from the local church (such clerics would indeed have an economic and cultural position which aligned them with this community rather than with the upper-class ecclesiastics attacked in, for example, Passus X 311–21). Langland's view of the dominant classes was not a flattering one, and there is no purely ethical or aesthetic reason to explain why those he castigates later (X 13–103) should not be represented here. The explanation is social and political. At this point his vision only notices lower-class people because his attention is on work and practical opposition to the work ethos as much as on any distinctly religious conversion. And what better location to symbolize this opposition than the pub? For this was a place endlessly castigated as the devil's anti-church, a place fostering solidarities and a culture hardly in harmony with the one recommended to plebeians by clerics and gentry. The wealthier families of late medieval Havering were typical enough of their social stratum in finding that 'Havering's ale-house and lesser inns posed a special threat to order and decency'.[57] In securing this judgement such respectable people would be familiar with the vivid pulpit attacks on the institution which competed with the Church for the time, attention, and money of lower-class people, those who tended to have 'mor haste to þe tauerne þan to holy chyrche'. As *Dives and Pauper* laments, 'þey han leuer gon to þe tauerne þan to holy chirche, leuer to heryn a tale or a song of Robyn Hood or of some rybaudye þan to heryn messe or matynys or onyþing of Goddis seruise', a sure sign of the dangerous threat they present to 'her souereyns, her doom & her gouernance'.[58] Langland himself presents Beton's ale house as a convivial, warm alternative to both work-discipline and official religion (V 296–306), a perspective cherished over 400 years later by Blake's 'The Little Vagabond' (*Songs of Experience*) – in very different contexts but ones where the 'indisciplined' labouring classes were viewed as a problem and threat to the possessing classes.[59] The pub represents a milieu in which the desublimation of the ruling groups' *official* culture takes place, in which an alternative is celebrated:

> There was lauȝynge and lourynge and 'lat go þe cuppe!'
> Bargaynes and beuerages bigonne to arise,
> And seten so til euensong and songen vmwhile
> Til Gloton hadde yglubbed a galon and a gille.
> Hise guttes bigonne to goþelen as two gredy sowes;
> He pissed a potel in a paternoster while,
> And blew þe rounde ruwet at þe ruggebones ende.
>
> (V 336–42)

This is a wonderful figuration of what respectable clerics, gentry, and burgesses see as the life of the 'wastours' first encountered in the Prologue. Here even the farting contrasts with the religious and latinate horn of Hope, *Deus tu conuersos viuificabis nos*, blown with the second penitential psalm, while the singing in the pub contrasts with evensong and the saints' singing for sinners later in the Passus (V 506–9). The contrast can doubtless be classified as 'satire' directed against those whom the more economically sufficient and respectable people of Havering saw as 'a special threat to order and decency', hence to religion. Yet the poetry involves something other than the respectable scheme of condemnatory judgement so familiar from sermons and confessional manuals. However hostile the aim, the poetry includes the projection of a profane, popular counter-culture in which the body, as Gloton's performance displays, is present and open.[60] Here we find communal solidarities, play, and laughter involving women and men together (medieval ale houses were far from being the 'predominantly male working-class pub' of later generations).[61] This contrasts eloquently with the official culture's latinate 'evensong' and 'paternoster' conducted in a setting sustained by compulsory and much resisted economic contributions (tithes). We also find 'ydel tales at þe Ale', 'rymes of Robyn hood', replacing holy-days, fast-days, and saints of the Church – of which the equally plebeian Norfolk Lollards made such hilarious mockery, to their cost in the ecclesiastical persecutions of 1428–31.[62]

By placing those he classifies as wasters and able-bodied beggars in the pub, the poet clarifies the range of matters at stake. Working people never did, after all, get for *nothing* the large quantities of drink and food the poet complains about. Like the gentry in Parliament and their clerical ideologues, the poem would have us forget that the so-called wasters are *labourers*, they are, in contemporary parlance, the 'winners'. As we noticed, the pub is full of people defined in terms of their labouring occupations (without which they could not be jugging it up) – cobblers, tinkers, road sweepers, diggers, and so on. Just the kind of list one finds in the Statute of Labourers and in the proceedings before the justices of the peace seeking to enforce it. In *Piers Plowman* (unlike *Winner and Waster*) the term 'waster' is developed to classify those who resist the pieties and discipline of the employers and the Good Shepherds. They are those who desublimate its most exalted ideals in profane parody and, crime of all crimes, are hostile to the work ethos the employers seek to impose.

Langland's construction of *wasters* is thus an ideological and partisanly class term. It is a quite identifiable part of specific social struggles in quite specific circumstances. So, as we shall see, are the ensuing agonized meditations on licit or illicit charity, on poverty, on the ethical status of wealth and work: their specific cultural significance can only be adequately grasped when seen in the circumstances outlined earlier in this chapter. We must remember that it is only *after* the demographic collapse that we find English writers in both pulpit and Parliament deploying the European disputes around poverty, work, and the friars: deploying them, that is, with very *practical* applications; namely, with the intention of getting as many people as possible to work as cheaply and as devotedly as possible in the face of the reduction in labour supply.

So preoccupied was Langland with the matrix of problems we have been examining that he decided to devote a whole Passus to it. This is the Passus normally known as 'the ploughing of the half acre', Passus VI. It might, however, more appropriately be called 'labour disputes and strikes on the manor', or, to use Langland's own language, strivings against the Statute (VI 320).

The Passus begins by reaffirming the traditional social model in the face of the challenges it has had to sustain, in the poem and in the poet's society. Here the knight so loves the peasant that he offers to share his manual labour and the peasant so loves maintaining the knightly class in its power and privilege that he quickly rejects the offer in favour of the status quo (VI 21–6). With a few strokes of the pen all contemporary struggles over villeinage, rents, fines, and rights of hunting are dissolved (VI 27–56).[63] A miracle has transformed peasant consciousness while leaving the systems of exploitation, power, and privilege untouched, safe in the hands of benevolent gentlemen in the current demographic collapse. The poet, however, was fortunately well aware of the crazy abstractionism this involved and once more submits his cherished social model to the unpalatable conflicts of his historical moment. The result is the breakdown of the good ploughman's enterprise and the collusion with the knight to which he had sought to commit his community.[64] Here I will focus on one aspect of this complex breakdown, the problems of the 'wastours' the knight was meant to repress (VI 28) together with those posed, to use Langland's terms, by bold big beggars and the unfortunate needy.

Before the breakdown the working people do just what the employers and their Statute demanded. They work hard and unquestioningly. The ploughman's task includes overseeing their work, fulfilling the role of the good reeves and bailiffs so essential to the gentry in its extractions from peasant communities. (Zvi Razi recalls how one year 'all men on the manor of Hales' were amerced ten pounds for refusing to elect a reeve for the Abbot's use [*ad opus abbatis*], an episode which symbolizes the place of such overseers.)[65] Piers, the ploughman, insists that only those who work best will be hired at harvest time. The specific direction of this threat is interesting. Middling and wealthy peasants, those with holdings of more than about thirty acres would not usually need to hire themselves out as wage-labourers – on the contrary, they would need some help from hired labour. It was the large group holding less than twelve acres who would certainly need supplementary or even the bulk of their income from wage-labour, and in most late medieval communities this seems to comprise at least 40 per cent of the population.[66] Piers's stick-and-carrot approach is thus plainly addressed to poorer peasant families and the many landless labourers who were totally dependent on wage-labour for their very survival. This distinction is important in grasping the real orientations of Passus VI. The point is that however resistant peasant families were to the extractions of gentry and state, they never needed urging to work their own holdings – their survival, let alone self-respect, self-identity, and relative comfort demanded it. The situation of those dependent on wage-labour was different, and this is what Langland addresses.

Contrary to their overseer's exhortations the 'werkmen' who have 'wroȝten ful faste' (VI 109) decide that they have done and got enough for their present wishes: 'Thanne seten somme and songen atte Nale/And holpen ere þe half acre wiþ "how trolly lolly"' (VI 115–16). In thus withdrawing to the pub, the 'werkmen' actually reject the tempo and labour discipline imposed on them; imposed on them by employers, not by nature – a different psychological and economic position to that of middling and substantial peasants. Already Langland has represented the village ale house as a demonic anti-Church, the location of 'wastours', and the present scene recapitulates the earlier one. In doing so it confirms the analysis offered above of the ideological nature of the term 'wastours' in quite particular social conflicts, sharpening our understanding of those who are repeatedly called wasters in the Passus (VI 25–6, 130, 133, 152, 161, 162, 173, 174, 201, 302, 323). As soon as 'werkmen' reject the employer's work ethic they are classified as 'wastours'. For these people, responding perfectly rationally to their place in the existing division of labour, land, and resources, work is no more than a means to acquire wages for immediate enjoyment of material comforts and the convivial pleasures found in the pub. Their work is in itself of no special concern, hardly the case for those working holdings which could be made to yield their families' subsistence and cultural needs. Nor will those who have to sell their labour-power at whatever rates current market conditions dictate have quite the same attitudes to work, time, and the future as those who do not.

Langland does not accept this fact and his response to the 'werkmen' become 'wastours' is to have Piers angrily warn them that unless they hurry 'to werche' now they will be starved out, to death if necessary (VI 117–20). At this moment the poet makes a move which was to have a long future before it. He turns the independent 'werkmen'/'wastours', those who have been seen both working and singing in the ale house, into able-bodied beggars, pseudo-cripples, and vagrants (VI 121–8). The shift inevitably involves a further implication: those who may *look* poor are likely in reality to be 'wastours', work-shy scroungers, to use the characteristic term from the fully-fledged ethos we now know so well. Piers responds by asserting a simple classification: either such people are physically disabled, in which case they are the deserving poor, or they are able-bodied vagrants who should be selling their labour-power 'as truþe wolde', not jugging it up 'in lecherie and in losengerie'. To the former alms are due, to the latter punishment (VI 129–51). The poem is plainly addressing the contexts and conflicts outlined in section I of this chapter. We quoted from the 1376 petition against 'wandering labourers' and have observed how useful it was for employers to classify migrant workers in search of the best wages on the current market as 'mendicant beggars' pursuing 'an idle life'. In this struggle against workers' mobility they demanded a law forbidding 'any sustenance and alms to be given to such false mendicants and beggars': 'let it be established by statute that all such false beggars as well as the said "staff strikers" shall be . . . placed in stocks or led to the nearest gaol, until they show themselves willing to submit and return to their own areas', thus accepting the wage-freeze imposed by employers at pre-plague levels.[67] The allegiances of the poem to the employers' work ethos and ideological imagery seem rather unequivocal, at this stage.

As it elaborates the scene in which Piers assures the 'werkmen'/'wastours'/mendicants that the employers' views represent 'truþe', the poem displays a prominent feature of those classified as 'undeserving' poor: their individual and collective self-agency, the very opposite quality to the passivized and deferential poor so pleasing to the pious:

> Thanne gan wastour to wraþen hym and wold have yfouȝte;
> To Piers þe Plowman he profrede his gloue.
> A Bretoner, a braggere, he bosted Piers als

And bad hym go pissen with his plowȝ: pyuysshe sherewe!
Wiltow, neltow, we wol have oure wille
Of þi flour and þi flessh, fecche whanne vs likeþ,
And maken vs murye þerwiþ maugree þi chekes
(VI 152–8)

Not surprisingly the poet has the secular élite summoned by the overseer to impose labour discipline, that is, the gentry's current labour legislation, 'þe statut' (VI 318, 320, 150–70). The knight, acting as a justice of labour or the peace, warns 'wastour' to do better, 'Or þow shalt abigge by þe lawe, by þe ordre þat I bere' (VI 166). His threat is made yet more explicit in the later C version of the poem: 'Or y shal bete the by the lawe and brynge þe in stokkes' (VIII 163). One recalls the new law: those who refuse to work at the wages fixed by the employing gentry 'shall be put in the stocks for three days or more by the said lords, stewards, bailiffs and constables of the vills or sent to the nearest gaol, there to remain until they are willing to submit to justice'.[68] The poem resolves this encounter not with the harmonious melodies heard by some nostalgic critics but in terms of the gentry's anxious perception of the current balance of forces illustrated in the parliamentary petitions of 1376 and 1377 against vagrants, malicious labourers, and bondsmen. So the worker-wasters reject the gentry's rhetoric and their law, as so many were to do in 1381 – and on many, many other occasions through the later Middle Ages. They 'leet liȝt of þe lawe and lasse of þe knyȝte' (VI 168).

At this point the poet hopes for a subsistence crisis. This would force working people into the kind of disciplined and docile labour force required by Piers and the gentry (VI 171–8). It does just this, and Langland allows himself the pleasure of imagining hungry wasters and able-bodied beggars turning into fanatically dedicated labourers, all content to work for minimal subsistence wages and ready to receive any bonuses with unquestioning gratitude (VI 183–201). We glimpse a vision of the new work ethos triumphant over rebellious labourers, an employer's utopia. In these circumstances the disciplinary dimension of 'charity' emerges as we watch its transformation into a discriminatory instrument of poor relief under lay control, itself an important part of the new ethos and its gradual institutionalization.[69] 'Of beggeris and bidderis what best to be doone' (VI 203)? Alms must be just enough to keep able-bodied labourers alive – 'lat hem ete wiþ hogges' (VI 181) – but certainly not enough to allow them any independence from the demands of the employers.

But Langland was deeply committed to traditional moral theory and could not remain happy with a solution in terms of the newer ethos. He now has Piers note that the reformed 'wasters' actually work so obediently and hard 'for defaute of foode': remove famine conditions and 'þei wol werche ille' (IV 204–6). That is, the production relations remain impersonal and fundamentally antagonistic, hardly a state of affairs congenial to Langland's traditional social model or equally traditional moral theology. As Piers points out, the labourers

> are my blody breþeren for god bouȝte vs alle;
> Truþe tauȝte me ones to louen hem ech one
> (VI 207–8)

The recognition of the Gospel's demands for Christian fraternalism will become increasingly prominent in the poem, and it had been foreshadowed in Repentance's moving oration.[70] Its social meaning and current potential, however, was far from simple, although John Ball had some challenging views on this. Whatever the difficulties here, Piers has lost confidence in the moral justification of solutions centred on hunger and forced labour. Hunger assures him that justification is available in the distinction between 'Bolde beggeris and bigge' and the impotent, deserving poor (VI 212–28). Yet in mid-stream Hunger seems to shift away from the emphasis on discriminatory and disciplinary charity. He tells Piers to feed and give money to the poor:

> Loue hem and lakke hem noȝt; lat god take þe vengeaunce;
> Theiȝ þei doon yuele lat þow god yworþe.
> (VI 225–6)

This could certainly be read as an abandonment of the punitive surveillance involved in the discriminatory relief from which he had begun, for now even *blame* of the 'undeserving' poor is to be left to God.[71] This wobble makes Piers's reaction open to more than one interpretation as he asks, 'Miȝte I synnelees do as þow seist?' (VI 230). Is he asking whether the solution centred on hunger, forced labour, and discriminatory charity is compatible with Christ's teaching in the Gospels? Or is he questioning the possible shift

Hunger has made from the newer ethos backed by gentry, clerics, parliament, law, and courts? It could well be that Langland himself was uncertain at this stage, an uncertainty he later resolved in the C version by eliminating Hunger's 'wobble'. That revision makes Piers's question unambiguously one about the evangelical authority of Hunger's defence of discriminatory charity and all that goes with that mentality.[72]

Hunger's reply to Piers is, however, clear, and it anticipates the C revisions of his speech. First he invokes God's curse on humanity in the third chapter of Genesis, adding to it. Where the Bible has 'In the sweat of thy face shalt thou eat bread' (3.19), the poem adds 'and swynk . . . And laboure'.[73] Next he uses another part of the Old Testament which contained some useful texts for those seeking Biblical underpinnings to the newer ethos, the 'wisdom' literature we saw FitzRalph using: the idle beggar shall not be relieved (VI 235–7; c.f. Proverbs 20.4). Then, seeking New Testament support he turns the parable of the talents, one that exhorts Christians to make full use of *spiritual* gifts, into a lesson on the divine punishment awaiting those who will not work (VI 238–46).[74] Pursuing his increasingly confident elaboration of the work ethos, Hunger wisely leaves the New Testament and makes the startling claim that,

> The freke þat fedeþ hymself wiþ his feiþful labour
> He is blessed by þe book in body and in soule
> (VI 25–52)

Theologically this seems very crudely Pelagian, but what interests me in the present discussion is the unqualified claim it makes for religious salvation as the reward of productive labour. As striking is the exegesis of 'þe book'. The passage quoted in the next line is Psalm 127.2, 'thou shalt eat the labours of thy hands'; yet it would hardly be more forced to read the Psalm as a verse promising devout Christian peasants that God will deliver them from the class that coercively extracts their labour and produce, thus at last enabling them to 'eat the labours of their hands' – a reading that would be congenial enough to radical Christian preachers like John Ball and to the communities which rose up in 1381 and formulated their demands at Mile End and Smithfield in June 1381. But as Hunger anticipates, *orthodox* Christianity was to continue adapting to the employers' changing needs and ethos, in its moral teaching as in its exegesis.[75]

Langland, however, was sure that whatever texts could be mustered in support of Hunger's doctrine, labourers would continue to resist, rejecting the work ethos propagated by justices of the peace, employers, and orthodox clerics. So he again presents their outlook as one in which work is solely a means to immediate enjoyments. As soon as their arduous labour completes the agricultural year and 'newe corn cam to chepyng' (VI 299), the labourers responses are unreformed and memorably imagined:

> And þo nolde Wastour noȝt werche, but wandred aboute,
> Ne no beggere ete breed þat benes Inne come,
> But Coket or clermatyn or of clene whete,
> Ne noon halfpenny ale in none wise drynke,
> But of þe beste and þe brunneste þat brewsteres selle.
> Laborers þat haue no land to lyue on but hire handes
> Deyneþ noȝt to dyne a day nyȝt olde wortes.
> May no peny ale hem paie, ne no pece of bacoun,
> But if it be fressh flessh ouþer fissh yfryed,
> And þat *chaud* and *plus chaud* for chillynge of hir mawe.
> (VI 302–11)

Once more, people who have been represented as the hardworking essential producers, the 'winners' of society, are reclassified as 'wastours', vagrants, and greedy labourers guilty of demanding 'excessive' wages to support living conditions better than those endured by preceding generations on the margins of survival.[76] The passage deploys the terms in which horrified gentry and clerics perceived working people's increased expectations and assertiveness, as quotations in the first section of this chapter illustrated. Again the poet locates the problems in the contemporary struggles over the price and terms of labour-power. He attributes the source of rebellion to *landless* labourers, that is to the workers most directly dependent on market fluctuations and incentives for their survival, as well as for relatively improved possibilities in the present. These opportunities could only be grasped if working women and men opposed the classes who sought to ensure that their own material privileges and power were not in any way eroded. Oppose them they did, and one should not forget that the poet writes this in the period immediately preceding the rising which involved representatives from 'the whole people below the ranks of those who exercised lordship in the countryside and established authority in the towns':[77]

But he be heiȝliche hyred ellis wole he chide;
That he was werkman wroȝt warie þe tyme.
Ayeins Catons counseil comseþ he to Iangle:
Paupertatis onus pacienter ferre memento;
He greueþ hym ageyn god and gruccheþ ageyn Reson,
And þanne corseþ þe kyng and al þe counseil after
Swiche lawes to loke laborers to chaste.

(VI 312–18)

These 'werkmen' see that what counts as practical 'Reason', labour 'lawes', and social virtue tends to be shaped by the current interests of the ruling classes, a tiny but immensely powerful fraction of the population. To the gentry (lay or ecclesiastic), views such as those expressed by Langland's labourers are not only rank sedition but blasphemous – the powerful have habitually found it difficult to distinguish a threat to their own privileges from a threat to God and all religion.[78] Langland concludes the Passus bemoaning how labourers strive 'ayeins þe statut' and threatening 'yow werkmen' with hunger and apocalyptic vengeance (VI 319–31). Perhaps not surprisingly, neither he nor the gentry see a benevolent divine hand shifting forces in favour of 'Laborers þat haue no land to lyue on but hire handes'!

Before leaving this fascinating Passus, I will offer one further observation. The struggle has been to get the best terms and price for labour-power in current market circumstances, 'But he be heiȝliche hyred ellis wole he chide', a powerful reminder that while we are dealing with a pre-capitalist society it seems to the poet a distinctly market-oriented one. It is appropriate to recollect Rodney Hilton's conclusion to his study of medieval peasant movements and the English rising of 1381: 'the leading social force in medieval peasant movements, even the most radical, seem to have been those elements most in contact with the market, those who in suitable circumstances would become capitalist farmers.'[79] Langland himself consistently identified those in most intimate contact with the market, whether small-scale commodity producers, labourers, or clerics, as forces subverting his idea of a good society. Certainly this market orientation, the employers' work ethos, and the labourers' response were to have a substantial future, and not only in Western Europe.

It is understandable that a writer who wished to support traditional versions of social organization should see market-centred relations and the contemporary practices of wage-labourers as dissolvents of fundamental pieties and forms of life. But there is an irony here. In opposing what he takes to be the subverters of tradition, the poet attacks lower-class reactions to changed circumstances by deploying a work ethos and moralizing vocabulary which is the *employers'* response to these same circumstances; a response designed 'to make the poor pay the costs of the fourteenth-century crisis' in a framework which itself made a rupture with 'tradition'.[80] The development of a self-righteous, moralistic language of attack on working people who resisted employers' rules and current needs was just one element in the development of an ethos that would prove appropriate to early capitalist societies. Little could have been further from Langland's overall values than to contribute to the evolution of such an ethos, yet at this point his poem was coming to do so.

The next Passus opens with a rather enigmatic claim that 'Treuþe' purchased Piers a pardon for himself, his 'heires euermoore after', and all that help his work (VII 1–8). In the contexts, it seems the pardon is at least initially viewed as a reward for work done within the framework of the employers' 'statute' and 'lawes' which Piers sought to uphold in Passus VI. This would be a striking secularization and politicization of pardons, but that is just the kind of effect one might expect from the work ethos pervading the previous Passus. Still, if the first 8 lines are ambiguous, those up to line 106 are not less so. They turn out to be someone's long and enthralling gloss on two lines from the Athanasian creed which are actually shown to be all that is written of the 'pardoun', 'þe bulle' Piers has obtained (VI 9–114).[81] The gloss seeks to conjure up the kind of social and moral order the poet longs for, predictably seeking to reimpose the traditional estates model. The first and second estates are addressed in lines 9–17, the third in lines 18–106. The disproportionate length is a fair indication of the domain most troublesome to the poet's ideology. First he imagines a form of merchant life that he and 'truþe' would be prepared to accept (VII 18–39). Next he tries to figure a legal community free from the encompassing world of the market and totally free from the conflicts over 'lawes' and 'þe statut', formulated by the gentry's lawyers, in Passus VI (VII 40–60).[82] After this he turns to lower-class groups. Those 'laborers þat lyuen by hir hondes' and become the employers' ideal work-force, with 'lowe' hearts and devotion to obedient work, those who reject the contemporary struggles of their communities against 'þe statut' and its beneficiaries, these people are no problem and will apparently receive Christian salvation (VII 62–4). But those classified (by the glossator? the gentry?) as 'Beggeres and bidderes' once again prove extremely vexing. Just as Hunger's lesson on alms in Passus VI (202–52) contained a 'wobble', so the present gloss on 'þe bulle' shows the presence of conflicting ideologies. On the one hand there is the newer Christian ethos which advocates a carefully discriminatory charity. Significantly this is now represented by the *pagan* Cato who advocated careful probing into the motives and means of those seeking material help (VII 72–5). On the other hand is the conflicting tradition represented here by a Christian of impeccable orthodoxy, St Gregory:

> Ac Gregory was a good man and bad vs gyuen alle
> That askeþ for his loue þat vs al leneþ:
> *Non eligas cui miserearis ne forte pretereas illum qui meretur accipere,*
> *Quia incertum est pro quo deo magis placeas.*
> For wite ye neuere who is worþi, ac god woot who haþ nede.
> (VII 76–8)

This is the position represented in the first section of this chapter by Clement of Alexandria, Richard of Maidstone, and *Dives and Pauper*. It is a demand for unconditional charity firmly rooted in Jesus's own unequivocal command, as we saw (e.g., Luke 6.29–30; Matthew 5.42). This assumes a detachment from the will to control and possess that has been habitually marginalized by most Christians, encouraged by convenient glossing of Jesus's hard sayings. Holy Church tells Will, before she disappears:

> The mooste partie of þis peple þat passeþ on þis erþe,
> Haue þei worship in þis world þei kepe no bettre;
> Of ooþer heuene þan here holde þei no tale.
> (I 7–9)

She and the poet should know something about Western Christendom. Now, however, the evangelical demand for unconditional charity was proving not merely uncongenial to 'natural' ('fallen') humanity, a perfectly understandable state of affairs to most of us, including the poet. It was also being crossed by the newer ethos outlined in our first section and exemplified here by the pagan Cato. The gloss soon shifts from the stark evangelical position to the more comfortable gentry and clerical pastime of exhorting labourers to be content with minimal subsistence rations and to enjoy reading saints' lives (VII 84–8). This shift leads into an attack on beggars introduced with the assertion, worthy of FitzRalph, that the Bible 'banneþ beggerie', supported by a line taken from Psalm 36, 'I have been young, and now am old: and I have not seen the just forsaken nor his seed seeking bread'. The exegetical methods here may be essential in shaping Christianity to accommodate the newer ethos, but they are precisely those for which Conscience abused Lady Mede (III 332–53). Had the glosser found 'a konnynge clerk þat kouþe þe leef han torned', he would have found a Psalm celebrating trust in God and the promise of punitive judgement against 'the wicked' who far from being beggars are immensely prosperous. Here, however, all the generosity and modesty called for in the tradition represented by Gregory is brushed aside. Begging is simplified, stereotyped, and assaulted in ways already encountered in the poem and in the first section of the chapter, ways which were to lead an extremely long life in our own culture:

> For þei lyue in no loue ne no lawe holde.
> Thei wedde no womman þat þei wiþ deele
> But as wilde bestes with wehee worþen vppe and werchen,
> And bryngen forþ barnes þat bastardes men calleþ.
>
> (VII 90–3)

The confidence of the description and the moral indignation in the judgement is almost overwhelming as we are invited to see 'beggerie' leading to rampant carnal lust and anarchy. Nevertheless, we should pause to recollect that while many labourers and smallholders were now less likely to suffer hunger than in the thirteenth century, severe rural and urban poverty, hunger, and existence on the margins of survival still abounded, and these people's lives were not helped by the newer ethos. The historian of changing patterns of charity and community in medieval Cambridge makes comments that are relevant to the present context:

> Even in this period when the lot of the labourers was improving, those who lived a precarious existence on the verge of subsistence, the *pauperisables* – workers and their families, dependants, and those unsuitably skilled – were affected by the shift in attitude on the part of those who were employers, and

> who were the traditional givers of charity. Now the poor were not to be helped but to be hunted down and put back to work, or into prison since they had no place within society and did not merit enjoyment of its benefits. They did not only cause a shortage of labour but defied social morality.

Here she cites the C-text version of the lines I have just quoted from the B-text, and goes on to recall some of the hostile, violent legislation against those classified as beggars in late medieval Europe.[83] The relations, however complex, between rhetorical classifications, image-making, demonizing, and the way these can encourage the cruellest forms of inhumanity should not be overlooked. We degrade and kill first in language. Certainly the rhetorical combat the poem takes part in, at this point, is inseparable from the daily conflict being fought out on the roads and markets, in the institutions of law and the stocks, as the massive numbers of surviving indictments under the Statute alone testify.[84]

In the image-making of the gloss's attack on vagrants one can discern yet another source of anxiety, equally social and yet perhaps even deeper for this poet. The suggestion offered here is a response to the poem's claim that these demonic vagrants destroy the nuclear family, already unquestionably traditional amongst the great majority of the population.[85] What could make the writer feel this anxiety in his England? The poet is disturbed by the contrast between traditional peasant households and the family formations of landless, mobile workers. In the former the nuclear family was the unit of primary *production* as well as of consumption. For those living within this family, essential access to the holding – the basic source of subsistence, self-identity, and the very condition of family reproduction – was controlled by marriage and inheritance patterns under parental, normally patriarchal domination. In the latter, the landless family was not a unit of production bound to a family holding. In so far as it was an economic unit, it depended on each individual selling her or his labour-power on the market as an autonomous worker. Under these circumstances traditional parental controls and sanctions were loosened, for the means of subsistence was attained by individual access to the labour-market, not to a family holding. Such changed conditions would lead to changed and more mobile patterns of household formation, among which marriage might become at least possible at earlier ages and undertaken more independently of parental wishes than had been customary. To traditional moralists like Langland such unions among the landless would certainly seem 'beggars' marriages'.[86] The poet's hostility would certainly not be diminished by observing their connections with migrant work and life oriented around the market.

Be that as it may, the attack on vagrant labourers and able-bodied beggars in Passus VII reinforces the denial of any need for more diversified and precise categories than those of bad, big beggars (*wastours*) and good, 'mekeliche' suffering disabled (VII 93–106). It also blocks out awareness of the cruel inadequacies in the accusation that *because* more physical deformity occurs among beggars than other people it *must* simply be the effect of malicious self-injury (VII 93–7). The tradition represented by Gregory in Passus VII is submerged in the ethos expressed by the non-Christian Cato. This, despite the 'wobbles' I have emphasized, seems the *dominant* tendency of Passus VI and VII. Langland's versions of work, the poor, and the good community had been seriously affected by the newer ethos.

There has, with good reason, been considerable commentary on Langland's attitudes to the friars, Adams actually identifying his position very closely with that of William of St Amour and FitzRalph.[87] But it is striking that just when Langland is elaborating his assault on vagrant labourers or able-bodied mendicants he does not launch one of his many attacks on the lives of contemporary friars, let alone develop a critique of their theological foundations. No William of St Amour or FitzRalph would have resisted such an opportunity. He could have introduced a friar to represent traditional defences of mendicancy and alms-giving to able-bodied beggars, thus linking official voluntary poverty with able-bodied 'wastours' and demonic beggars. He would not be brushing historical developments against the grain. But Langland did nothing of the sort. Instead he did something antithetical.

He began a dramatic disengagement from the newer ethos and the attempt to give it religious sanctifications, the attempt to make Jesus speak the language of the vagrancy petition, of the newer positions on poverty, beggary, and the able-bodied poor. A priest appears wanting to read the pardon itself. However unsympathetic a figure, however motivated by the wish to defend clerical monopolies, his scepticism towards the long gloss allegedly contained in 'þe bulle' forces the poem towards new perspectives. The status of the gloss becomes completely uncertain as it disappears before two extremely generalized lines from the creed – salvation for those who 'do wel', damnation for those who 'do yuel' (VII 109–18). The priest's intervention stimulates a startling transformation in the ploughman's outlook and a major rupture with the dominant tendencies of Passus VI and VII which we have been analysing. Quoting from Psalm 23 to affirm his trust in divine providence, he tears up 'þe bulle':

> 'I shal cessen of my sowyng', quod Piers, '& swynke noȝt so harde
> Ne aboute my bilyue [bely ioye] so bisy be na moore;
> Of preieres and of penaunce my plouȝ shal ben herafter,
> And wepen whan I sholde werche þouȝ whete breed me faille.'[88]
> (VII 122–5)

Clearly the transformation is a religious conversion forcing an abandonment of attempts to equate the work ethos, now so favoured by employers and their clerical allies, with Christian moral theory and faith.[89] In justification of this change the ploughman invokes Jesus's own denunciation of any form of work ethic, so memorably elaborated in Luke 12 (22–31) and Matthew 6 (25–34):

> And but if luc lye he lereþ vs anoþer
> By foweles þat are noȝt bisy aboute þe bely ioye;
> *Ne soliciti sitis* he seiþ in þe gospel
> And sheweþ vs by ensample vs selue to wisse.
> The foweles in þe firmament, who fynt hem at wynter?
> Whan þe frost freseþ fode hem bihoueþ;
> Haue þei no gerner to go to but god fynt hem alle.
> (VII 129–35)

These lines, taken up in Passus XIV, are not only a generalized upgrading of the contemplative life, an aspect often discussed by scholars. In context they are a decisive retreat from the dominant tendency in the ethos of the previous two Passus. The terms of *that* tendency would positively encourage the followers of Jesus's teaching to be charged with familiar accusations: 'wastours', 'able-bodied beggars', 'scroungers'. It would encourage commentators with FitzRalph's sympathies to recall arguments that renunciation of dominion and possession is the cause of more 'solicitude' rather than less. It could even provoke a counter-exegesis of the relevant Gospel texts designed to make them more congruent with the newer ethos, the kind of exegesis we earlier noted in FitzRalph. An example of how this could be done here is offered by the late medieval preacher Geiler who claims that the hard, utopian words of Jesus, cited by Piers in the passage just quoted, are actually an *attack* on the idle who will not work. He arrives at this stunning interpretation by saying that the birds of the air do all in their power to get food from early morning onwards, and that Jesus is telling men to do likewise, that is to work hard.[90] Far from resorting to such exegetical stratagems, Piers lets Jesus's text stand against his own previous approach, and, as his development in the poem conveys plainly enough, his creator blessed this move, whatever fresh problems that might make. He did so, in my view, because he grasped that the dominant tendency of Passus V–VII would promote an ethos in which productive work and the employers' imposition of labour discipline (in their own material interests) was becoming the official goal and informing end of human existence.[91] His own wish to defend traditional theory in changed communities was gathering consequences he could not accept. These Passus had perhaps suggested to him how the much abused wage-labourers, wasters, or vagrants and those who fought against them, the hiring, wage-fixing employers and legislators, actually cultivated the same terrain, actually constituted a diabolic unity destroying the social model and morality Langland wished to perpetuate and impose. Piers's and Langland's retreat is thoroughly intelligible and, with perhaps a few inconsistencies, sustained for the rest of the poem.

The disengagement from the prevailing ethos of Passus V–VII, from the attitudes expressed in the Statute and vagrancy petition, leads to changed perceptions of poverty, the poor, and work. These we shall now explore. Certainly the disengagement did not entail an abandonment of preoccupations with the practices of contemporary communities and social morality – nor did his intense concern with theological problems, nor his increasing focus on Christ and salvation history. He remains a poet of history and incarnation (not of some individualistic mystical journey of the alone to union with the alone), the poet of a 'creatour weex creature', one who took 'Adames kynde' to learn the feel of human experience, 'To wite what all wo is þat woot of alle ioye', one for whom the only irrevocably fatal sin finally seems to be 'vnkyndenesse' within one's own community (XIV 215; XVIII 222–5; XVII 254–60).

Passus IX emerges from the poet's search to discover how the good life might be led in his own world, 'How dowel, dobet and dobest doon among þe peple' (VIII 114). He comes to contrast mutual help and human solidarity in Jewish communities with the 'vnkyndenesse' he finds in the contemporary Christian 'commune' (IX 66–96). It is hardly surprising that this consideration should raise issues we have been following in earlier Passus. Having observed that clerical misuse of ecclesiastical wealth, '*patrimonium christi*', deprives the poor, 'þe beggere', he returns to the material reproduction of communities. Here the basic unit of production is represented as the family, 'trewe wedded libbynge folk' who must 'werche and wynne and þe world sustene', as well as perpetuating the species (IX 110–20). This traditional model of a world resting on landholding peasant family units is immediately contrasted with a group of figures so prominent earlier in the poem, the dreaded 'wastours', those who 'Wandren as wolues and wasten' (IX 121–2, 198). Here, however, the poet shifts his diagnosis of the problem. What turns 'werkmen' into 'wastours' and vagrants is no longer simply identified with opposition to the employers' laws and work ethos. Rather these figures are now seen as the product of a breakdown in the traditional family unit – an anxiety we found in Passus VII and discussed above. They are, allegedly, what they are because they have been born 'out of wedlok' or into what seem disordered marriages, to a traditional moralist (IX 121–33, 195–201). If the traditional family unit was collapsing (what a long and politically charged life this story has had), then wage freezes, labour legislation and the employers' work ethos would hardly be sufficient remedy.

If Passus IX shifts the main diagnosis of 'wastours' and vagrants, does it offer any explanation for this apparent disintegration of traditional family formations? It does. The trouble, Langland maintains, is that these days marriage is dominated by the market, a view shared by many contemporaries and perfectly compatible with his vision of English communities throughout the poem.[92] So working harder within the framework provided by the market would merely exacerbate the trends the poet disapproves. An ironic commentary on the failed solutions of Passus VI. As for work totally independent of market transactions, this was already becoming the object of nostalgic fantasy, of myth, as his own poem suggests with great force.[93]

Fresh perspectives such as these certainly reinforced Piers's conversion, but they also prompted another look at the place of the knightly class in the vision of Christian community the poet is still trying to compose. In Passus VI it was represented as unambiguously benevolent but powerless to enforce 'þe lawe' and 'þe statut' against assertive labourers. Passus X, however, displays the gentry as themselves an incorrigible part of the basic problems (X 13–116). Drawing on traditional clerical criticism of upper-class 'vices', the poet implies that the only difference between these people and the 'wastours' he found in ale houses is the scale of the former's 'gaynesse and glotonye', enabled by the 'rentes' they extract from the peasantry.[94] Worst of all, this privileged group is apparently the 'moost vnkynde', the least charitable to the poor and to beggars. Piers's transformation enables the poet to see the people who moralize so indignantly about greedy labourers, exemplified in the Statute and vagrancy petition, as those who 'welden þe welþe of þis worlde' and yet reject the traditional demands of a Gregorian charity in alms-giving, refusing to be 'plenteouse to þe pouere as pure charite wolde' (X 24, 83–7). Movingly, he now comments: 'Ne were mercy in meene men moore þan in riche/Mendinaunt3 metelees my3te go to bedde' (X 65–6). No anxiety about discriminatory tests and disciplinary charity can be detected here, any more than in Scripture's insistence that love and generosity must be shown in social practice, 'in commune' (X 357–63). Unless it is so fulfilled:

> It shal bisitten vs ful soure þe siluer þat we kepen,
> And our bakkes þat moþeeten be and seen beggeris go naked,
> Or delit in wyn and wildefowel and wite any in defaute.
> For euery cristene creature sholde be kynde til ooþer.
> (X 365–8)

The effects of Piers's conversion, inseparably religious and social, are clear. Whatever resistances they encounter, even from the poet's self-projection, they now pervade the visions.[95]

They are forcefully present in Will's recovery from his collapse into a despairing hedonism in Passus XI. Scripture's views on charity are reaffirmed by Trajan, and saving love is identified with indiscriminate giving in the individual's community (XI 171–84). The newer ethos whose marks were stamped into the poem, is again challenged as the poet increasingly stresses the unity of Christ and the poor. They now become the special images of Christ, in the present:

> For oure Ioye and oure Iuel, Iesu crist of heuene,
> In a pouere mannes apparaille pursueþ vs euere,
> And lokeþ on vs in hir liknesse and þat wiþ louely chere
> To knowen vs by oure kynde herte and castynge of oure eiȝen,
> Wheiþer we loue þe lordes here bifore þe lord of blisse
>
> (XI 185–9)

The verbs' tense here fuses time past and time present in a way which demands the contemporary application of evangelical perspectives. As Jesus's voice intervenes, 'for the pouere I shall paie' (XI 195–6), we should not miss either its cultural resonance in the debate on poverty, or the presence of the Last Judgement in the form given in Matthew 25.34–7. It now seems that Christian community entails a fraternalism which calls unceasingly for unconditional generosity and the recognition that the Christ who travelled about in 'pouere apparaill' has often been met and is still present 'in þe apparaille of a pouere man', but not, apparently, in the employing classes and their ethos (XI 199–278). The poet reinterprets the story of Martha and Mary, turning it from its conventional exegesis as an allegory of the superiority of the contemplative life to one showing poverty as the highest state (XI 250–8). Contrary to William of St Amour, John XXII, and their followers it is affirmed that poverty, and abandonment of possessions by those who have them, *does* nourish freedom from anxious attachment to things, helping people annihilate the selfhood which shuts them from their 'kynde'.[96] The poem's support of Piers's conversion at the close of Passus VII thus flourishes.

Yet Langland decided to organize an encounter between this evangelical, utopian line of development and what now poses in his culture as common sense, a practical work-oriented alternative. So he invents the memorable figure of Haukyn to represent the latter. A follower of the *earlier* Piers, he is an advocate of hard productive labour and its exaltation. He hates all 'ydelnesse' and produces commodities essential to the community, earning his livelihood in the sweat of his face as 'Genesis þe geaunt' had commanded in Passus VI. He is an impressive representative of the work ethos without which there would be, he assures us, 'a careful commune'.[97] The poet, however, sees differently. He shows his readers how this ethos is now inextricably bound up with market energies that subvert the traditional models of community and morality he wishes to affirm. It now even seems a graver threat than the lower-class resistance which had preoccupied the sixth Passus, a view which the end of Passus XIX will confirm.[98] What Langland evokes is the way a culture of work zealously oriented around a dynamic market creates new desires, transforms 'kynde', and positively encourages behaviour which has traditionally been viewed as sin, as 'vnkynde', as 'cruwel'.[99] Because the poet believes he is dealing with pervasive tendencies in his culture, it makes excellent sense that Haukyn should not only figure forth small-scale commodity producers and traders. He also represents substantial merchants involved in overseas trade, these powerful members of urban oligarchies, and bold, migrant, mendicant minstrels, like the figure of the poet.[100] Whether small-scale or grand, the consequences are an aggressive individualism in which the person's sense of identity is as one 'singuler by hymself', 'an order by hymself'.[101] These are cultural forces the poet opposes, however deeply he and his own work are affected by them. The task he sets himself is to imagine their conversion, to persuade Haukyn to follow the path of Piers.

He therefore has Patience quote the evangelical texts informing Piers's conversion, assuring Haukyn that to abandon the work ethic, even 'pouȝ no plouȝ erye', will be liberating (XIV 29–33; compare VII 122–35). Perhaps thinking about the current labour legislation, certainly secure in his own culture of discourse, Haukyn laughs at this teaching, promising that whoever followed it would be far from blessed, a view that FitzRalph, vagrancy petitioners and many others would share (XIV 34–5). It is perfectly cogent that Haukyn, in these contexts, goes on to ask whether 'richesse riȝtfulliche wonne and resonably despended' are not more pleasing to God than even 'paciente pouerte' (XIV 102–3).

To this challenging antagonist Langland's responses are shrewd. He has not forgotten, as Haukyn suspects, that people starve to death, that though they certainly do not live by bread alone they do not live without it (compare I 14–26). He now argues that the real source of devastating material deprivation is 'vnkyndenesse' and lack of 'mesure' in the community (XIV 71–3). Contrary to current views, so powerfully represented by Haukyn, the work ethos is no solution. On the contrary, the poem has claimed, in present society it fosters boundless desires which rupture the webs of community. The effect of famine is thus grounded in the structure and ethos of the community, as its differential attack along lines of economic class plainly confirms. In its own idiom, the poem asserts against Haukyn, that economic growth will not in itself even eliminate poverty, let alone create anything Langland could recognize as a just community. Not only has the poet decided that the hard sayings of Jesus on wealth and poverty must be reasserted in the face of their current marginalization or exegetical evaporation, but that their practical relevance to contemporary communities should be appreciated. We can see just why Patience greeted Haukyn's resistant question about the benefits of 'richesse riȝtfulliche wonne and resonably despended' with such hilarity: 'Ye? *quis est ille*? . . . quik, *laudabimus eum*!' (XIV 102–4). Inexorably the argument insists that the greatest impediment both to a community in which *kyndenesse* will flourish and to salvation is 'richesse', the 'riche', and the very ethos Haukyn embodies (XIV 104ff.). The way forward is for communities to be 'in commune riche, noon coueitous for hymselue' (XIV 201).

What then of the spectre of vagrant labourers and able-bodied beggars striding through Passus VI–VII and the Prologue? They have not vanished from the poem but are viewed in a rather different light. A 'beggeris bagge' is now contrasted with 'Almaries and yren bounden cofres', the recalcitrant labourers' lack of means and will to accumulate wealth contrasted with those who have the wealth and power to exploit market relations, legal institutions, and the labour of others. The social typology of mortal sinners is revised.[102] In this revision, there can be no space for outlooks fostered or legitimated by the newer ethos outlined in our first section and seen pressing its way even into *Piers Plowman*.

Striving to convert Haukyn, and all he stands for, the poet returns to the unity of Christ and the poor, the very hallmark of a tradition we have seen under threat in the later Middle Ages. This theme stimulates some extremely powerful writing which can be represented by the following passage:

For muche murþe is amonges riche, as in mete and cloþyng . . .
Ac beggeris aboute Midsomer bredlees þei soupe,
And yet is wynter for hem worse, for weetshoed þei gange,
Afurst soore and afyngred, and foule yrebuked
And arated of riche men þat ruþe is to here.
Now, lord, sende hem somer, and som maner ioye
(XIV 157, 160–4)

There are a number of memorable statements of this kind between Passus X and XV, attributed to different speakers and all carrying the commitment of the poet's full sympathy.[103] Without any sentimentalization they all force readers to shift outside the ethos in which able-bodied vagrants are swiftly classified as drunken scroungers, drones, wasters. Such poetry evokes the physical state of miserable poverty with sharp specificity, as it does the stigmatization to which its victims were increasingly subject. He himself joined with employers and 'foule yrebuked/And arated' the itinerant poor, but passages like the one just quoted overwhelm the poem's contribution to the iconology of what was still an emerging ethos.[104] It is worth recalling when St Francis found a friar abusing an 'idle beggar who had asked for alms' he insisted that anyone 'who curses a poor man, does an injury to Christ, because he bears the noble sign of him who made himself poor for us in this world'.[105] It is precisely this vision Langland is affirming. In the midst of his emblems of deadly sin, he now insists that even the slothful, idle poor person, 'bereþ þe signe of pouerte/And in þat secte oure saueour saued al mankynde' (XIV 254–9). He also reiterates that the closest follower of Christ (*contra* William of St Amour, John XXII, FitzRalph, and others) is the person who abandons possessions, 'And for goddes loue leueþ al and lyueþ as a beggere', one:

> þat possession forsakeþ
> And put hym to be pacient and pouerte weddeþ,
> The which is sib to god hymself, so neiȝ is pouerte.
> (XIV 264, 271–4)

The speaker here is Patience and is certainly not subjected to critical undermining by the poet. On the contrary, the view has emerged through different voices, is rooted in Piers's conversion, and comes to dominate the poem's vision. In this passage, as some commentators have noted, the poet actually seems to recall St Francis's marriage to holy poverty as the expression of the deepest form of Christian piety.[106]

Could such arguments and such visions shape human history, nourish the reformation of communities and their individuals? Could they check the forces of market energies so powerfully figured in the poem, check the emergence of newer ideologies which would legitimate these forces, and drive evangelical attitudes to charity, poverty, and the poor into the wilderness? In Haukyn's moving response at the end of Passus XIV, his sorrow and the signs of conversion, the poem answers these questions affirmatively. This is a utopian act of great faith but far from the individualistic and ultimately desperate fideism that closed Passus X and led into the temporary abandonment of moral questions in despair at the beginning of Passus XI. Here the faith has come through the long processes of debate and contradictory image-making we have been following and tries not to ignore the webs of relationships that constitute human communities. The poet has sought to join evangelical teaching on poverty with his own concepts and images of *kyndenesse* and a Christian fraternity where all are 'in commune riche', all 'breþeren as of oo blood' (XIV 202; XI 200). Piers's conversion is confirmed, its meanings, including its social meanings, unfolded. There is to be no sustained return to the newer ethos behind the break at the close of Passus VII.[107]

Here it may be asked whether the controversial figure of Need opposes the developments I have been describing.[108] In my view, it does not: the figure confirms Langland's rejection of the newer ethos that had threatened to assimilate his ploughman's vision, his own, and the active life itself, Haukyn. At the opening of Passus XX the poet is still travelling:

> Heuy chered I yede and elenge in herte.
> I ne wiste wher to ete ne at what place,
> And it neghed neiȝ þe noon and wiþ nede I mette
> (XX 2–4)

He is still the poet who declared earlier, 'forþ gan I walke/In manere of a mendynaunt many yer after' (XIII 1–2), still the man whose form of life 'fewe' could allow (XV 4–10), the figure around whose life a haunting debate is added in the C-version of the poem (V 1–108). However deep the anxiety about this form of life and its place in the poet's favoured social model, one aspect should be made clear, as it is in the C-version. There the poet tells Reason 'y begge/Withoute bagge or botel but my wombe one' (V 51–2), aligning his life with those who reject all forms of accumulation and organized self-protection.[109] Whether it turns out to be licit or not in his culture it has, at least, some vital signs of a genuine acceptance of the renunciations made by Piers in the pursuit of evangelic poverty. As for the judgement of such signs, we have learnt the 'wil' in which charity resides is finally known only by 'Piers þe Plowman, *Petrus id est Christus'* (XV 209–12). Furthermore, the lines quoted above from Passus XX confirm that the poet's vagrancy is the sort that leads to 'nede'. When the poet describes his hunger as he meets 'nede' we should remember an earlier passage:

> And in þe apparaille of a pouere man and pilgrymes liknesse
> Many tyme god haþ ben met among nedy peple
> Ther neuere segge hym seiȝ in secte of þe riche.
>
> (XI 243–5)

Only a very rash reader would now sit in judgement on the figure of the 'nedy' poet, 'in þe apparaille of a pouere man', so choosing to ignore not only the prevailing vision of the poem but also the poet's own anxious self-criticism.

Need, in fact, berates the poet (the dreamer, 'Will', the complex projection of William Langland) for feeling such shame at his voluntary dedication to a mendicant pursuit of religious understanding in preference to a conventional form of work and life, whether manual or nonmanual. His shame, not surprisingly, is based on hostile attitudes to able-bodied vagrants and so-called 'wastours', ones he appreciated only too well. Langland now uses Need to reaffirm the *rights* of those in need, in contrast to the newer ethos which, as we have observed, advocated a discriminatory and punitive poor relief as a component of labour discipline, rather than part of the pursuit of an evangelical life.[110] Even in Need's irritated speech, however, there is nothing that could be judged as self-indulgence or abuse of others' kindness by anyone who has not completely internalized the newer outlook figured forth and decisively rejected by *Piers Plowman*. The legitimate rights in question, Need emphasizes, are to the necessities for physical survival disciplined by temperance.[111] The defence Need offers is actually part of the major strands of the poem we have discussed in this chapter. They are quite contrary to the views of William of St Amour and FitzRalph, and to the emerging common sense of Western culture, which will doubtless be moved to laughter or incredulity with the unconverted Haukyn. But they are quite congruent with Franciscan perspectives (XX 35–50). Once more God in Christ is identified with the 'nedy', the contemporary 'nedy' poor with Christ, and the most devotedly Christian form of life is voluntary poverty, the deliberate decision 'to be nedy': 'Siþ he þat wroȝte al þe world was wilfulliche nedy,/Ne neuere noon so nedy ne pouerer deide' (XX 48–50).

This voluntary poverty, so prominent from Passus XI through to XVIII, is both theological, the self-emptying of the deity in mysteriously generous identification with humanity, and social, the divine identification with the dispossessed. This, in turn, has implications for moral theory and practice in historical communities. We recall, for example, that even the slothful poor 'bereþ þe signe of pouerte/And in þat secte oure saueour saued al mankynde', much more so the voluntarily poor who 'for goddes loue leueþ al and lyueþ as a beggere' (XIV 258–64). Need has ample precedence within the poem to reassure the needy poet that there is indeed some justification for his own peculiar life, so long as he takes no more than he needs for survival – following the ascetic path of St Francis.

It is in its own contexts that one must read the statement, 'nede haþ no lawe' (XX 10). Provocative as it may be in a world where the 'newer' ethos became the dominant one, in itself it was traditional enough. As *Dives and Pauper* observes, 'it is a general reule in þe lawe þat nede hat no lawe' (citing as an example the actions of the disciples in Matthew 12.1–4). As for laws concerning property, they are suspended: 'in gret myschef, nede excusiþ hym from þefte & fro synne ȝif he do it only for nede & nout for couetyse.' In the writer's tradition, 'in grete nede alle þing is comoun'. This is not as challenging as Patience's demand, 'cristene sholde be in commune riche' (XIV 202), but still too challenging to survive in the mainstream of the capitalist world's elaboration of the newer ethos.[112] To this older Christian tradition Langland's Need belongs, the 'family resemblance' with the view in *Dives and Pauper* plain enough. Its quite distinct dramatic, theological, and social depth, the disturbing quality of its energetic reproach to the poet's guilt and anxiety, these are the products of its particular place in *Piers Plowman*, that extraordinary exploration of so many conflicting forces in its culture.

This consideration of the controversial figure of Need gives us one of the numerous perspectives from which to assess Langland's criticism of the friars and his final suggestions about their future. Instead of collapsing Langland into FitzRalph or William of St Amour, we should give full weight to his exaltation of voluntary poverty, his celebration of the poor Christ, and to shifts in the poem's treatment of able-bodied beggars. This will help us see how the late medieval friars are attacked from a stance which is very different from John XXII's or FitzRalph's, however many particular complaints about specific abuses are common to Langland and a satiric anti-mendicant tradition with roots in William of St Amour and Jeun de Meun's part of the *Romance of the Rose*.[113] They are *not* attacked for following a mistaken ideal or for misunderstanding the nature of Christ's life or orthodox Christian doctrine or the respective merits of poverty (voluntary or involuntary), riches, alms-giving, or dominion. Far from it, the prevailing line of criticism after Piers's conversion, as Skeat long ago noted, is that they are apostates to the traditional valuation of absolute voluntary poverty in the pursuit of holiness through imitating Christ's life.[114] Need, returning later in the Passus, summarizes Langland's vision of contemporary friars in the very midst of its final representation:

Nede neghede þo neer and Conscience he tolde
That þei come for coueitise, to haue cure of soules.
And for þei are pouere, parauenture, for patrymonye hem failleþ,
They wol flatere to fare wel folk þat ben riche.

(XX 232–5)

Throughout *Piers Plowman* friars have been treated as especially distressing symptoms of religion's immersion in the nexus of lordship, patronage, worldly power, and the market, with even the sacraments becoming commodities.[115] Need's mockery in the following lines is within the terms of this framework, an attack not against voluntary poverty but against these people's travesty of it, a sarcastic reminder of the ideals of their founders, ones cherished by the author (XX 236–41). It is in line with this that Conscience too invokes St Francis and St Dominic, abandoning dominion: 'For loue lafte þei lordshipe, boþe lond and scole' (XX 251–2). The bitterly gamesome stance of Need, with Conscience's milder exhortation, has the support of the poem's most emphatic developments since Piers's conversion.

The twentieth Passus, however, shows that its maker did not finally believe that either mockery or encouraging exhortation and instruction were sufficient to the present circumstances. The friars, he dramatized at some length, would not withstand the current cultural forces the poet wished to resist. He had to acknowledge that in his own world the ideas of St Francis seemed more and more hopelessly anachronistic. The vision of the pauper Christ, present in the contemporary poor, however mobile or 'slothful', was waning and even directly challenged from a number of directions, including from within those officially committed to it.[116] Langland's own solution to a contemporary reality he found so uncongenial and so intractable is a *compromise*. In the spirit of compromise he advocates that modern friars be given 'a fyndyng' (XX 383). This, he claims, might dissuade them from treating the sacrament of penance as a commodity for exchange in the market. The point about the 'fyndyng' is that contemporary friars apparently do not have the commitment to endure genuine poverty with the rigours of an imitation of Christ and St Francis which would involve destitution, 'need'. The final Passus shows that for them, in the poet's view, need works just as William of St Amour and others claimed, aggrandizing instead of annihilating selfhood and its anxieties. The solution now put forward is thus very far from ideal for Langland but the best he finds possible within the apparently prevailing forces of his culture. The only way forward at the end of the poem, with the collapse of those who carry the traditions of St Francis and of the clerisy as a whole, is to continue the wandering search for Piers Plowman and Grace outside the now enchanted official 'chirche' (XX 294–386). The implications of this conclusion for orthodox Catholic assumptions and pieties are, in my view, profoundly subversive, a view that will remain unpalatable to some but whose grounds the poem has made clear.[117] Here, however, I wish to conclude with some considerations closer to the concerns of the present chapter.

Piers Plowman actually conveys the doomed, anachronistic nature of the neo-Franciscan ethos it cherishes. The conclusion we have just been discussing is a particularly sharp example of this, while its position at the end of the long poetic search gives it added weight. So, perhaps, does its alignment with the end of the poet's life, at least in his moving self-projection (XX 183–202). But some important and recurring evasions also contribute to this effect. Langland's revitalization of a traditional ethos towards the poor, poverty, and related issues, together with his commitment to traditional versions of community, is accomplished with great poetic power and scope. Yet it continually dissolves the drastic social and economic problems his poem continually returns to, problems so disturbing to his contemporaries, himself, and indeed to *Piers Plowman*. Elsewhere I have illustrated this process from the treatment of patient poverty in Passus XIV and XV.[118] There is neither need nor space to go over that material again, and the relevant point here is that Langland's passionate recreation of traditional and neo-Franciscan perspectives in this part of the poem constantly leads to an imaginative *withdrawal* from the field of material production at the basis of all human spiritual life as of all human relations.

Within the terms and preoccupations of a prophetic, self-consciously reforming poem like this one, such withdrawal is not a mark of consummate 'faith' but of evasion. And perhaps evasion is the very opposite of faith, whether in religious or secular domains. The poet does figure forth all that he opposes in the market and the work ethos, showing its ultimate incompatibility with evangelic traditions; he does come to exalt voluntary poverty, the itinerant poor, and the image of Christ in even the 'slothful' poor; and he does convert Haukyn. But he cannot imagine an alternative social and ecclesiastical order to the dynamic, mobile, market society and culture he realizes so impressively in *Piers Plowman*. True enough, he tries again and again to develop a version of Christian community around the concepts of *kyndenesse* and fraternity. He even has Christ himself present these terms in Passus XVII and XVIII: salvation depends on eschewing 'vnkyndenesse', acknowledging *in practice* how 'we beþ breþeren of blood' depending ultimately on Christ's own refusal to be 'vnkynde' to those who through his incarnation have become his 'kynde', his 'breþeren'.[119] The vision is a stirring affirmation of human solidarity, one whose survival now seems bound up with the very survival of the earth and its people.

Nevertheless it does not seem grudging to ask again what sense of community the poem is able to imagine, to ask how these values of *kyndenesse* and fraternity are to be sustained in his culture, indeed, to ask what they entail. For example, does Christian fraternal kindness mean freeing villeins from traditional forms of bondage which took 50 per cent of their produce? Does it mean supporting the demands of peasant communities and labourers formalized at Smithfield and Mile End in June 1381? There is every reason to believe that Langland answered 'certainly not' to such pressing *contemporary* questions. Unlike so many peasants, he simply takes it for granted that no 'cherl' should be allowed to make a 'chartre' to sell his 'chatel/Wiþouten leue of his lord', nor be free to leave the manor of his lord (XI 127–30). Neither he nor Piers envisage the end of serfdom that 'bondemen' and economic forces were urging.[120] Does Christian fraternal kindness mean allowing working people to use current economic opportunities and migration to raise their levels of subsistence above customary margins of survival? Again, there is no doubt that Langland answers 'certainly not'. Yet from these concepts and hints that at least ideally fraternity demands that 'cristene sholde be in commune riche' (XIV 202), very different social meanings can be drawn. In Froissart's famous account of John Ball's preaching, 'wherefore many of the mean people loved him', we also find a version of fraternity and some views about how to create the basis for kindness in the community:

> the matters goeth not well to pass in England nor shall do till everything be common, and that there be no villains nor gentlemen, but that we may be all united together [*tout-unis*] and that the lords be no greater masters than we be. What have we deserved, or why should we be kept thus in servage? We be all come from one father and mother, Adam and Eve: whereby can they say or shew that they be greater lords than we be, saving by that they cause us to win and labour for that they dispend? They are clothed in velvet and camlet furred with grise, and we be vestured with poor cloth: they have their wines, spices and good bread, and we have the drawing out of chaff and drink water: they dwell in fair houses, and we have the pain and travail, rain and wind in the fields; and by that cometh of our labours they keep and maintain their estates . . . if we go together, all manner of people that be now in any bondage will follow us to the intent to be made free; and when the king seeth us, we shall have some remedy.[121]

Walsingham's account of Ball's preaching, if more violent, highlights the same fraternal vision and some of the same demands which emerged in more practical terms in and around London in 1381.[122] One can see how powerful elements in *Piers Plowman* could well attract radical Christians in Langland's England, however shocking this has proved to scholars and probably to the poet himself. This is obviously not to say that the use of *Piers Plowman* in the enigmatic letters emerging from the rising represent reliable exegesis of the poem.[123] The point is that such reception, and what it discloses about the heterogeneous contexts of *Piers Plowman*, suggest how the articulation of kindness and fraternity are left far too vague to fulfil the role they are given in the poem's version of desirable community. For in the case of these terms Langland has written as though the deep social and ideological conflicts the poem addresses can be set aside. Here he *assumes* that a historical community with a common project exists, a common project with a shared teleology which enables a common vocabulary with a common meaning. But this was just not so in his society, as his own poem grasps so tellingly and often so despairingly. The cost of evading these unpleasant realities was to make the key terms of community as appropriate to the radical Christian framework of a John Ball as to the enraged abuse of the allegedly demonic peasantry and labourers in Gower's *Vox Clamantis*. Undecidability is not always a writer's highest achievement, as Langland himself would agree.

It should be emphasized that the emptiness in the terms 'kindness' and 'fraternity' is not at all the product of aesthetic deficiencies. On the contrary, I have pointed to the poetic and emotional power with which the terms are endowed. It is rather a product of dislocations, deep changes, and conflicts in post-plague English society, marked as it was by unprecedented mobility. These changes were experienced very differently in Langland's society: what to many peasants and labourers was beneficial, liberating, a Godsend, to gentry and clerical allies was malevolent, anarchic, and satanic. The notion of common profit was as profoundly contested as was the title to being the 'true' commons of England. In such circumstances even the greatest act of will and the most benevolent sentiments cannot create a common project – even the practical meaning of 'benevolence' will become contested, as the story of alms-giving and charity illustrates so well.

These are the contexts which account for the emptiness in Langland's key terms. It seems to me thoroughly symptomatic that he turned his back on one of the most prominent uses of the vocabulary of 'fraternity' in his society – the craft and religious *fraternities* which so multiplied and flourished in late medieval England.[124] Why did he do so? The answer seems to be that fraternities brought out something else that Langland's own usage of the term is designed to dissolve. Namely, that the solidarity and community offered by fraternities was not only a reassuring extension of the bonds of family and kin, nor only a much-needed substitute in the face of the greatly increased mortality and mobility of the plague years.[125] It was also part of a system in which the existence of most brotherhoods was bound up with principles of *exclusion* and competitive display. In a brilliant discussion of 'Ritual, drama and social body in the late medieval English town', Mervyn James notes that images of society as a body, 'were in historical fact projected by societies which were deeply divided – riven by intense competitiveness: by the struggle for honour and worship, status and precedence, power and wealth'. His exemplification of competition between craft fraternities leading to riots, law-suits, and bloodshed, sometimes accompanying the Corpus Christi processions and plays themselves, may sound strange to certain ears.[126] But those who strive to understand something of the social and economic realities of Langland's England, rather than substituting for it clerical ideology, homilies, and the texts of rituals, will see the representative nature of James's materials. One should not need the witness of the French Revolution to understand that Fraternity is capable of social meanings quite the opposite to the benevolent generalities Langland ascribes to it.[127] The poet did indeed have Grace in the apostolic Church teaching, 'eche a craft loue ooþer,/Ne no boost ne debat be among hem alle' (XIX 250–1); this is a utopian negation of the present world where the poet has to separate his language of 'fraternity' from actually existing 'fraternities' – at the grave cost of social and ethical emptiness, or, at best, a plangent anachronism.

As the poem abandons its final attempt to imagine the continuation of a Christian community modelled on apostolic principles (XIX–XX) the poet himself acknowledges how the social world which stimulated his dogged and passionate explorations negates his traditional categories. The negation, explicitly, is at all social levels and involves both laity and ecclesiastics. Its gist may be exemplified by a memorable and aggressive challenge to Conscience who is attempting to follow the traditional teaching of Grace and Piers:

> 'Ye? baw!' quod a Brewere, 'I wol noȝt be ruled,
> By Iesu! for al youre Ianglynge, with *Spiritus Iusticie*,
> Ne after Conscience, by crist! while I kan selle
> Boþe dregges and draf and drawe at oon hole
> Thikke ale and þynne ale; þat is my kynde
> And noȝt hakke after holynesse
>
> (XIX 396–400)

The brewer, one of those many small-scale commodity-producers so troubling to Langland throughout his poem, returns us to the unconverted Haukyn and to the world of 'Rose þe Regrater', breweress and huckster (V 217–25). Rose has recently been considered with cases in contemporary court records, showing how they and their fictional analogue are part of a late medieval world 'dominated by petty production', in which petty retail traders were important and common: 'Langland's world was not a world of low life, but of normality.'[128] To have such an image of current 'normality' at the end of Passus XIX seems far more shocking than receiving it as an emblem of deadly sin in Passus V. For since then the poem has elaborated its version of kindness, fraternity, and the exemplary life of Christ, allegedly securing at least the recognition of kindness and fraternity as crucial values among Christians. Nor does the poet again turn away from the 'normality' the brewer represents, one in which, as the 'lewed' vicar observes, value and action is determined by 'wynnyng' (XIX 451–3).[129] This emerging normality was to prove quite as intractable to the revolutionary version of fraternity articulated by John Ball as to that in the poet's more traditional conservatism – hardly any consolation for Langland.

But then let us very briefly consider his self-projection in the poem – vagrant, immensely mobile, poet, dreamer, minor cleric, figure of Will.[130] It most starkly emphasizes the *lack* of fraternal bonds and the *lack* of a traditional community in which the 'I' would have a stable place in a stable web of relationships. This isolated figure is continually criticized in the poem, and frequently moralized against by scholars. Understandably. And yet these attacks mistake the disturbing individual symptoms of social dislocations and changes for the causes. We tend to become what we behold; moving in the same culture as what we oppose, that too will partly shape us. Just so the figure of the poet shares much with those he and his author most strongly oppose. As the poet himself makes so clear. The identity of the poet is every bit as 'singular', quite as much 'an ordre by hymselue' as that market-oriented winner, Haukyn (XIV 281–5). But where is the fraternal community into which he can transcend this individualism? By the poem's own account, as we have found, nowhere. The emerging world rejects the poet's categories and they turn out to be ones he himself cannot inhabit. To me it seems that in the post-plague world he wrestles with, the poet who had so much to say about fraternity, about lived *kyndenesse* and about community, feels himself to be something of an orphan.[131] It is the greatness of this wonderful poem, its religious vision inseparable from its powerful historical imagination, to have been able to dramatize just how, and so often just why, it is not and could not be everywhere equal to the greatest force and to all the consequences of its questions. Nor have we proved to be.

Chapter Two

THE MAKING OF MARGERY KEMPE: INDIVIDUAL AND COMMUNITY

ȝe arn no good wyfe

(John Kempe to Margery Kempe)

'Why gost þu in white? Art þu a mayden?'
Sche, knelyng on hir knes be-for hym, seyd, 'Nay, ser, I am no mayden; I am a wife.' He comawydyd hys mene to fettyn a peyr of feterys & seyd she xuld ben feteryd, for sche was a fals heretyke.

(Archbishop of York and Margery Kempe)

forsake þis lyfe þat þu hast, & go spynne & carde as oþer women don.

('men of þe cuntre', in Yorkshire, to Margery Kempe)

Margery Kempe belonged to a cultural domain which Langland viewed with dismay. But the mercantile world that seemed such an ominous deviation from traditions he cherished, was Margery's 'natural' and unquestioned element. Born about 1373, she was the daughter of a very powerful burgess in Lynn, one of England's largest towns and part of a European economic system. Her husband, though lacking the prominence and wealth of her father, came from the same class, and with him she had fourteen children. She herself was, for a time, an independent businesswoman, but gradually became as mobile as the fictional Wife of Bath or the figure of the poet in *Piers Plowman*, a pilgrim to Jerusalem and Europe, a visionary and a mystic. She dictated what she considered the most significant experiences of her life in a work from which she hoped readers would derive 'gret solas and comfort', witnessing the divine mercy and revelation she felt her life exemplified.

Her book, as Sarah Beckwith notes, 'contains an account of its own difficult genesis and Margery's difficulties in persuading her male scribe to take down her revelations: "for þer was so mech obloquie & slawndyr"'.[1] It is one of the most fascinating English texts of the later Middle Ages, a precious work for anyone interested in the history of gender, subjectivities, and English culture. More than any other writing from this era, Margery Kempe's draws attention to many of the complex processes through which female identity might be made in a particular community and class. The book resists conventional sublimations of such processes and the painful conflicts they entailed. This resistance makes it often an extremely moving text, after all these years, across the most thorough transformations of economic systems and mentalities. Thorough, undoubtedly, but perhaps less than total: could it be that at least some of her struggles resonate in our own domestic culture and have not been transcended?

Sadly, but predictably, the book's very resistance to sublimation has been the main reason it has aroused such condescension and hostility among medievalists, ones quite able to keep a calm, scholarly respect when writing about texts exhibiting pathological anti-feminism or dehumanizing class hatred. The hostility has been amply documented in Clarissa Atkinson's indispensable study of Margery Kempe and well analysed in an important essay by Sarah Beckwith. Commentary, the two critics show, has been dominated by terms such as these: 'terrible hysteria', 'neuroticism', 'a hysteric, if not an epileptic', a sufferer from 'morbid self-engrossment', lacking in 'spiritual wisdom' or 'true [!] mystical experience', 'quite mad – an incurable hysteric with a large paranoid trend'.[2] Still emerging in the 1980s one continues to find the extraordinarily uncritical deployment of such obscure but loaded terms by critics: 'a hysterical personality organization', 'a woman whose preoccupation with herself and pervasive hysterical fear come close to insanity'.[3] From their very different theoretical perspectives both Atkinson and Beckwith disclose the resentment of such commentators against Margery's engagement with the social world, her refusal to obey the wishes of the monk at Canterbury: 'I wold þow wer closyd in an hows of ston þat þer schuld no man speke wyth þe' (27). They analyse the way modern scholars, like the medieval monk, have desired to lock her up, to deprive her of her social mobility, her relative independence of masculine control (as we shall see, relative must be stressed). Those disapproving scholars explicitly prefer the path of negative mysticism, the mysticism of the pseudo-Dionysius or *The Cloud of Unknowing*, to the affective or positive mystical tradition to which Margery belongs, and Beckwith's comment on this preference is very illuminating: 'Negative mysticism, by insisting on the unrepresentability of the Other (God) refuses the return to the social sphere.'[4] This can hardly be said of Margery. Even though her 'return' is very different from Langland's, her book, like the self or selves projected in it, actually works over and is produced by cultural forces and problems which are of great significance, in her own time and, so it seems to me, beyond.

I

It was just this awareness that led Sheila Delany to begin her stimulating essay on Margery Kempe and Chaucer's Wife of Bath 'by placing Margery Kempe in her social milieu'.[5] Eight years later, during which time Delany's essay seems largely to have been ignored, Clarissa Atkinson included an outline of the social, economic, and political features of Lynn, paying due attention to the place of women in the merchant class. Given the accessibility of these excellent descriptions of Margery's Lynn, now to be used with the invaluable documentary survey edited by Dorothy Owen, there is no need to go over this ground here.[6] What seems worth recalling, however, is the significance and representativeness of such a community in late medieval culture and society. Late medieval England contained, and had done for many years before Margery Kempe, many communities governed by men whose wealth came from trade, industry, and renting out of property in town and country. In such communities, which varied greatly in size, markets were central – urban markets, rural markets, and, in Lynn's case, international markets. Their élite was driven by the desire for economic success and security, for political power and social recognition. Perceptions, desires, and discourses were shaped by a web of economic and social relationships organized around market transactions and values.[7]

Few observations about Margery Kempe's book are more just than Delany's: 'one is kept constantly aware of the "cash nexus"; it pervades her consciousness as it pervaded her world, part of every human endeavour and confrontation. No one is immune from money consciousness.'[8] The accuracy of this remark suggests how her work resisted the sublimation of its enabling community. In the account of 'conversion' something emerges of her experience as a female within an urban class which fostered a strong sense of class identity and self-value.[9] This is the ground of her 'grett pompe & pride', her 'pompows aray', the head dress and cloaks she described in such vivid detail (5, 9). As much as for the aristocracy or rural gentry the maintenance of oligarchic identity in towns depended on maintaining social and class differentiations expressed through display.[10] This had to be very visible and aggressively competitive, 'þat it schuld be þe mor starying to mennys sygth and hir-self þe mor ben worshepd'. As befits those who attempted to control the townspeople, 'Alle hir desyr was for to be worshepd of þe pepul'. She was also acutely conscious of gradations within the ruling class, sharply reminding her husband 'þat sche was comyn of worthy kenred – hym semyd neuyr for to a weddyd hir, for hir fadyr was sum-tyme meyr' (9).

She indicates the personal and psychological drives within her class and community when she recalls how she seemed compulsively driven to accumulate: refusing to 'be content with þe goodys þat God had sent hire' she 'evyr desyrd mor & more' (9). The trouble with such conventional moralizing is that it quite fails to engage with the complexities of the situation. For the goods that God had sent her were only sent through the competitive practices and mercantile mentality of her successful father, without which neither goods nor status could be retained. So while she came to judge her motives hostilely, 'for pure covetyse & for to maynten hir pride', she proved herself a true daughter of her class in her drive to become 'on of þe grettest brewers in þe town' (9), more than Langland's Rose the regrator.[11] When this successful business collapsed after three or four years she defied her husband's 'cownsel' and set up a milling enterprise (9–10).

It is important that we understand how normal were the values she exhibited in these episodes, and how marginal the moralizing clerical grid she later applied. Nor are they utterly alien to our own infinitely more intensive and extensive market society where the pursuit of economic self-interest and the accumulation of commodities are perceived as the greatest human good, one which should determine collective decision and personal values. However, in that pre-capitalist and predominantly agrarian society such market values were far from achieving the virtual hegemony they have acquired in contemporary capitalist societies. Granted, historians such as Toussaert, Thomas, and Delumeau have demonstrated an immense disparity between the religion of a tiny clerical élite and the religion of the vast majority of people, suggesting how there never was a 'golden age' of medieval Christianity preceding some post-medieval 'fall'.[12] Nevertheless, whatever the current cultural tendencies, aspects of the Gospels could still be heard – at least enough to induce some anxiety amongst urban middle classes and élites about the final justice of their form of life. It is in this framework that Margery interpreted the collapse of her second business enterprise as a divine warning that she should forsake 'hir pride, hir coueytyse, & desyr þat sche had of þe worshepys of þe world' (11). As usual such condemnation attacks the individual sinner without bringing into question the system of relationships which organizes social life in a way that demands the behaviour judged as sinful if the existing order is to be maintained. Here, understandably, Margery does not put the habitual practices and values of her own class into question. Even if God judges her own enthusiastic participation in her class's practices as sinful, they themselves remain fundamental and untroubling presuppositions of her world, a naturalized part of her daily experience.

It is hardly surprising, then, that they played a decisive role in shaping her identity through all transformations. One of the potential effects of the thirteenth-century expansion of markets for those not too destitute to enter the circuits of exchange, was to encourage the exercise of individual choice, one that potentially instigates a development of individual consciousness, responsibility, and *relative* autonomy (all 'autonomy' always being thoroughly relative).[13] One of the consequences of the mid-fourteenth-century demographic collapse, as we observed in the previous chapter, was to make this potential more widely available, much to the chagrin of employers and their allies. Appreciation of potential advantages of free access to markets, including the freedom to sell labour-power, was among the motivations of those rising in 1381, a rising that was concentrated in 'the most industrialised and commercialised part of the country' where the peasant market and its potentials were most developed.[14] Despite being a woman, Margery's own access to the market as owner of money enabled her to act as a relatively free agent, and to act in the public sphere of production and exchange. She invested capital, organized public work, employed men, defied her official domestic master, made thoroughly individualistic and independent choices (within the current horizons), and exercised power which was inextricably bound up with her specific class and its position in a pre-capitalist market economy. This power even, as we shall see, enabled her to *buy* the sexual and physical autonomy from her husband that she longed for, a longing itself, perhaps, fostered by the class outlook and practice just outlined.

Nowhere is Delany's observation that the 'cash nexus . . . pervades her consciousness' more explicitly illustrated than in the categories and metaphors through which Margery Kempe thinks about and experiences some of the basic interactions between God and humanity. While St Paul certainly uses symbolism drawn from the transactions of slave markets, there is nothing approaching the scope and detailed literalism with which Margery applies market models. As Clarissa Atkinson remarks: 'Unlike the feudal lord of Anselmain theology, Margery's God, who controlled the economy of salvation, functioned as a great banker or a merchant prince.'[15] Some of the passages now to be considered may seem idiosyncratic, but Margery's outlook is perfectly representative of versions of consolation and salvation sponsored in conventional religious practices and discourses in her culture. Her writing suggests the feelings involved in the formulaic evidence concerning what Rosenthal called the 'purchase of paradise' and Chiffoleau 'la comptabilité de l'au-delà', evidence found copiously in wills, indulgences, sermons, and conventional verses, like those on Gregory's trental.[16]

When Margery Kempe records how she wished to go back to Jerusalem 'to purchasyn hir mor pardon' (75) we witness an example of the links between someone's religious consciousness and their culture's profane economic practice, so habitual as to be naturalized. As her class fostered restless drives to acquire money enabling power over consumption (rather than capitalist accumulation) so the religion it supported and paid for fostered the congenially congruent idea that 'mor' was better, could be purchased and would afford efficacious credit on distant shores where the final accounts would be settled. True enough, the restless drive for economic gain was in a system where failure or refusal to compete entailed decline, decay, and the disaster of downward declassment for self and family: not to pursue 'mor' would inevitably breed anxiety and insecurity, yet the very pursuit of 'mor' was itself a cause and source of anxiety and insecurity, as moralists safely removed from direct participation had always noted. This dialectic has a potentially disturbing religious form. The very drive for 'mor' that Margery's wish on the road from Jerusalem illustrates (more pardon, more absolution, more indulgences), is potentially both effect and cause of a compulsive discontent, a haunting anxiety which seeks alleviation from the very processes that stimulate it. It is the economic, institutional, and psychological matrix that Chaucer mediates as his pardoner mockingly invites the Canterbury pilgrims to give thanks for having an ecclesiastical official with them, one who possesses the means to ease their passage through purgatory:

> taketh pardoun as ye wende,
> Al newe and fressh at every miles ende,
> So that ye offren, alwey newe and newe,
> Nobles or pens, whiche that be goode and trewe.
> It is an honour to everich that is heer
> That ye mowe have a suffisant pardoneer
> T'assoille yow, in contree as ye ryde,
> For aventures whiche that may bityde.
> Paraventure ther may fallen oon or two
> Doun of his hors, and breke his nekke atwo.
> Looke which a seuretee is it to yow alle
> That I am in youre felaweshipe yfalle,
> That may assoille you. . .

The very means for attaining 'seuretee' is the means for inducing anxiety and guilt which in turn drives the penitent to seek or purchase more securities in the matrix which induces more guilt and anxiety.[17]

For Margery Kempe, however, a return to Jerusalem 'to purchasyn hir mor pardon' is made unnecessary by Christ's direct intervention to tell her that by saying or thinking reverend sentiments about those holy places, she will receive the same pardon as if she went physically (75). While this could sponsor a significant deinstitutionalization of pardon, not for the first or last time in the book, it still shows the effects of Margery's market model since the 'mor' pardon granted her can now be put to further philanthropic uses, charitably bestowed on others – the only justification Langland could find for mercantile wealth.[18]

Saved the journey back to Jerusalem, Margery travelled on, coming to Assisi in late summer 1414 where the model we are considering is clearly exemplified: 'Sche was þer also on Lammes Day, when þer is gret pardon of plenyr remyssyon, for to purchasyn grace, mercy, & forȝeueness for hir-self, for alle hir frendys, for alle hir enmys, & for alle þe sowlys in Purgatory' (79). Here we meet the ecclesiastic underpinning of Margery's vocabulary, as of Chaucer's pardoner. The special indulgence she refers to was tied in with pilgrimage to the chapel of the Portiuncula.[19] Outlining the history of indulgences, R. W. Southern traces their development from Urban II's use of them to encourage men to join the Crusade to the later medieval extension of grants of plenary indulgence to individuals purchasing them from confessors. He shows that by 1344 'this free use of the papal power had grown to massive proportions' and from the later fourteenth century plenary privileges extended to local churches, as the one Margery visited in Assisi, 'had become very common', as had individually obtainable plenary indulgences.[20] Whereas this situation was scandalous or hilarious to some, it caused no qualms for Margery and the public setting she evokes in Assisi reminds us of the utter normality of her mentality and the scene: '& þer was a lady was comyn fro Rome to purchasyn hir pardon. Hir name was Margaret Florentyne. & sche had wyth hir many Knygtys of Roodys, many gentyl-women, & mekyl good caryage' (79). Her own son, after his conversion, 'went many pilgrimagys to Rome & to many oþer holy placys to purchasyn hym pardon' (224), and it is appropriate that one of the final events in the book is Margery's visit to Syon Abbey in 1434 'to purchasyn hir pardon'.[21] Continually accumulating, continually spending, continually needing to purchase 'mor', the model of the market and the relationships it sponsors determines this version of guilt, forgiveness, and salvation.

The market's permeation of religious consciousness can be seen in Margery's conversations as clearly as in her approach to pardons. For example, the one with a widow in Lynn who asked Margery to find out if the husband had any need of help. After an answer from the deity Margery told the widow, 'Ȝyf ȝe wyl don almes for hym iij pownd er iiij in messys & almes-ȝeuyng to powyr folke, ȝe schal hyly plesyn God & don þe sowle gret esse'. If not, the soul should 'be xxx ȝer in Purgatory' (46–7). Whatever the theological sophistications woven in scholastic Latin, there can be no doubt that this simple conversation is perfectly representative of conventional late medieval piety: financial investment has as tangible purchasing power in the afterlife as in the markets which played a major role in shaping language and consciousness of lay people who could afford such investments. For Margery and her peers, masses are measured in financial terms, just as they were in medieval wills.[22] Indeed, the multiplication of masses for the dead, all of which had to be bought, is one of the marked features of late medieval piety, or rather, its usual qualification, among the sectors whose economic and social situation enabled them to participate in this enterprise. For those, Norman Tanner has described the arrangements in his invaluable study of Norwich wills and religion in the later Middle Ages:

> The arrangement most favoured by the testators from Norwich, and the one upon which much the largest amount of money was spent, was the employment of a priest to 'celebrate' or to 'sing and pray' for the testator's soul for a specified period of time or – the phrase normally used before about 1425 but rarely thereafter – to 'say an annual of Masses' (*annuale Missarum*). They normally left £5.6s.8d (eight marks) for a priest to 'celebrate' or 'sing and pray' for a year but normally rather less, frequently between five marks and £4, for an annual of Masses.[23]

The significance of this for our attempts to understand the common religious mentality in Margery's social milieu can hardly be overemphasized. Yet the situation in which a very wealthy man such as William Setman, mercer and former mayor of Norwich, might even purchase 4,000 masses to be said immediately after his death, together with a perpetual chantry, manifests what seems a rather obvious problem. Tanner describes it as a theological problem fundamental to the multiplying of masses when, as the 1281 Council of Canterbury at Lambeth affirmed, the eucharistic sacrifice, Christ, 'is of infinite merit'. And he comments most helpfully on the wills he studied:

> Nobody from Norwich explicitly faced up in his will to this problem, of why many Masses should be said for a soul when a single Mass was thought to be of infinite value. But the fact that those requesting Masses almost invariably asked for more than one clearly implies that they thought the merit gained would be proportional to the number said. A Mass was regarded very much as a unit of merit which could be assigned

> to dead persons at will. There generally seems to have been a fairly direct correlation between the wealth of a testator and the number of masses requested.[24]

Neither Norwich testators nor Margery Kempe faced up to the problem because it simply was not a problem to those whose perceptions were organized around the production and exchange of commodities in their markets. In such a context Margery's desire 'to purchasyn hir mor pardon' and the testators' confidence that investment in 'more' masses would purchase more security would seem perfectly 'natural'. And not only in masses or pardons, but also, for example, in pilgrimages: Richard Baxter, a former mayor of Norwich, left £40 to a hermit 'to make a pilgrimage for me to Rome, going round there fifteen times in a great circle, and also to Jerusalem, doing in both places as a true pilgrim does' – not long after Margery's own pilgrimage there. In fact thirty-one of Tanner's wills contained bequests for pilgrimages, and this was certainly a common enough feature in medieval wills coming from this class.[25] The context and its complex ramifications is nicely represented by the alderman whose will contained a bequest for a priest to go to Rome to buy a bull, 'if it could be purchased for less than £5 – which granted 300 days of pardon to every well disposed person who prayed at his grave for his and his two wives' souls'.[26]

That ecclesiastics such as the rector of Grimsby (the Abbot and Convent of Wellon) and the local Austin friars could get locked in competition over parishioners' bequests for annuals and trentals is another eloquent indicator of the interaction of religion and economy.[27] As is the conflict over the status of St Nicholas's chapel in Lynn, where Margery observed that the parishioners striving to get it new privileges 'haddyn gret help of lordshyp, & also, þe most of alle, þei wer ryche men, worshepful marchawntys, & haddyn gold a-now, which may spede in euery nede, & þat is rewth þat mede xuld spede er þan trewth' (59). This is one of the rare instances in which it occurs to Margery that 'mede' might block 'treuth', although, rather predictably, those defending the monopolies of the parish church against St Nicholas's chapel were hardly journeymen, labourers, and the dispossessed. Both factions were members of the same class, sharing the same religious and social outlook.[28] It is no surprise that Margery's Christ, the Christ of this community, should perceive the processes of salvation in a wonderfully congruent manner. He tells Margery, for instance, that her current confessor, Master Robert Spryngolde, will have 'halfe' the meritorious tears and works Christ had 'wrowt' in her (216), thus supporting her earlier will: 'I make þe [Christ] myn executor of alle þe god wekys þat þow werkyst in me . . . it is fully my wyl þat þow ȝeue Maystyr R. halfyndel to encres of hys meryte' (20–1). Once more the mechanisms and quantifications at work here are plainly projected from the financial interactions of the community's market, ones to which Christ is as fully reconciled as Margery.

The assimilation of Christianity to the market and the mentalities it fostered seemed as natural to Margery as it seemed agonizingly problematic to Langland, with his contrasting social experience and his neo-Franciscan vision. So different to the writing of both these virtual contemporaries, Chaucer's *Canterbury Tales* disclosed some of the ways in which social and economic categories, together with a markedly possessive individualism encouraged by market relations, shaped consciousness and current practices, including religious ones. He denaturalized what Margery and her conventionally pious fellow-Christians naturalized. Yet, unlike Langland, he accepted the market and its apparent consequences. In my view, the rich vintner's son and civil servant was moved by no vision of a reformed community, no vision of a possible 'common profit' in a common project, no traditional vision of community at all and no nostalgia for one – for him, as I have argued elsewhere, an undogmatic ethical stoicism seemed the appropriate response to his social experience.[29] The future, as argued in the last chapter, did not lie with Langland.

II

When Margery Kempe 'was xx ȝer of age or sumdele mor, sche was maryed to a worschepful burgeys' (6), and to this realm I shall now turn. Having seen that her book does not open with a passivized female figure, we will now see how that glimpse of free agency in a market world related to the passive voice in the statement just quoted – 'sche was maryed to a worschepful burgeys' – a formulation which assumes the distribution of power in the organization of marriages among members of the more affluent, more substantial property-owning classes. Her book offers a rare evocation of basic aspects of human experience habitually obscured from our attention to the past, not least of all by the gendered horizons of those who constructed written traditions, their selection of what was worth writing, and the composition of genres and modes within which to write. 'By God! if wommen hadde writen stories' (*Wife of Bath's Prologue*, 693).

Margery breaks this traditional silence to recall the physical miseries of her first pregnancy and childbirth, culminating in the expectation of death and the fear of damnation. Part of this fear was caused by the fact that this female member of the Lynn oligarchy had already begun to resist the pressures of male authority before she took on her husband. Apparently she had not heeded the conventional warnings of the contemporary prior of Mount Grace whose extremely popular translation *The Mirrour of the Blessed Lyf of Jesu Christ* has been likened to Margery's book in the meditative forms it proposes.[30] Love, preoccupied as he often is with the threat from Lollardy, warns his readers that whatever the Church's officials teach must be accepted, 'and be buxome to hise [God's] vikeres that ben in holy chirche thy souereynes, not only gode and wele leuynge, bot also schrewes and yuel lyuynge'. Unlike Lollards, Margery had not rejected the sacrament of confession, but she had sought a potentially Lollard-like autonomy of her 'souereynes' and the institution. She apparently decided that 'hir nedyd no confessyon but don penawns be hir-self a-loone, & all schuld be forȝouyn, for God is mercyful j-now' (7).[31] But to sustain such individualistic practices against spiritual 'souereynes', against the institutional apparatus whose authority had been reinforced by education and daily experience, especially to sustain them under the pressing fear of the torments of the afterlife so vividly invoked by the clergy, this proved overwhelmingly distressing for one who, unlike Lollards, accepted the Catholic Church's own version of its powers. In the face of death, the result of this contradictory movement of both individualistic negation and orthodox affirmation of the institution was a dreadful guilt culminating in the determination to fulfil the letter of ecclesiastical doctrine and make a good confession.[32]

However, the man standing in for the deity manifested an aggressive impatience with results which offer some insight to the pressures of the system on an earnest layperson who took it seriously (7):

> &, whan sche cam to þe poynt for to seyn þat þing whech sche had so long conselyd, hir confessowr was a lytyl to hastye &

gan scharply to vndyrnemyn hir er þan sche had fully seyd hir entent, & so sche wold no mor seyn for nowt he mygth do. And a-noon, for dreed sche had of dampnacyon on þe to syde & hys scharp repreuyng on þat oþer syde, þis creatur went owt of hir mende & was wondyrlye vexid & labowryd wyth spyritys half ȝer viij wekys & odde days.

At this stage of her life, in this crisis, her confidence proved extremely vulnerable to priestly judgements. Its power silenced her, with dreadful consequences for Margery. The habitual practices of her 'mende' which enabled her to live within her community now became transformed into frightening forces – satanic (7):

þe deuelys . . . bodyn hir sche schuld forsake hir Crystendam hir feyth, and denyin hir God, hys Modyr, & alle þe seyntys in Heuyn, hyr goode werkys & all good vertues, hir fadyr, hyr modyr, & alle hire frendys. And so sche dede.

These torments are not presented simply as external impositions on an integrated, homogeneous self but the guilty product of her own struggles for an identity which would enable a relative autonomy in relation to priest, husband, and others. The cost of this individual struggle is a terrifying isolation combined with immense aggression against her husband, her community, and the self formed by conflicting tendencies within it (7–8):

Sche slawndred hir husband, hir frendys, and her owyn self; sche spak many a repreuows worde and many a schrewyd worde; sche knew no vertu ne goodnesse; sche desyryd all wykkydnesse; lych as þe spyrytys temptyd hir to sey & do so sche seyd & dede. Sche wold a fordon hir-self many a tym at her steryngys & a ben damnyd wyth hem in Helle, & in-to wytnesse þerof sche bot hir owen hand so vyolently þat it was seen al hir lyfe aftyr. And also sche roof hir skyn on hir body a-ȝen hir hert wyth hir nayles spetowsly, for sche had noon oþer instrumentys, & wers sche wold a don saf sche was bowndyn & kept wyth strength boþe day & nygth þat sche mygth not haue hir wylle.

Such alienation from the web of relationships which sustained her inevitably entailed massive guilt and violent hatred of 'hir-self'. That which the attacked self rejects is also desperately needed for survival as a human, that is, social individual. No wonder that she turned her pain and anger against 'hir-self', biting her hand 'so vyolently' that the scar remained all her life, tearing her skin with her nails and seeking self-slaughter as the only resolution of these intolerable conflicts. The 'decentred' subject, past or present, may be far more like this Margery than its anti-'humanist' celebrants proclaim, neither liberating nor revolutionary.[33]

The community resisted the violence Margery turned against 'hir-self' by using greater force – 'sche was bowndyn & kept wyth strength boþe day & nygth'. Yet it dealt more angrily with another woman suffering from chronic despair after the birth of a child, one 'alienyd of hir witte' and also rejecting husband and 'neyborwys' (177–8):

> Sche roryth & cryith so þat sche makith folk euyl a-feerd. Sche wyl boþe smytyn and bityn, & þerfor is sche manykyld on hir wristys . . . to þe forþest ende of þe town in-to a chambyr þat þe pepil xulde not heryn hir cryin. & þer was sche bowndyn handys and feet wyth chenys of yron þat sche xulde smytyn no-body. . .

Perhaps there is an anxiety in this isolating confinement of the female victim which Foucault's history of 'madness' might not lead one to expect in this period. Nevertheless this is certainly not 'the great confinement' and it is suggestive that the woman in the medieval attic was apparently able to talk gently, 'wyth good wil', to Margery, gradually returning to 'hir witte & hir mende a-ȝen' and, perhaps the same thing, reintegration in their community (178). Margery's recovery from her own despairing conflicts was also through a visitor from outside the immediate circle of family, neighbours, and ecclesiastical authorities. But in her case another male displaced confessor and husband in a nurturing, accepting intimacy (8):

> as sche lay a-loone and hir kepars wer fro hir, owyr mercyful Lord Crist Ihesu, euyr to be trostyd, worshypd be his name, neuyr forsakyng hys seruawnt in tyme of nede, aperyd to hys creatur whych had forsakyn hym in lyknesse of a man, most semly, most bewtyuows, & most amyable þat euyr mygth be seen wyth mannys eye, clad in a mantyl of purpyl sylke, syttyng up-on hir beddys syde, lokyng vp-on hir wyth so

> blyssyd a chere þat sche was strengthyd in alle hir spyritys, seyd to hir þes wordys: 'Dowtyr, why hast þow forsakyn me, and I forsoke neuyr þe?'

This non-judgemental yet male acceptance of her divided, highly differentiated, and guilt-ridden self enables her reincorporation in the community; supported by her husband's 'tendyrnes & compassyon', she again 'knew hir frendys & hir meny & all oþer þat cam to hir' (8).[34]

But this reincorporation suggests just how the position of bourgeois wives could generate contradictions between the subject's class and gender leading to serious difficulties. We have observed how her class position gave her independent access to the market, as investor, producer, and consumer, and how this shaped her identity, including her religious consciousness. It is not entirely implausible to speculate that her attempt to retain some independence of the confessional, some autonomy in her settling of accounts with God, was itself part of the particular kinds of consciousness and aspiration fostered, or at least enabled, by this class position. Yet although a member of the dominant urban class she was marked by gender. Her culture trained the biological female into a 'woman' whose existence was to be fulfilled (except for the tiny number of nuns) by becoming a wife: that is, in her class, a 'piece of valuable property' over which 'the laws of religion and society' gave the husband overwhelming power, massive domestic, legal, and political privileges many of which turned women into non-persons or at best gave them the same status as infants.[35] Wives in the merchant élite generally seem to have been in a far more passivized and domestically powerless position than those of lower-class urban and rural families. This would be because in Margery's class wives' work, and the relative increase in autonomy and domestic power this could bring, was *not* an economic necessity. John Kempe, we recall, *opposed* his wife's business enterprises (10). As Sylvia Thrupp has pointed out, the primary role of the merchant-class wife was to be 'amenable to male authority' and useful within the family unit under the husband's rule.[36] This male ideology was remorselessly reiterated in a wide range of genres, and clerics insisted that women did indeed constitute a subordinate social group, whatever their economic and overt social status. So in *Dives and Pauper* we find this typical demand:

> iche man in his owyn houshold schulde don þe offys of þe buschop in techinge & correctynge of comoun þingis. And þerfor seith þe lawe þat þe offys of teching & chastysyng longyth nout only to þe buschop but to euery gouernour aftir his name & his degre, to þe pore man gouernynge his pore houshold, to þe riche man gouernynge his mene, to þe housebond gouernyng his wif . . . to the kyng gouernynge his peple.[37]

This treatment of the household displays features that have often been attributed to the Reformation and its allegedly innovatory elevation of 'the authority of lay heads of households'.[38] There can be little doubt about the place ascribed to woman under her resident bishop and king, the source of divine wisdom and secular authority. There was plainly no distinction in such a scheme between the female servant, the mayor's wife, and the king's wife. How a man of Margery's own class might represent this ideology to his wife is exhibited in a contemporary work translated by Eileen Power as *The Goodman of Paris*. It contains a fascinatingly detailed account of the wife's duties and the household organization, but the aspect of most relevance in the present discussion is epitomized in the following quotation:

> For to show what I have said, that you ought to be very privy and loving with your husband, I set here a rustic example. . . . Of domestic animals you shall see how that a greyhound or mastiff or little dog, whether it be on the road, or at table, or in bed, ever keepeth him close to the person from whom he taketh his food and leaveth all the others and is distant and shy with them; and if the dog is afar off, he always has his heart and his eye upon his master; even if his master whip him and throw stones at him, the dog followeth, wagging his tail and lying down before his master to appease him, and through rivers, through woods, through thieves and through battles followeth him.[39]

The implications of the demand for a wife 'amenable to male authority' are well illustrated. Any autonomy must be denied the woman: to convey this the image of the 'domestic', utterly subservient, and totally dependent dog is well chosen. It also offers a model which negates female subjectivity and imagination. The woman/dog only exists in terms of the husband's desires, needs, and whims, her 'heart' and 'eye' obsessively fixed on the 'master'. He can exercise absolute authority supported by control of her food and backed up by physical violence, the 'whip' legitimated by church doctrine and secular law. Yet whatever he does, the wife will continue to need and serve him, loving him and wagging her tail, perhaps like the wife at the end of Chaucer's *Shipman's Tale*. Indeed, this domesticated, subjugated person is supposed to offer the husband the human intimacy and warmth so conspicuously absent from the male world in which he competes for economic and political power. It is no coincidence that the Goodman of Paris, and John Kempe, men of a leading class, should seek to prevent their wives from participating in their own world of work, the market, keeping them in the sphere appropriate to 'domestic animals'. This containment would be a sign of the male's social status. But it would also undermine the potentials of female autonomy: by depriving these women of any economic self-determination it would make them more dependent than female wage-labourers, certainly than those without children, and perhaps more dependent than the merchant's dog. No more Wives of Bath.

Such commonplace utterances as those by the cleric and the merchant do not tell us about the complexities of actual relationships. Plainly enough, they express masculine desires for a total control over women which could never be attained, as Othello found. They are legitimations of male fantasy and it is true that they were perfectly compatible with proclamations of 'affection' and 'love'. Othello is profuse with such declarations and the Goodman's 'affection' for his younger wife is clear. Nor is there any reason to doubt that such declarations could manifest themselves in behaviour which the woman would experience and value as affection. Margery herself described her husband as 'euyr hauyng tendyrnes & compassyon of hir' (8), despite the treatment we are about to consider. Sharp contradictions pervade most human attitudes. Nevertheless, the masculine fantasies of dominion in the household were at least part of the way men perceived themselves ('master'), their wives, and women in general. Furthermore, they had considerable underpinning in the legal, political, and religious domains. They mattered, as fantasies, especially group or collective fantasies, always do. For Margery, and other women, they posed appalling problems. To this fact we shall now turn.

The starkest manifestation of such female subjection in Margery Kempe's book is in the most intimate sphere, the sexual. Despite her ability to exploit her class advantages against her husband's authority ('sche answeryd schrewdly & schortly & seyd þat sche was comyn of worthy kenred . . . for sche wold not folwyn hys cownsel'), despite her insistence on investing her capital in business enterprises of her own choice, her *gender* demanded extreme self-subordination before the husband's desires. She is thus forced to endure years of compulsory sexuality, what Sheila Delany rightly names as 'legal rape', against which Margery expresses the deepest repugnance and pain.[40] This is another common area of traditional female experience habitually blocked from literary record and exploration, hence from many admiring versions of the past shaped by the ideological and experiential horizons of its male producers. Where it does get mediated is, significantly, in the comic modes of fabliaux, habitually around a man satirized for misrecognition of his excessive age rather than for his violation of another human being's subjectivity.[41] Margery's book does not allow the collusions or evasions offered by comic fabliaux but forces us to confront this aspect of traditional sexual arrangements (11–12):

> And aftyr þis tyme sche had neuyr desyr to komown fleschly wyth hyre husbonde, for þe dette of matrimony was so abhominabyl to hir þat sche had leuar, hir thowt, etyn or drynkyn þe wose, þe mukke in þe chanel, þan to consentyn to any fleschly comownyng. . . . He wold have hys wylle, & sche obeyd wyth greet wepyng & sorwyng.

Across the years, the pain and degradation can be felt. Out of this legalized rape, she continued to conceive and bear children. How the mark of gender contradicted the promises of class she had taken so enthusiastically.

The Church's collusion with such behaviour should not be overlooked. Chaucer's translation of standard penitential material in his *Parson's Tale* summarizes the relevant Catholic dogma:

> for thre thyngs a man and his wyf flesshly mowen assemble. The firste is in entente of engendrure of children to the service of God; for certes that is the cause final of matrimoyne. Another cause is to yelden everich of hem to oother the dette of hire bodies. . . . The thridde is for to eschewe leccherye and vileynye.[42]

The first is meritorious, the second is too, 'ye, though it be ageyn hir likynge and the lust of hire herte' (940). The third definitely involves venial sin, but, the text asserts, 'scarsly may ther any of thise be withoute venial synne, for the corrupcion and for the delit' (941). This is conventional teaching, manifesting the habitual degradation of human sexuality in Christian tradition, a degradation which entailed a consequence succinctly stated in the major history of theologians' teachings on marriage and sexuality by J. T. Noonan: 'The failure to incorporate love into the purpose of marital intercourse.'[43] While the text given to the Parson associates all marital sexuality with 'corrupcion' and a 'delit' involving at least venial sin, it pursues the traditional attack on married couples who make love 'oonly for amorous love', to pursue mutual 'delit': this is deadly sin. This endlessly repeated formula, still being regurgitated in Calvin's *Institutes*, branded such marital sexual love as adultery (939, 942, 848). No wonder then that the safest marital sex is the most unenjoyable, one where 'it be ageyn hir likynge and the lust of hire herte' (940). In this scale of Christian values Margery's painful subjection of her body to marital rape, as she says, 'only for obedyens' (12), would score high marks as a model of meritorious marital sexuality. It did not take Victorians to invent the idealized model of female sufferance of sexual violence. Jesus himself confirms this orthodox teaching to Margery when she observes that the marital sex imposed on her 'is to me gret peyn & gret dysese': he replies, 'þerfor is it no synne to þe, dowtyr, for it is to þe raþar mede & meryte' (48). *Therefore* . . . how resonant is that chain of reasoning. Margery's description of her own feelings, however, the recollection of how 'very peynful & horrybyl' this virtuous marital subjection actually was for her (14), discloses at least something of the experiential reality, the human costs of such ideology and sexual arrangements, ones which theological abstractions occlude.

Christian dogma did more than sanctify such female subjection in marital sexuality: its degradation of human sexuality inevitably contributed at least one powerful element to the identity of anyone who happened to take it seriously during their lives (as opposed to merely at the terminal point). The quotation above from Chaucer's translation of penitential instructions displays the general fear and disgust at human sexuality which the clergy felt and sought to instil: even if one did not embrace one's spouse 'oonly for amorous love', thus avoiding the deadly sin of adultery, even if one only acted sexually within the clerical prescriptions for meritorious intercourse, still, we recall, 'scarsly may ther any of thise be withoute venial synne, for the corrupcion and for the delit.' This was the attitude mediated through confession, an institution designed to organize the most intimate aspects of life, to fashion the self. As Thomas N. Tentler writes in his scrupulous study of confessional literature:

> Sexual organs and functions are called *turpia*, shameful things; and authors deprecate indiscriminately the immoral, the ugly and the unseemly. . . . Popularly, sex became identified not only with sin, but the devil himself, and theologians suggested that God gave Satan a special measure of freedom to intervene in the realm of sexual activity. . . . That marital intercourse had to be 'excused' is evidence enough of the magnitude of the difficulty Christian theology had created.[44]

Tentler's detailed analysis of the literature on the sinfulness of marital sex whose end is mutual joy, literature which also includes elaborate restrictions on the legitimate times and positions for marital sexuality (sinful in menstruation, probably sinful during many 'holy' seasons and times, sinful before communion – three to seven days before some argued – probably sinful unless the man was on top the woman underneath), makes us see just why he should conclude that 'The language of de Butrio, Denis [the fifteenth-century Carthusian], and Foresti had untold capacity for harm to consciences', and that the rigoristic condemnations of 'too ardent' marital lovers could create 'grave distress' for married penitents.[45] That we mostly have to imagine the effects of such teaching on people's versions of themselves and human sexuality is a limitation of surviving sources to which Margery's book is a rare exception. Like so many others, Margery had undoubtedly come across such instruction, teaching people to search out the minute particulars of marital pleasures in making love: 'If one was too immodest in touches, embraces, kisses and other dishonourable things (*inhonesta*), it sometimes might be mortally sinful because these things are not consonant with sacred matrimony. . . . If he knew his wife not for offspring or paying the debt . . . he has exposed himself on account of this kind of intemperance to the dangers of serious sin.'[46] She would have encountered confessors working with standard examination formulae for their penitents such as this: 'I have not had a godly attitude with respect to birth. Or that I have paid the debt but have had too much pleasure.'[47] Or by the attitudes of even the relatively non-rigoristic Gerson:

> After enumerating in a brief sentence [in *Regulae Morales*, 'De Luxuria'] the ways the conjugal act can be mortally sinful – during menstruation, outside the proper organ, desiring someone else, from evil motives – he concludes pessimistically: 'Complete abstinence from carnal acts – as in virgins and widows – is often easier than exercising conjugal rights, just as a fever by drinking, a fire by blowing, and an itch by scratching ultimately become more inflamed.'[48]

No wonder that saints' lives, religious literature for popular consumption, should reproduce such attitudes, as in the life of St Cecilia, translated by Margery's contemporary East Anglian, friar Osbern Bokenham.[49] There the saint goes to her marriage wearing 'nexst hyr skyn an hayre', warning her spouse that an angel will strike him 'ful cruelly' if, 'þou me touche wyth vnclene love/Wyth wyl me to defoulen flesshly' (see 11: 7,466–7, 7,500–7). Marital sexual love is 'vnclene', a source of contamination.

Margery's 'conversion' shows the potentials of such teaching in the fashioning of individual feeling amongst those prepared to accept the authority of the Church in this sphere. Her rejection of marital sex coincides with a conversion which, understandably enough, seems to have transformed her sense of her own sexuality. Fending off the now repugnant sexual activity of her husband she actually presents herself as a belated St Cecilia, with Jesus himself replacing the angel and assuring her that 'I schal sodeynly sle þin husbonde' (21):

> þan on þe Wednysday in Estern Woke, aftyr hyr husbond wold have had knowlach of hir as he was wone be-for, & whan he gan neygh hir, sche seyd, 'Ihesus, help me,' & he had no power to towche hir at þat tyme in þat wyse, ne neuyr aftyr.

Like Bokenham's St Cecilia, Margery had already been secretly punishing her body by wearing 'an hayr of a kylne swech as men dryen on malt', something her husband had not noticed although 'sche lay be hym every nygth in his bedde, & weryd þe hayr every day, & bar chylderyn in þe tyme' (12). A striking image of intimacy in holy matrimony, it also displays the self-punitive guilt fostered by aspects of orthodox teaching.

For one of Margery's problems was that *before* her conversion she had enjoyed making love with her husband, one whose affection, as we noted above, she had valued. This now became a source of guilt and shame, judged as 'inordynat lofe & þe gret delectacyon þat þei haddyn eyþr of hem in vsyng of oþer' (12). Even many years later her disgust at having to look after the incontinent and demented old person her husband had become was turned into a sense of pleasure when she saw it as a peculiarly well-designed divine punishment (181):

> [she] had ful mech labowr wyth hym, for in hys last days he turnyd childisch a-ȝen & lakkyd reson þat he cowd not don hys owyn esement to gon to a sege, or ellys he wolde not, but as a childe voydyd his natural digestyon in hys lynyn clothys þer he sat be þe fyre er at þe tabil, wheþyr it wer, he wolde sparyn no place. And þerfor was hir labowr meche þe mor in waschyng & wryngyng & hir costage in fyryng & lettyd hir ful meche fro hir contemplacyon þat many tymys sche xuld an yrkyd hir labowr saf sche bethowt hir how sche in hir ȝong age had ful many delectabyl thowtys, fleschly lustys, & inordinat louys to hys persone.

This characterizes her book's resistance to processes of sublimation and is also a moving example of the power of clerical doctrine to induce self-disgust over an individual's sexual joy within marriage. Such guilt about her own natural urges and sexual affections could not be without painful consequences. These can be seen in the self-punishing hair worn next to her body, in the language of self-loathing with which she refers to her own sexuality, in her painfully 'confusyd' responses to the sexual invitation from 'a man whech sche louyd' (14–15), and above all in the tormenting twelve-day visions she recalls from a later period (144–5):

> owrys of fowle thowtys & fowle mendys of letchery & alle vnclennes . . . horybyl syghtys & abhominabyl, for anythyng þat sche cowde do, of beheldyng of mennys membrys & swech oþer abhominacyons. Sche sey as hir thowt veryly dyuers men of religyon, prestys, & many oþer, bothyn hethyn & Cristen comyn be-for hir syght þat sche myth not enchewyn hem ne puttyn hem owt of hir syght, schewyng her bar membyrs vn-to hir. & þerwyth þe Deuyl bad hir in hir mende chesyn whom

> sche wolde han fyrst of hem alle & sche must be comown to hem alle. & he seyd sche lykyd bettyr summe on of hem þan alle þe oþer. Hir thowt þat he seyd trewth; sche cowde not sey nay; & sche must nedys don hys byddyng, & yet wolde sche not a don it for alle þis worlde. But ȝet hir thowt þat it xulde be don, & hir thowt þat þes horrybyl syghtys & cursyd mendys wer delectabyl to hir a-geyn hir wille.

Once again the text refuses all the available strategies of sublimation. The anguish and the cultural sources of her divisions are clear in Margery's attempt to fashion an identity in accord with clerical versions of purity and sanctity. The would-be ruler of desire becomes its slave as the repressed returns to plague the repressor in malignant forms. To Catherine of Siena, too, the 'devil' had brought 'vile pictures of men and women behaving loosely'.[50] Such visions mirror the clerical representation of human sexuality. As pornographic representation, whether secular or in the pursuit of holiness, fragments and fetishizes the body so in Margery's vision humans are reduced to mutilated objects of the spectator's gaze, arousing deeply ambivalent feelings. Turned to 'bar membyrs', people's bodies are seen as 'horybyl syghtys & abhominabyl' yet also as 'delectabyl to hir a-geyn hir wille'. The 'gret delectacyon' of early marital sexuality (12) becomes the reified and deformed sexuality envisioned in so much orthodox teaching.[51] Perhaps Blake's questions in the *Visions of the Daughters of Albion* could be asked not only of eighteenth-century Protestantism: 'Are not these the places of religion? the rewards of continence?/The self enjoyings of self denial?' (7: 8–9).

Margery was not St Cecilia, John Kempe not Valerian, and the merchants' world of Lynn not the fantasy one of saints' legends. Yet it held its own means for her relative emancipation. In the end her inherited money and the permeation of her milieu with market assumptions offered Margery freedom from the legalized, sacralized rape which was the starkest manifestation of subjection on the grounds of gender. The key transaction here is among the most memorable episodes in the Book, 'up-on a fryday on Mydsomyr Evyn in rygth hot wedyr, as þis creatur was komyng fro-ȝorke-ward beryng a botel wyth bere in hir hand & hir husbond a cake in hys bosom' (23). John raises the issue of Margery's repugnance towards sexual union with him, indeed of her wish that he should be killed rather than permitted to force 'vnclennesse' on her, a wish which elicits the comment, 'ȝe arn no good wyfe'. As to his rape of her, he comments, 'now may I vsyn ȝow wyth-owtyn dedly synne' (23–4). Nevertheless he is prepared to negotiate, as a good merchant. The key item in the contract he offers is that if she will pay his economic debts he will, in exchange, release her from 'þe dette of matrimony' she now found so 'abhominabyl' (24, 11). If not, 'þan schal I medyl ȝow a-geyn' (24). After consulting Jesus, Margery agrees to the exchange: 'Grawntyth me þat ȝe schal not komyn in my bed, & I grawnt ȝow to qwyte ȝor dettys . . . so þat ȝe neuyr make no chalengyn in me to askyn no dett of matrimony aftyr þis day' (24–5). For Sheila Delany this transaction is merely a distressing mark of Margery's 'perception of herself as property, and the alienated quality of her relationships'.[52] It seems to me, however, that this underestimates the liberating potentials of the market in that society. Margery acts as one merchant with capital negotiating with another to buy a commodity that had been purchased from her merchant-father in the Lynn marriage market. The practice of market relations carried with it opportunity for those with enough financial resources to enter the circuits of exchange, opportunity, as noted above, to increase the scope of choices, to act on them and to foster at least the *potential* for increasingly differentiated identities and liberties. In considering these marital negotiations a reader's hostility to the commodification of intimate relations (a subject that already fascinated Chaucer) should not block out the fact that this is just what enabled Margery Kempe to dissolve bonds of most painful subjection imposed and naturalized through identity bestowed according to gender. The promises of the market in *that* culture should not be obscured by confusion with the operations of the market and its ideologues in contemporary capitalist societies dominated by massive multinationals and industrial–military complexes. Nor should it be obscured by the moralizings of traditional writers such as Langland.

III

Negotiating this exchange was not sufficient for Margery's emergent identity. Life within the nuclear family was still the life of female service to husband, children, and home. There was only one daunting way forward. Against a weight of social and psychological pressure Margery struggled to release herself from the nuclear family. Her wish to gain autonomy from the children she was compelled to produce was an essential part of this and she found a powerful and thoroughly practical ally (48):

> owyr Lord seyd to hir, 'Dowtyr, þow art with chylde.' Sche seyd a-ȝen, 'A, Lord, how xal I þan do for kepyng of my chylde?' Owir Lord seyd, 'Dowtyr, drede þe not, I xal ordeyn for an kepar.'

It is of considerable interest that we can already find a wife in this class expressing the wish for freedom from the sacralized demands that married women's existence should be dominated by their traditional reproductive and nurturing roles within the family, and finding Jesus ready to help with the provision of infant care. Indeed, she hears Jesus assuring her that her aspirations are far from unique. Apparently 'many wifys' desire the autonomy from the patriarchal family that she is struggling for, the desire to live 'frely fro her husbondys' (212). Perhaps Jesus is as good a guide as any to desires and pressures for cultural change in the domestic sphere of Margery's class and community, an area about which we are extremely ignorant, and may have been much misled by the masculine horizons of surviving sources from all institutions, levels, and genres of the society. Even if medieval literature were responsive to such pressures within the domestic sphere it would mediate them through the prevailing anti-feminist models and images of a world turned upside down by un-'feminine' females.[53] Perhaps then a cultural historian aware of the clear evidence for the prominently active role of women in Lollardy, aware of the pressures Margery both brought to bear and claimed to represent, will suspect that Hoccleve's anti-feminist rant about the women's 'paart', during his attack on Oldcastle, was responding to rather more specific pressures than its conventional idiom might at first sight suggest:[54]

> Some wommen eeke, thogh hir wit be thynne,
> Wole argumentes make in holy writ!
> Lewde calates! sittith doun and spynne,
> And kakele of sumwhat elles, for your wit
> Is al to feeble to despute of it!
> To Clerkes grete apparteneth þat aart
> The knowleche of þat, god hath fro yow shit;
> Stynte and leue of for right sclendre is your paart.

Our knowledge of such contexts will advance as more people orient their research in these directions, but it seems at least plausible to suggest that Margery and her Jesus know something about some women in her community, their frustrations and aspirations. Furthermore, these aspirations may well be a significant dimension to the writings that comprise the materials studied in 'literary criticism', writings permeated by anti-feminism and its definitions of what constitute legitimate or illicit identities for females. For Margery herself, a major part of the struggle for a viable identity was inevitably against many of these definitions and against the traditional bonds of the nuclear family.

We can see how these difficult divisions between herself and the community, as well as within herself, continued late into her life. Long after she had been living separately from her husband, he fell and cracked open his head so that 'men wend þat he xulde a be deed'. Her community's aggressive response exemplifies the kind of hostility that is perhaps still discernible in our own culture towards those who are perceived as a threat to the vestigial sacredness of the nuclear family's bonds, especially if they are women: 'And þan þe pepil seyd, ȝyf he deyd, hys wyfe was worthy to ben hangyn for hys deth, for-as-meche as sche myth a kept hym & dede not' (179; see, similarly, 180). For these people Margery has failed to fulfil the very criteria by which her identity as a wife is constituted: namely, a subordinate servicer of man's domestic and intimate needs, a mother/nurse both to infants and to adult males whose infantile dependence on woman, however chaotic the resulting feelings, never seems outgrown but merely transposed into the patriarchal family.[55] By dissolving the bonds of the conventional family unit, by refusing to identify herself with the traditional models of woman/wife/mother, she could be seen as a threat to the foundations of Law and Order, to Man and God. The fact that Margery and John 'dwellyd not togedyr . . . for, as is wretyn be-forn, þei bothyn wyth on assent & wyth fre wil' had agreed to the arrangements, seemed no mitigation in the community's view. Perhaps too the aggression over her separation from John and her rejection of the 'nurse' role expresses not only anxiety at the spectre of female autonomy and its consequences in the community (for both sexes), but also anxiety prompted by ambivalent feelings towards the sacred family itself which could not be directly acknowledged. Perhaps, that is, Margery functions as a screen onto which such repressed feelings together with guilt about them could be self-righteously projected – a common enough propensity of human beings, individuals and collectives, in very different social formations.[56] Jesus, we recall, had his suspicions on this score.

Nevertheless, it is hard to imagine Margery being free of divided and guilty feelings herself. A member of the community from which she had never been walled off, whatever the wishes of the monk of Canterbury, she had been trained to identify with the model she rejected, one 'þe pepil' so heatedly defend. It can come as no surprise then that she seeks a compromise. She asks Jesus to let her husband live for just a year in which she can act out the community's definition of 'good wyfe', one her husband had long ago accused her of failing (23, 180). Jesus obliges by delivering John from immediate death and ordering Margery to take him to *her* home and look after him. Even here Margery's will is still divided, as she complains, 'Nay, good Lord, for I xal þan not tendyn to þe as I do now' (180). Conformity with conventional female life goes against the grain of her own religious identity. The conflict within is resolved in a thoroughly suggestive way. Margery is reminded by Jesus that John 'mad þi body fre to me þat þu xuldist seruyn me & leuyn & clene, and þerfor I wil þat þu be fre to helpyn hym at hys nede': that is, because John released her from her 'marital debts' (at a price and in immediate self-interest Jesus kindly overlooks) he is to be cared for now. Because he agreed to the dissolution of marital and familial bonds he is to be praised and rewarded. Even so, Margery can only endure the conventional role of wife/nurse to the now literally reinfantilized husband by seeing it as a divine punishment for her youthful sexual passion (181). There thus seems much that is misleading in the view that, 'It is one of Kempe's glories that she successfully managed to incorporate her family sentiments into a quest for personal holiness', or that her book generates 'the ideal of domestic service' as a 'new spiritual ideal'.[57] For Margery's religious identity involved a *rupture* with the earthly family, an energetic struggle *against* the nuclear family, its bonds, its defences in the lay community, and its legitimating ideologies. This was clearly how 'þe pepil' in Lynn saw her project in the episode just examined and I now wish to consider some related and striking examples of other communities' responses to her.

Let us take the events in Leicester, a major Lollard centre and one of the seven towns where she records certain people demanding that she should be burnt to death, the fate of many who refused to accept the dogmatic authority of the Church.[58] Here the secular authority initiated the attack on the travelling woman: 'þu art a fals strumpet, a fals loller, & a fals deceyuer of þe pepyl, & þerfor I xal haue þe in preson' (111–12). The terms of abuse are not random. They assert that Margery subverts the dominant powers' official version of correct sexual, religious, and social order, a threat to major and interlocking areas of control. The religious charge is shown to be absurd by theological experts who interrogate her formally, apparently asking questions that would have easily exposed Lollard sympathies. Nor need we doubt Margery's account, for had she not answered 'ryth wel', so that the clerics declared themselves 'wel plesyd', she would certainly not have remained at liberty in that period (after Oldcastle's rising), her life given the seal of approval by Archbishops and Bishops. As for the charge 'fals strumpet' it takes us into the familiar realm of male projections onto women, ones given full indulgence in the anti-feminist tradition as well as in the daily life that sustains this. It seems to have proved difficult for men to treat women as fellow human creatures.[59] Here the Mayor who immediately charges her as a 'strumpet' shows the male propensity to sexualize all that a woman can do or say, something he would not do to a male. It is also characteristic of such projectionism that it should culminate in one of the leading men, the Steward of Leicester himself, using his authority to take her by the hand and lead her 'in-to hys chawmbyr' where he begins to attack her sexually, both verbally and physically. She tries to fend him off by invoking her official status as 'a mannys wife', but 'he strogelyd wyth hir, schewyng vn-clene tokenys & vngoodly cuntenawns' (113). For Margery to sustain a sense of self free from such powerfully supported projections, under such pressures and dangerous isolation, was a massively demanding task.

One of the most startling and revealing accusations the Mayor makes comes later, after Margery has gained the doctrinal approval of the clerics. Before the Abbot, Dean, canons, friars, priests, and many lay people gathered to hear the case in the Church of All Hallows, he claims: 'I trowe þow art comyn hedyr to han a-wey owr wyuys fro us & ledyn hem wyth þe' (116). Startling, but disclosing fears that are now quite recognizable. Margery catalyzes specifically masculine anxieties about potential female autonomy, the potential freedom of will to select life-projects in which servicing males is not on the agenda. It is indicative of the psychological depths of such masculine fears that they should be manifest even in a society where the economic, religious, legal, political, and military institutions, at all levels, are under absolute male rule, depths so wonderfully dramatized in Shakespeare's *Othello*. To the respectable layman Margery represents a way of life which will detach women from the patriarchal family: this would deprive adult males of emotional and physical resources infancy taught them to expect only from females and which had been secured in adulthood by prevailing gender arrangements and ideologies. These teach men to see women

> as naturally fit to nurture other people's individuality; as the born audience in whose awareness other people's subjective existence can be mirrored; as the being so peculiarly needed to confirm other people's worth, power, significance that if she fails to render them this service she is a monster.[60]

These assumptions are basic to traditional representations of women, and the threat Margery's identity poses is the source of fear, the fear played with in the Towneley Noah play. After receiving some conventional wife-beating, the woman turns to the audience:

> Lord, I were at ese, and hertely full hoylle,
> Might I onys haue a measse of wedows coyll.
> For thi [her husband's] saull, without lese, shuld I
>   dele penny doyll;
> So wold mo, no frese, that I se on this sole
> Of wifys that ar here,
> For the life that thay leyd,
> Wold thare husbandys were dede.

The husband's response is to advise 'wedmen' to 'chastice' women and their tongues, if they love their own lives and hope for bliss.[61] One understands why the Leicester man wants to imprison or burn Margery, a woman whose form of life breaks through the bonds that Noah's wife relies on mortality to unfasten. That the man fears Margery's unending, dangerous struggles could prove more attractive to the wives of Leicester than marriage to respectable citizens such as himself and the Steward is a striking example of masculine acknowledgement that marriage was neither a big deal for women nor experienced as such. And who are we to contradict the Mayor? Jesus, as observed earlier, did not. And nor did Chaucer.[62]

This is not the only place Margery triggers off such fears. In Beverley, for example, she was brought before the Archbishop of York who had already interrogated her, finding her an orthodox Catholic. Now 'a Frer Prechowr whech was Suffragan wyth þe Erchebischop' accused her of visiting Lady Westmorland, daughter of John of Gaunt and Catherine Swynford, where 'þu cownseledyst my Lady Greystokke to forsakyn hir husbonde, þat is a barownys wyfe & dowtyr to my Lady of Westmorlonde, & now hast seyd j-now to be brent for' (133). The extraordinary, violent aggression in this conclusion displays as deep an anxiety about female commitment to the marital household as that shown by the Mayor of Leicester. And a friar had more intimate and general knowledge than most men of the grounds for such anxiety through his confessorial role. The exhibition of such anxiety about female autonomy in a class where women could hardly organize around any kind of emancipatory programme calls for explanations to include a psychoanalytic framework able to put questions about the construction of 'masculinity' (from infancy), about masculine dependency and aggression, about masculine fantasization of the female in a distinctly male psychodrama.[63]

Two other contrasting incidents in Yorkshire will close this part of my reflections on responses to Margery's identity. Arrested and abused as a Lollard woman who should be burnt (129), accused of being Oldcastle's daughter carrying seditious letters about England (132), she also meets many 'men of þe cuntre' who advised her to 'forsake þis lyfe þat þu hast, & go spynne & carde as oþer women don' (129). Their response is no different to the civil servant Hoccleve's or to the Mayor of Leicester's, nor are its psychological and economic sources. But for Margery to forsake this disturbing form of life to return to the pinfold of an unwelcome domesticity under husbandly rule would be to risk the collapse of her painfully evolved identity into the appalling psychic chaos she experienced after her first childbirth. The second incident possibly gives further hints of the grounds for male anxiety about the security of female identifications with traditional models. Imprisoned in Beverley, Margery acts in a way that a male establishment might have found very hard to distinguish from the preaching they had forbidden to females – as 'a gret clerke' had reminded her at her trial in York (126):

> þan stode sche lokyng owt at a wyndown, tellyng many good talys to hem þat wolde heryn hir, in so meche þat women wept

> sor & seyde wyth gret heuynes of her hertys, 'Alas woman, why xalt þu be brent?' Than sche preyid þe good wyfe of þe hows to ȝeuyn hir drynke, for sche was euyl for thryste. And þe good wife seyde hir husbond had born a-wey þe key, wherfor sche myth not comyn to hir ne ȝeuyn hir drynke. And þan þe women tokyn a leddyr & set up to þe wyndown & ȝouyn hir a pynte of wyn in a potte & toke hir a pece, besechyng hir to settyn a-wey þe potte preuyly & þe pece þat whan þe good man come he myth not aspye it.
>
> (130–1)

The image here tantalizingly reminds one how thoroughly most medieval writing occludes the lives, interactions, and responses of half the human beings in all social classes. Very rare are such figurations of a community of women unmediated by anti-feminist projections and ideology.[64] Particularly noticeable is the way female support and sympathy for Margery entails just the female autonomy and mutual collusion against male authority that the men in the preceding examples so feared. How would the Mayor of Leicester, 'þe good man' of Beverley, or the countless host of anti-feminist homilists have responded to this episode? The contrast between such support and the masculine aggression reminds one of Jesus's claim that many wives would like to 'be as frely fro her husbondys as þu art fro þyn' (212). Perhaps they would have envisaged such freedom within the *secularized* terms of the egalitarian vision of mutual liberty, love, and 'suffrance' so delicately formulated at the opening of Chaucer's *Franklin's Tale*. If so, they were utopians whose vision would become a remote historical possibility, although one involving as great conflicts and psychological distress as Margery herself lived with.

Margery did not share the secular dreams at the opening of the *Franklin's Tale*. But she did, nevertheless, replace the two families she had been part of, the first under Mayor John Brunham, the second under that 'worschepful burgeys' John Kempe. She replaced them in the imaginary realm of the Holy Family.

This was a nuclear family but, most significantly, with an *absent* father. Joseph is only mentioned four times in the book, and that merely in passing, while Jesus's other father is conspicuously absent. When he does appear, it is to propose marriage to Margery in Rome, and the proposal is not at all welcome, 'for al hir lofe & al hir affeccyon was set in þe manhode of Crist' (86). Within the single-parent family Margery celebrates, Mary is the devoted and idealized mother of late medieval Catholicism, while at the centre of this family is the mother–son relationship.[65] So dominant is this model that Jesus's prophetic life, his preaching of the imminent Kingdom, and the Passion and Resurrection narratives are all perceived in its terms – all is turned into a domestic drama focusing particularly on the mother–son affections (187–97). So in the crucifixion Margery attends to the interactions between mother and son, her 'beheldyng' (191, 192); in the deposition, to how the mother 'kyssyd hys mowth . . . ' (193); in the resurrection, even the Gospel narrative is rewritten to prioritize the mother–son relation – Jesus now first appears to his mother and Margery watches the mother 'felyn and tastyn owr Lordys body al a-bowtyn & hys handys & hys feet' (196). Margery's own closest identification is with the mother, whom she serves as domestic intimate – 'whan owr Lady was comyn hom & was leyd down on a bed, þan sche mad for owr Lady a good cawdel & browt it hir to comfortyn hir', telling the grieving Mary, 'ȝe must nedys comfortyn ȝowr-self & cesyn of ȝowr sorwyng'. The mother's reply perfectly sums up the text's orientation, hardly idiosyncratic in its culture, rejecting comfort on the grounds that 'þer was neuyr woman in þis world bar a bettyr childe ne a mekar to hys modyr þan my Sone was to me' (195).[66]

If one sets this against the Gospel's eschatological preacher of the Kingdom, rather than against her contemporary Nicholas Love's immensely popular *Mirrour of the Blessed Lyf of Jesu Christ*, one is struck by the passivization of Jesus and especially his reinfantilization. A characteristic vision is the appearance of Mary, 'holdyng a fayr white kerche in hir hand & seyng to hir, "Dowtyr, wilt þu se my Sone?" & a-non forth-wyth sche say owr Lady han hyr blissyd Sone in hir hand & swathyd hym ful lytely in þe white kerche þat sche myth wel be-holdyn how sche dede' (209). Perhaps this 'white kerche' was among the 'fayr whyte clothys & kerchys for to swathyn in hir Sone' that Mary had been given by Margery earlier in the book (19). Jesus himself sponsors such reinfantilizations of his risen self as he thanks Margery because, 'þu clepist my Modyr for to comyn in-to þi sowle & takyn me in hir armys & leyn me to hir brestys & ȝeuyn me sokyn' (210). Perfectly conventional in terms of late medieval piety, and perfectly intelligible within a Kleinian framework, it is strikingly remote from the representation of Jesus in the Gospels. There he has absolutely no commitment to the nuclear family, patriarchal or matriarchal. In fact his references to it are often extremely harsh, treating it as one of the impediments to the repentance and conversion he demands. For example:

> And his mother and his brethren came and, standing without, sent unto him, calling him. And the multitude sat about him. And they say to him: Behold thy mother and thy brethren without seek for thee. And answering them, he said: Who is my mother and my brethren? And looking round about on them who sat about him, he saith: Behold my mother and my brethren. For whosoever shall do the will of God, he is my brother and my sister and mother.[67]
>
> (Mark 3.31–5)

Or the following: 'If any man come to me, and hate not his father and mother and wife and children and brethren and sisters, yea and his own life also, he cannot be my disciple' (Luke 14.26; see also Matthew 10.35–6). How should one interpret the cultural and psychological meaning of an infantilization of Jesus so alien to the Gospels? How, with any precision, seek to explain the differences between the representations of Jesus in Margery Kempe or Nicholas Love and those in Langland, or in contemporary Lollard piety, male and female? Here it must suffice to offer a few very tentative suggestions about Margery's own reinfantilization of Jesus.

It enabled Margery to identify with the 'good' mother in a way that her experience in the earthly family had denied. This identification made reparation possible for her objections to traditional female roles and tasks while it offered an idealized object for her 'maternal' care – 'a bettyr childe ne a mekar to hys modyr' was never found in the world (195). Because the identification is through Mary, it facilitates transcendence of the clerically induced guilt about her own sexuality, allowing the imaginary identification with a mother who remains a virgin, thus uncontaminated by sexual union and human processes of reproduction.[68] Perhaps mediation through Mary also creates a distance which safeguards her from any fears of assimilation or being taken over by the 'maternal' functions. One recalls the dialogue with Jesus about another unchosen addition to her progeny: 'A, Lord, how xal

I þan do for kepyng of my chylde? . . . Dowtyr, drede þe not, I xal ordeyn for an kepar' (48). Identification with the 'good' mother could be made without any such problems and 'drede', in the imaginary realm.

Reinfantilization has at least one other possible effect. It offers an image of the one sphere in which the woman obviously controls males.[69] Only when a husband becomes like a child, as John Kempe 'turnyd childisch a-ȝen' (181), is such power ever available again to a woman in relation to an adult male. That early power and its possible reactivation certainly terrified Blake: 'What may Man be? who can tell! But what may Woman be?/To have power over Man from Cradle to corruptible Grave' (*Jerusalem*, 56. 3–4). The quest for such power or even the fear of such a quest is a sign of a culture in which relations between women and men are rather unhappy. There seems to be some ground for wondering whether the anonymous knife-wielder in a vision such as this, preceded by guilty weeping, projects an aspect of the female spectator's feelings (208):

> sche saw wyth hir gostly eye owr Lordys body lying be-forn hir, & hys heuyd, as hir thowt, fast be hir wyth hys blissyd face vpward, þe semeliest man þat euyr myth be seen er thowt. And þan cam on wyth a baselard-knyfe to hir syght & kytt þat precyows body al on long in þe brest.

However one reads such haunting reworkings of the killing of Jesus the prevailing ambience within the Holy Family is one where the woman's pursuit of individual holiness is combined with 'homly' intimacy and affection.[70]

Here the conflicts and contradictions of earthly life are resolved. Even an already commonplace male assumption whose practical consequences had caused Margery such pain, within the family and the community, could be uttered in this realm without the slightest unease to her: 'it longyth to þe wyfe to be wyth hir husbond & no very joy to han tyl sche come to hys presens' (31). Had Margery consistently felt anything like this, John Kempe would doubtless not have lamented, 'ȝe arn no good wyfe' (23). Also superseded in this realm were contradictions between her desires for sexual intimacy and disgust at sexuality, between her desire for autonomy from husbandly power, culminating in separate housing, and her wish to be cared for by a distinctly male but non-coercive figure. Indeed the 'semly, most bewtyuows, & moꞩt amyable' man (8) whom she marries, it seems, during November 1414 in Rome, tells her that 'þer was neuyr childe so buxom to þe modyr as I xal be to þe' (87).[71] Once more it seems as though the only cultural image for a non-coercive male in relation to a woman is that of the child. Simultaneously the imaginary frees Margery to enjoy the intimacy of a sexual relation chosen in guilt-free mutuality. Jesus himself says to her (90):

> it is conuenyent þe wyf to be homly wyth hir husbond. Be he neuyr so gret a lorde & sche so powr a woman whan he weddyth hir, ȝet þei must ly to-gedir & rest to-gedir in joy & pes. Ryght so mot it be twyx þe & me.

In terms of banishing all traces of guilt about human sexuality the imaginary realm is especially effective, for it legitimates the language of sexuality, and whatever intimate connotations this resonates with, while insisting that it is allegorical, insisting that whoever feels familiar evocations of embodied sexuality is a wicked literalist, quite unlike the 'pure' spiritual exegete.[72] Perhaps the fact that Margery's visionary mode does not exactly encourage allegorical sublimations with which the language of human sexuality can be simultaneously enjoyed and denied, is among the reasons it has not endeared itself to pious scholars (90):

> Þerfore most I nedys be homly wyth þe & lyn in þi bed wyth þe. Dowtyr, thow desyrest gretly to se me, & þu mayst boldly, whan þu art in þi bed, take me to þe as for þi weddyd husbond, as thy derworthy derlyng, & as for thy swete sone, for I wyl be louyd as a sone schuld be louyd wyth þe modyr & wil þat þu loue me, dowtyr, as a good wife owyth to loue hir husbonde. & þerfor þu mayst boldly take me in þe armys of þi sowle & kyssen my mowth, myn hed, & my fete as swetly as thow wylt.

Intimacy and reciprocity, once more the mother–child relationship is preserved in that of wife–husband. Here the passage also resolves the contradictions between Margery's desire for freedom from traditional versions of motherhood in Lynn and her wish to identify with that role. Furthermore, it legitimates female sexual initiative ('whan þu art in þi bed, take me to þe . . . boldly take me . . .

kyssen'). The clerical grids which Margery knew as well as Chaucer's Parson, and their effects rather better, are suspended. Clericalizing readers are left free to persuade themselves that they read spiritually and simply pass through the bodily shell to the allegorical kernel – or to condemn the 'misplaced concreteness' of Margery Kempe and advocate other forms of mystical writing.

Be that as it may, the imaginary realm superseded the irresolvable contradictions of domestic life determined by class, gender, and religious doctrine, mediated between her real flight from the family and her need of it. This realm enabled both an affirmation of her community's conventional stereotypes and their negation. Pure negation, if this is even conceivable, would make the maintenance of any viable identity impossible, while a more unqualified affirmation would have produced neither Margery Kempe nor her book.

While we noted how Margery's first recorded crisis was catalysed by a priest, and have examined some of the effects of clerical teaching about human sexuality in Margery's sense of self, it seems right to conclude this chapter by briefly recalling how prominent the contemporary Church was in the making of Margery's identity. As Clarissa Atkinson has argued:

> Acceptance and support from clerical authorities were essential to Margery's inner and outer peace. Even with God's private assurance, she could not have maintained her eccentric existence without the sanction of the Church. At first she needed the archbishop's permission to live apart from her husband; later, clerical authorization was necessary for her to wear white clothes, to go on pilgrimage, to receive communion weekly – in other words, to live the life God commanded and she wanted for herself. Besides, her life on the boundary of Church and society was psychically and physically dangerous and exhausting, and she needed the support and reassurance of respected persons in order to maintain her determination and self-confidence.[73]

This is well put, and Atkinson's chapter on 'Church and Clergy' in her study of Margery Kempe shows how Margery's piety was contained within the boundaries of Catholic orthodoxy and obedience. This was so despite the deity assuring her that any cleric who spoke against her was 'þe Deuelys clerk' (158), and that any cleric who spoke against her spoke against God (85). The extra-ecclesiastical and anti-ecclesiastical potentials of her vision were never realized. Both Clarissa Atkinson and Anthony Goodman have rightly emphasized the 'support and protection' Margery received from clerics, offering a timely corrective to those who have sought to marginalize her historical significance by turning her into a 'case history' of 'hysteria' within a naively desocializing and sexist psychoanalysis.[74] One feature not stressed in the admirable work of Goodman and Atkinson, however, is worth attention. Namely, that among the diverse and complex contexts in which Margery's version of herself was formed, combative interactions with clerics played a notable part. In this connection, it is also noticeable that we get an image of a clerical community whose responses to her were so far from homogeneous that they could range from the most intimate and reverential support to the most aggressive dismissal.[75] One example of such formative interaction must stand for the many contained in the book. It is also almost extensive enough and generically similar enough to bear comparison with the moving account the Lollard Thorpe gave of his stand before Archbishop Arundel.[76]

During a pilgrimage to York, where she had been for a couple of weeks, Margery was summoned to the Chapter-house for examination before many clerics (121–2). Despite her doctrinal orthodoxy and submission to Church authority she was ordered to appear before the Archbishop, one already involved in the persecution and burning of Lollards. The intimidatory nature of such proceedings is plain, and the Archbishop's retinue display the effects of power and a 'McCarthyite' outlook: 'despisyng hir, callyng hir "loller" & "heretyke," & sworen many an horribyl othe þat sche xuld be brent' (123–4). As the trial opened Margery encountered the same aggression from the Archbishop (124):

> scharply he seyd to hir, 'Why gost þu in white? Art þu a mayden?' Sche, knelyng on hir knes be-for hym, seyd, 'Nay, ser, I am no mayden; I am a wife.' He comawndyd hys mene to fettyn a peyr of feterys & seyd sche xulde ben feteryd, for sche was a fals heretyke.

This is a clerical version of the Mayor's anger in Leicester, anger at someone who undermines conventional classifications intrinsic to traditional social control and individual identifications. Her heresy lies in confounding the categories virgin (white clothes) and wife, as well as in her mobility and autonomy.[77] The wish to fetter her expresses the same sentiment as the Canterbury monk who said, 'I wold þow wer closyd in an hows of ston þat þer schuld no man speke wyth þe' (27). The woman's subjectivity and the marks of free agency seem dangerous. Margery stands, as she recalls, 'a-lone', very vulnerable: '& hir flesch tremelyd & whakyd wondirly þat sche was fayn to puttyn hir handys vndyr hir cloþis þat it schulde not be aspyed' (124). This touching detail is not the fantasia of superpersons with which saints' legends are packed. It helps the reader appreciate the kind of pressures brought to bear on her, the combination of isolation and interaction in which her identity was tested and made. Certainly she had models which allowed her to assimilate even attacks from the Church – as her favourite confessor had told her of a substitute who sought totally to undermine her sense of herself, 'God for ȝowr meryte hath ordeynd hym to be ȝowr scorge & faryth wyth ȝow as a smyth wyth a fyle' (44). If she could stand against such power and hostility could she not identify with St Paul himself? 'I please myself in my infirmities, in persecutions, in distress, for Christ. For when I am weak, then am I powerful' (2 Corinthians 12.10).

Through her fear of the powerful men threatening her, the truth of an earlier comment in the Book becomes manifest: 'here most dred was þat sche xuld turnyn & not kepyn hir perfeccyon' (43). Such turning would leave her as 'decentred' as she had once been before, and she knew it would herald no paradise. Challenged 'ful boystowsly' by the Archbishop about her gift of weeping she counterattacks in prophetic style: 'Syr, ȝe xal welyn sum day þat ȝe had wept as sor as I.' And similarly when he tells her 'I her seyn þu art a ryth wikked woman' she replies, 'Ser, so I her seyn þat ȝe arn a wikkyd man. And, ȝyf ȝe ben as wikkyd as men seyn, ȝe xal neuyr come in Heuyn les þan ȝe amende ȝow whil ȝe ben her' (125). The Archibishop, however 'boistowsly', takes up this reply, 'Why, þow, what sey men of me', allowing Margery the lofty retort, 'Oþer men, syr, can telle ȝow wel a-now'. In this perilous exchange Margery presents herself as wresting the initiative from the hostile examiner and in doing so confirming her own threatened identity. So much so that 'a gret clerke wyth a furryd hood' intervenes to protect the bullying senior colleague: 'Pes, þu speke of þi-self & late hym ben'. She then refuses to leave his diocese as 'hastily' as he wished, '& I must, ser, wyth ȝowr leue, gon to Brydlyngton', the 'must' registering a source of higher authority than the prelates 'leue', so tactfully mentioned (125). Even when he makes the conventional enough demand that she, a female, promise not to teach or 'chalengyn' people in his diocese,[78] she refuses, reinventing her speech in memorable fashion (126):

> Nay, syr, I xal not sweryn . . . for I xal spekyn of God & vndirnemyn hem þat sweryn gret oþes wher-so-euyr I go vn-to þe tyme þat þe Pope & Holy Chirche hath ordeynde þat no man schal be so hardy to spekyn of God, for God al-mythy forbedith not, ser, þat we xal speke of hym. And also þe Gospel makyth mencyon þat, whan þe woman had herd owr Lord prechyd, sche cam be-forn hym wyth a lowde voys & seyd, 'Blyssed be þe wombe þat þe bar & þe tetys þat ȝaf þe sowkyn.' Þan owr Lord seyd a-ȝen to hir, 'Forsoþe so ar þei blissed þat heryn þe word of God and kepyn it.' And þerfor, sir, me thynkyth þat þe Gospel ȝeuyth me leue to spekyn of God.

Such a claim, in the face of a Church engaged in a long struggle to burn Lollardy out of the community, could easily have been taken as a sign of Lollard advocacy of the priesthood of all believers, or at least as an assertion of laypeople's right of independent access to a vernacular Bible.[79] The clerical reaction is unequivocally hostile, 'her wot we wel þat sche hath a deuyl wyth-inne hir, for sche spekyth of þe Gospel' (126). On the face of it, a peculiar piece of logic for Christian clerics, but one that becomes perfectly intelligible in this context. Margery's confidence in her prophetic identity, strengthened in the exchange, is emphasized by her decision to highlight gender. She moves from a bisexual 'we' ('we xal speke') to a specific assertion of *women's* religious rights: again, in her own contexts, she was evolving 'clerical apprehensions about assertively devout women', about women who were reputed to be claiming, even appropriating, the priestly powers monopolized by the male clerisy, and, once more, about Lollard communities, where women were particularly prominent.[80] No wonder 'a gret clerke' immediately reaches for St Paul to prove 'a-geyns hir þat no woman xulde prechyn' (126). Doubtless the comforting text was this:

> Let women keep silence in the churches; for it is not permitted them to speak but to be subject, as also the law saith. But if they would learn anything, let them ask their husbands at home. For it is a shame for a woman to speak in the church.
> (1 Corinthians 14.34–5)

What Margery thought of these inspired instructions to ask John Kempe 'at home' of anything she wished to learn we can only guess. Rather wisely, if not with prophetic abandon, she apparently did not play off her own experience against this solemn utterance; nor quote the Wife of Bath's view that, 'Experience, though noon auctoritee/ Were in this world, is right ynogh for me/To speke of wo that is in mariage' (*Wife of Bath's Prologue*, ll. 1–3). Nevertheless, she does respond: 'I preche not, ser, I come in no pulpytt. I vse but comownycacyon & good wordys, & þat wil I do whil I leue' (126). Any Lollard woman or man could, of course, have said the same. One can see why clerics who conceded that her dogma was utterly orthodox, after the Archbishop 'put to hir þe Articles of owr feyth', should proclaim 'we wil not suffyr hir to dwellyn a-mong vs, for þe pepil hath gret feyth in hir dalyawnce, and perauentur sche myth peruertyn summe of hem' (125). Such men felt threatened by someone who seemed, however marginally, to 'usurp' not only priestly but gender prerogatives;[81] here the celibate élite could find a common cause with husbands like the Mayor of Leicester. The level of clerical anxiety is further suggested by the doctor of divinity who claims Margery propagated anti-clerical stories, 'þe werst talys of prestys þat euyr I herde' (126). Margery relates a standard enough *exemplum* and explains that like any conservative satire she 'spak but of o preste be þe maner of exampyl', not a fiction undermining the authority of the institution and its officers. In the trial scene, the Archbishop accepts Margery's interpretation of the 'exampyl', but the doctor's response is another reminder of the aggressive and defensive contexts established by what Hope Emily Allen, in her exceptionally helpful annotations to Margery's book, called 'the Counter-Reformation in fifteenth-century England'.[82]

Margery's identity was made in these contexts, in such encounters. The menacing aggression, with the flames of Smithfield in the background, played an important role in testing and substantiating this identity. Surviving in the manner she did strengthened her sense of self and its legitimate existence within the community. The opposition was as important in her self-differentiation as the intimate and unequivocal support of the Dominican confessor, her friend Master Aleyn of Lynn, or Richard Caistyr of St Stephen's Norwich. As for the Archbishop, he concluded the interrogation by paying a man to lead Margery 'owt of þis cuntre'. Although he prays her to pray for him and blesses her (128), he wished to get rid of someone who however orthodox at least seemed a potentially disturbing challenge to fundamental aspects of gender arrangements and clerical power.

Yet this challenge was interwoven with a form of affirming the Catholic Church which few of its officials could totally fail to appreciate in that 'counter-reformation' context. It can be illustrated by an episode in Lynn during January 1421 (162–4). The Guild Hall was burnt down by 'a gret fyer . . . an hydows fyer & greuows' which seemed about to consume the splendid parish church. In this situation the often hostile laypeople, 'for enchewyng of her bodily perel', encourage Margery's cryings and the clergy consult her over a thoroughly revealing action (163):

> Than cam hir confessowr to hir & askyd ȝyf it wer best to beryn þe Sacrament to þe fyer er not. Sche seyd, 'Ȝys, ser, ȝys, for owr Lord Ihesu Crist telde me it xalbe ryth wel.' So hir confessowr, parisch preste of Seynt Margaretys Cherche, toke þe precyows Sacrament & went be-forn þe fyer as deuowtly as he cowde & sithyn browt it in a-geyn to þe Cherche, & þe sparkys of þe fyer fleyn a-bowte þe Cherch.

This is a world in which the Church and the Sacrament it makes has immense magical power, one that is as great 'for enchewyng of her bodily perel' as for helping peoples' passage in the afterlife.[83] Margery's form of piety unequivocally confirms such magic and the source of its mediating human agency, the official clergy. In this instance, supported by her own advice and intercession, God responds with a 'myrakyl', a snow storm which quenched the fire.

This episode precisely matches the 'myracles' Nicholas Love recounts in his treatise defending Catholic dogma about the Sacrament against Lollards, miracles in which the Sacrament delivers prisoners' bonds, saves from drowning in tempests, converts sceptics, delivers from purgatory, and so on. Against 'the disciples of Antecrist that ben clepid lollardes', Love insists that in Catholic practice, 'is none perile of ydolatrie', and that even if Catholic dogma 'were not sothe: ȝit the siker parte were to byleue as holy churche techeth with a boxome drede'.[84] Idolatry or not, Love's commonplace account of miracles which allegedly 'prove' the dogma, and the episode in Lynn, demonstrate a fetishization of the Sacrament Margery identifies with completely. It was one that could only reinforce clerical power against what Nicholas Love, in the *Mirrour* itself, described as the derision of 'the lewed lollardes': 'heere lawheth the lollarde and skorneth holy chirche in allegeaunce of such myracles haldynge hem bot magge tales and feyned illusiouns.'[85] One can see why the Mount Grace monks kept Margery's book.

In this context the so-called 'concreteness' of Margery's piety would neither seem 'misplaced' nor an example of 'bad' Catholicism to the clerisy.[86] Whatever potential danger her identity held for gender arrangements and the priestly monopoly of the means of grace and correct knowledge on everything, whatever its inner conflicts, its dependence on the web of ecclesiastical 'practices, abhorred by Lollards', was a welcome support for orthodox Catholicism.[87] Indeed, it was the visible, spectatorial, ritualistic, iconic aspects of late medieval Catholicism that often triggered off Margery's most overwhelming religious experiences. Sometimes this was at ecclesiastically sanctified shrines spread across England, Europe, and Jerusalem, part of a conventional piety devoted to visiting 'holy reliqwiis' such as 'owr Ladys smokke' (237) or 'þe Blod of Hayles' (110); more frequently still at major moments of the ecclesiastical year. For example (184):

> Many ȝerys on Palme Sonday, as þis creatur was at þe processyon wyth oþer good pepyl in þe chirch-ȝerd & beheld how þe preystys dedyn her obseruawnce, how þei knelyd to þe Sacrament & þe pepil also, it semyd to hir gostly sygth as þei

> sche had ben þat tyme in Ierusalem & seen owr Lord in hys manhod receyued of þe pepil as he was whil he went her in erþ. Þan had sche so meche swetnes & deuocyon þat sche myth not beryn it, but cryid, wept, & sobbyd.

This centralizes Church ritual and the privileged clerical actors, 'þe prestys' through whom the visionary's experience is mediated as she *beheld* and *watched* with 'þe pepil'. Even 'þat tyme in Ierusalem' was the time organized through ecclesiastical legend, liturgy and iconography, as we can see from Margery's own time in Jerusalem (67–75) or her meditations on the Passion (187–94); it was not the grid through which Lollards encountered Jesus. It is a related and significant fact that Margery's devotion is both focused on the eucharist and continually expressed in terms of *seeing* the Sacrament, as in the passage just quoted, or the following one where she is describing what evoked her communion with God (172):

> And most of alle whan sche sey þe precyows Sacrament born a-bowte þe town wyth lyte & reuerens, þe pepil knelyng on her kneys þan had sche many holy thowtys & meditacyons, and þan oftyn-tymys xulde sche cryin & roryn as þow sche xulde a brostyn for þe feyth & þe trost þat sche had in þe precyows Sacrament.

The scene in many ways characterizes popular religious sentiment described with such memorable specificity by the Catholic historian Jacques Toussaert.[88] Once again it centralizes the ecclesiastic ceremony, the religious object which only its officials could make, the priests processing: laypeople kneeled and *watched*, Margery saw the Sacrament. Margery is thus part of a piety well suited to block off any critical, ironic reflections of the faithful, whether sponsored by women like Margery Baxter of Martham or men like the great evangelist William White, both condemned by the Church in East Anglia, White being burnt on ground Margery would have trodden.[89] This normal enough mode, found in Nicholas Love's immensely popular *Mirrour of the Blessed Lyf*, precludes the agonizing theological, ethical, and social reflections of Langland's equally visionary work; above all, it precludes the *iconoclastic* discourses of

Lollard Christianity, with its interest in the relations between Catholic mythology, dogma, and clerical power, including economic power, its suspicion and often hilarious mockery of what seemed spectatorial religion (icons, relics, pilgrimages, a eucharist which can appropriately be taken to put out fires or processed round towns).[90] In 'the battle against Lollardy' one can see how Margery's 'concreteness' could seem not at all 'misplaced' and how her conflict-ridden identity could find a supportive context in her heterogeneous community.

Chapter Three

MASCULINE IDENTITY IN THE COURTLY COMMUNITY: THE SELF LOVING IN *TROILUS AND CRISEYDE*

> But almost every knight is a slave to love now, and waits at its doors to receive his fate.
>
> (John Gower, *Vox Clamantis*, V 4)

> Incidentally, it may be remembered that in discussing the question of mourning [in *Mourning and Melancholia*] we also failed to discover why it should be such a painful thing.
>
> (Freud, *Inhibitions, Symptoms and Anxieties*, VII)

In her illuminating study of 'politics, faith and culture' in Anglo-Norman and Middle English romances, Susan Crane's final chapter is devoted to changes in 'the social context of courtly writing' and the genre's adaptations:

> In the later Middle Ages courtly literature provided scripts for noble endeavour – for behavior between lovers, among knights, to prisoners, and to enemies in war. . . . A rich culture grew around knighthood in these centuries. Tournaments imitated those of romances, as did feasts and pageants. . . . Secular chivalric orders. . . . The pomp and the literary cast of these new practices should not mislead us into thinking they were only games or poses.

As for the heroes of the later insular romances they are 'imitable and useful models' in cultivating a courtly ethos embraced by the knightly class. In the romances, 'aesthetic dimensions carry important meanings in the world as well as in the text'.[1] This writing, 'scripts for noble behavior', is one of the contexts in which *Troilus and Criseyde* was produced and received. Its imagined community is the court; the version of love and chivalry, albeit set in Troy, is at least within the general literary domain Crane describes. Yet the poem has plainly not attracted its massive commentary because of its typicality in the general domain of courtly romance. What comprises its extraordinary distinction is often as disputed as questions about what may and may not be appropriate ways of reading the work.

This is not the place to offer a history of such commentary, let alone to join debate with the wide range of ideological presuppositions informing its diverse results.[2] My own general perspectives on the poem's peculiar distinctiveness have not changed much since I argued in *Chaucer, Langland and the Creative Imagination* that whatever else it does, which is doubtless a great deal, it developed a social psychology which comprised a profound contribution to the understanding of interactions between individual and community. In the making of Criseyde, the poem explores the complex ways in which individual action, consciousness, and sexuality are bound up with specific social and ideological systems.[3] Since then Stephen Knight has maintained that Criseyde should be seen as 'a figure of a new self-consciousness' in a poem of exceptionally powerful 'historical imagination':

> The poem does bear in on fourteenth century human relations and realize, in tremendous detail and with extraordinary feeling, the experience not of one couple but of people, at a time when the collective patterns of social structure, behaviour and feeling were in a process of radical changes.[4]

Knight concentrates on the poem's attention to the 'relations of public and private life and values', its 'ground-breaking' moves 'to internalize the conflicts of private and public and to write a romance which actualizes the personal feelings of love' in line with 'love as it is now understood, an inescapable attraction between *individual* human beings' imagined in a very different mode to the lover of the *Romance of the Rose*, Yvain, Tristan, or Isolde. In this inevitably controversial reading the poem itself (not just an allegedly wicked knight and an allegedly wicked woman) marginalizes the disturbing public world while evoking constant awareness of its forces as those 'against which the newly and polemically privatized genre is operating'.[5]

Bearing these earlier studies in mind, I now wish to address another aspect of the historical and psychological imagination displayed in this wonderful poem – namely its exploration of heterosexual love in the making of masculine identity in a particular class and culture. To what extent such history is, like Petrarch, 'deed and nayled in his cheste', to what extent, and why, it is part of contemporary cultures, seem questions worth pursuing, although here they will not be confronted.

The festival near the beginning of the first book of *Troilus and Criseyde* introduces Troilus as part of a knightly community seen from a position which makes invisible all those outside this tiny social élite (I 162–322). The Trojan scene would evoke familiar forms of public worship to any medieval audience. In these, community, class, and occupational solidarities were affirmed, ones intrinsic to individual identities. As Mervyn James has described so well in relation to Corpus Christi festivals, they also sought the negotiation and symbolic control of potentially divisive competition, within and between groups.[6] It is in this context that we encounter the 'fierse and proude knyght' (I 225), a paragon of his class, Prince Troilus. He is leading young knights up and down in the temple, 'Byholding ay the ladies of the town', praising and criticizing them, 'On this lady, and now on that, lokynge' (I 183–9, 269–70). As Stephen Knight writes, Troilus is represented in this sequence as a 'fully feudal figure':

> Like any baron he leads a band of young knights and deplores any tendency to desert the collective group for the private pursuits of love. He is a model of the noble life, 'The worthiest and grettest of degree' [I 244], both 'proud' and 'debonaire' [I 214].[7]

Yet it should be added that this subcommunity of males partly defines itself in relation to women, whatever the potential threat this poses to male-bonding and 'the collective group' led by the royal knight. As they eye up the static women the males constitute their own sense of identity as mobile, active, powerful. Rosalind Coward's comments on men eyeing women on contemporary streets seem relevant to the scene here:

> Men can and do stare at women; men assess, judge and make advances on the basis of these visual impressions. The ability to scrutinize is premised on power. Indeed the look confers power; women's inability to return such a critical and aggressive look

> is a sign of subordination, of being the recipients of another's assessments.[8]

This 'subordination' simultaneously confirms the male supremacism which, by definition, depends on constituting another as subordinate. Troilus's performance as he leads the 'yonge knygthes' is a representative one, part of the confirmation of gender relations and power in his culture, part of the daily making of 'masculine' identity as active, free, predatory subject, an identity dependent on the simultaneous construction of 'feminine' identity as passive, powerless object. Perhaps our own culture's habituation to such scenes explains why critics so rarely comment on the aggression which the poet himself emphasized in his choice of a violent, even sadistic language with which to describe Troilus's gaze at the woman: 'His eye percede, and so depe it wente/Til on Criseyde it smot, and ther it stente' (I 272–3). The terms I am pointing to are 'percede', 'depe' and 'smot'. The language, in the scene Chaucer represents, is part of the situation Susanne Kappeler describes in *The Pornography of Representation*:

> Turning another human being, another subject, woman into an object is robbing her of her own subjectivity. The systematic representation of women–objects is not a question of a single subject representing to himself another subject, who happens to be a pretty woman, as an object. In cultural historic terms, it is the male gender unified by a common sense, who assumes the subject position: as the authors of culture, men assume the voice, compose the picture, write the story, for themselves and other men and *about* women. . . . *Men act* and *women appear*.[9]

The behaviour of the young knights is an aspect of a cultural project through which 'masculine' subjects are made, and, as we observed a little earlier, a subordinate other produced without subjectivity, one whose sole purpose is to stimulate the subject's feelings. But *Troilus and Criseyde* does not invite an uncritical identification with Troilus's conventional enough behaviour. Already it implies that while the females are indeed simply objects in the field formed by the male gaze, these objects are actually subjects having to negotiate these threatening situations within the limited strategies available to 'respectable', 'womanly' women, ones who do not wish to be classified like the Wife of Bath, or worse. So the poem shows the woman as a subject reacting to Troilus's public gaze:

> . . . she let falle
> Hire look a lite aside in swich manere,
> Ascaunces, 'What! may I nat stonden here?'
> (I 290–2)

But even this can be interpreted by the gazer in the light of fantasies about women which continue to negate their subjectivity, fantasies as culturally formed as the railway-system. At once we find Troilus simply assimilating Criseyde's downward look to his own pleasures, making it a catalyst to 'gret desir' (I 294–8). Probably only female figures as idealized and as socially superior as Blanche, daughter of the great Duke Henry of Lancaster, could even be imagined dealing with knightly gazers in effortless self-possession and confident power.[10]

Yet the development of masculine identity in the knightly class demanded more than the cult of a public face of invulnerable mastery (I 227–8, 190–2), backed up by the capital-intensive skills appropriate to mounted soldiers. It involved what is already very much on Troilus's tongue – 'love', with its courtly 'observaunces', its 'servyse', its 'ordre', its 'lay' (I 195–201, 330–50). The poet shows Troilus prying into his companions' feelings about 'love' and abusing their 'love' immediately before his own conversion. This suggests, as does the whole poem and its genre, the importance of 'love' in courtly culture. The discourse of which 'love' is a major term has already been learnt by the courtly male, an essential strand in his identity. What we now witness is how it creates a sense of lack in the young knight. His mocking curiosity towards his male companions turns out to be nearer rivalry and anxiety than indifference or genuine detachment. At some level the worthy knight has grasped that to fulfil the demands of the ego-ideal intrinsic to his class and gender identity he needs to participate in what he calls the 'observaunces' of love. He 'needs' a woman as marker of his own subjectivity and worth as an adult knight. This 'need' is only confused with a supposedly simple instinctual drive for copulation by readers whose impatient and abstract moralism prevents them from attending to the poem's own grasp of the *cultural* formation of knightly love and the social construction of specific forms of sexuality.[11] Troilus's class and its culture prepares him to inhabit the same language and structure of feeling as the husband of Blanche, a figure whose social status corresponds to the Trojan's:

> Syr, quod he, sith first I kouthe
> Have any maner wyt fro youthe,
> Or kyndely understondyng
> To comprehende, in any thyng,
> What love was, in my owne wyt,
> Dredeles, I have ever yit
> Be tributarye and yiven rente
> To Love, hooly with good entente,
> And throgh plesaunce become his thral
> With good wille, body, hert, and al.
> Al this I putte in his servage,
> As to my lord, and dide homage;
> And ful devoutly I prayed him to,
> He shulde besette myn herte so
> That hyt plesance to hym were,
> And worship to my lady dere.
> And this was longe, and many a yer
> Or that myn herte was set owher,
> That I dide thus, and nyste why;
> I trowe hit cam me kyndely.
> (*The Book of the Duchess*, 11. 759–78)

This passage clearly indicates how initiation in the discourse of love long preceded the existence of any specific relationship: it is the culture of discourse which produces the particular form of desire. So internalized is the education which makes a courtly male of him that he can assert it must be a product of nature, 'I trowe hit cam me kyndely', confirming a characteristic move in the self-representations of the dominant class, attributing features that are the product of a training based on massive privileges of economic and social power to 'natural' qualities beyond the potential of 'common' people. The rich vintner's son who wrote the poem, however, makes it as clear here as he does elsewhere, that love is a 'craft' (1. 791), a discipline which was one of the markers of full membership in that upper-class community, one to which he himself gained access but was not to the manner born.[12] That this 'craft' was a major strand in the constitution of masculine identity in that community did not, of course, mean that it was without its problems for men, as both the melancholic knight in *The Book of the Duchess* and Troilus witness.

It is within this received courtly culture of discourse that the poem represents Troilus's withdrawal to the privacy of his bedroom. Here he works on the image of the woman retained in his 'mynde', composed by the gaze which 'percede' and 'smot' its object (I 358–434).[13] It is unfolded in the language of love, so central to the identity of the complete courtier. All the familiar terms are well known to Troilus: 'To love . . . To serven . . . grace . . . oon of hire servantes . . . travaille . . . grame . . . desir . . . pris'. So too are the references to secrecy, to a private realm opposed to the public, the complex opposition treated with great skill by Stephen Knight.[14] As for the woman, in a conventional formula we shall return to later, she is invoked as the man's healer (I 461–2, 469, 484–7), and Monica McAlpine's view that Criseyde is 'a mere image serving Troilus' fantasy life' is incontestable.[15] Nevertheless it would be a mistake to ignore the poem's lucid representation of the way Troilus's 'private' fantasy is a product of a public culture, a product that exemplifies how culture is sustained by countless private acts which may well be experienced as unique and spontaneous. In this fantasy Troilus keeps good male company and proves himself to have come of age in courtly society. The poem comments on his fantasy: 'Thus took he purpos loves crafte to suwe' (I 379), echoing the decision of the knight in *The Book of the Duchess*, 'I ches love to my firste craft' (1.791). The more skilled in 'loves crafte' the more complete the achievement of the knight, as lengthy passages at the close of the first and third books insist. There we learn that Troilus's pursuit of 'loves crafte' led him to fight like a lion in defence of Troy, while becoming the friendliest, 'gentilest', and most generous of knights in the town. After Hector he becomes its toughest defender and all 'this encrees of hardynesse and myght' is a product 'of love'. Indeed, all the accomplishments which make him a supreme model for men of his class can be attributed to 'Loves heigh servise', one that drives out everything that counts as 'vice' in his culture (I 1,072–85; III 1,772–1,806). The formation of 'love' is thus a decisive part of a successful upper-class masculine identity, one that simultaneously and designedly excludes the lower classes. As Andreas Capellanus notes in a chapter concerning peasants, they 'can scarcely ever be found serving in Love's court. They are impelled to acts of love in the natural way ['naturaliter'] like a horse or a mule.' So for them, 'regular toil and the continuing uninterrupted consolations of ploughshare and hoe are enough': even if it were possible, initiation in the languages of 'love' would be dangerous since it might encourage them to follow forms of life which would remove their toil from 'our' service and result in 'unfruitful' estates 'for us'. As for peasant women, the appropriate treatment is 'compulsion', rape, not 'love'.[16]

'Love' is certainly a powerful way of binding the individual into the class. It offers a system through which the cultural standards and ideals of the class are internalized. They are assimilated both to the individual's ideal self-image and to basic sexual drives which may now only be legitimately acted out within the terms of this system. As for the woman, she is primarily the eroticized repository of the values and standards of the male's social group. The passages describing how Troilus's 'love' makes him a class paragon are intelligible precisely and only because the woman represents the masculine self-image and class ideal. To 'love' is to become fused with the most revered values in the community where the male's identity emerges. With great shrewdness Pandarus tells the converted Troilus to say after him, 'for now myself I love' (I 934): the ambiguity in the phrase is wonderfully appropriate, conjuring up Narcissus's discovery that he burns for love of himself, that what he desires is himself.[17] Here, however, the apparently individualistic and 'desocialized' narcissism of the male lover is a narcissism *with* an object, a particular social construct with specific social functions. The way the poem explores this is just one delicate example of Stephen Knight's claim that it manifests 'both a theoretical grasp of sociocultural patterns and also a deeply imagined recreation of human life'.[18]

In Book V the poem introduces another representation of masculine identity and the genesis of 'love' within classic forms of courtly language. A strand which has actually woven its way through the text now emerges – namely, inter-male competition within the knightly class. While the class is divided along national lines, the poet has both Troilus and Diomede stress the shared values and practices among both Greek and Trojan knights.[19] It is this continuity, rather than any nationalistic differences, that the poem examines. In doing so it alludes to a potentially dangerous feature in the formation of the knightly ruling class, one we shall return to in the next chapter and which has been described by Mervyn James in his invaluable study of the mentality defined by the concept of 'honour':

> This, emerging out of a long-established military and chivalric tradition, is characterized above all by a stress on competitive assertiveness; it assumes a state of affairs in which resort to violence is natural and justifiable. . . . From honour's self-assertion there also followed its competitiveness and aggressivity . . . always latent in the relationships of men of honour.[20]

One of the functions of courtesy and courtly ritual was to contain this aggressive competition 'within acceptable limits', though 'even courtesy did no more than demarcate the battlefield'.[21] How precarious are the restraints on 'competitive assertiveness' in the male lover the poem makes startlingly clear.

Diomede's orientation towards Criseyde begins in an episode which reflects the male-gazing scene in Troy. Turned into a commodity by Trojan males, as Hector objects (IV 179–82), Criseyde is sold to the Greeks, cruelly cut off from her home. The Greek knight watches her miserable separation from Troilus, reads the signs of love, moves in 'and by the regne hire hente', leading her 'by the bridel' (V 74–92). This position of domination brings traditional imagery of male supremacism into play, one that the Wife of Bath had to invert in her battle with the monologic anti-feminism of the fifth husband – 'He yaf me al the bridel in myn hond'.[22] From this position of power Diomede begins to display his mastery of courtly language, including the familiar discourse of love. All the key terms are produced as the man 'gan fallen forth in speche', no novice in the 'craft', as the poet notes (V 107, 89–90):

> as a knyght . . . preyede hir . . . 'I swor you . . . To ben youre frend . . . I pray yow . . . Comaundeth me, how soore that me smerte,/To don al that may like unto youre herte . . . as youre brother . . . my frendshipe . . . O[ne] god of Love in soth we [Greeks and Trojans] serven bothe . . . beth nat wroth with me . . . serve . . . Youre owene aboven every creature . . . I loved never womman herebiforn . . . ne nevere shal no mo . . . beth nat my fo . . . I am nat of power for to stryve/Ayeyns the god of Love . . . mercy . . . grace . . . serve . . . til I sterve'.
>
> (V 106–75)

These are the familiar terms of the courtly composition of 'love' which we find not only in Troilus, Palamon, Arcite, Aurelius,

Absalon, and other Chaucerian males but in fifteenth- and sixteenth-century makings of 'love'. Its remote descendants are still alive today, commonplace and popularized, as in so many Mills and Boon romances. The male protests his subjugation, his self-disciplined and reverential service of the commanding woman, but the poet has preceded this with the figure which emblematizes the actual power relations – the isolated woman, handed from one group of males to another, led 'by the bridel'.[23] The female whom the knight addresses is as imperialistically constituted as the women in the earlier scene of the gaze.

One fresh motif, however, is added. For Diomede explicitly mentions the competition for women in his own knightly community, a competition involving shared self-images embodied in woman and one which binds the men together even as it seems to divide them (V 169–75). This dialectic was one Chaucer treated in *The Knight's Tale* and *The Franklin's Tale*, just as he did in the different idiom of *The Miller's Tale* and *The Merchant's Tale*. As Stephen Knight writes of *The Knight's Tale*:

> Chaucer's story, by having two lovers of one woman, makes conflict central and overt, creating much more sharply than usual 'competitive assertiveness', that inherent acquisitive aggression which was the real core of the medieval knight's quest for wealth and honour.[24]

Women, like Emily in *The Knight's Tale*, certainly become 'the symbol of competition', as Troilus himself acknowledges;[25] but simultaneously they are the symbol of a common knightly project. The competition Diomede makes so explicit becomes a dominant motif in Book V, and the poem comes to suggest how it permeates the formation of masculine love in this culture.

Just as Troilus had 'argumented' to himself after his gaze had 'percede' the woman at the festival (I 377, 272), so Chaucer has Diomede arguing 'withinne hymself' between his bridel-taking encounter with Criseyde and his second meeting. The passage recalls the urgent demands Troilus made to Pandarus and the men's plotting to involve Criseyde in the knight's 'love' through the poem's first three books:

> This Diomede, of whom you telle I gan,
> Goth now withinne hymself ay arguynge
> With al the sleighte, and al that evere he kan,

How he may best, with shortest taryinge,
Into his net Criseydes herte brynge.
To this entent he koude nevere fyne;
To fisshen hire, he leyde out hook and lyne.
(V 771–7)

Like most love-poems this one has been replete with commonplace male claims about cruel females fishing for 'gilteles' men, with 'nettes' in which the male heart is 'narwe ymasked and yknet' (II 327–8; III 1,353–5), only it has attended with unusual care to the consequences this inversion of reality entailed for women.[26] It also attends with care to the psychological grounds of such inversions, and to those I return below. Here, however, the masculine introspective language receives its most overt critique. Chaucer encourages us to consider the levels of aggression in this conventional formation of masculine desire, foregrounding not only the 'net' but the 'hook' with which the male plans to 'fisshen hire', the hook which will penetrate the fish's mouth. The image is commonplace and one finds it elaborated near the beginning of Andreas's book on love.[27] But unlike much traditional literary history, Chaucer's poems rarely ask us to think that by identifying something as 'conventional' we have even begun to understand its human significance. At this point his work unpacks the sadism habitually naturalized in the language of love and in commentaries which accept and use its terms as unproblematic. Diomede moves on from the 'hook' image to argue that: 'whoso myghte wynnen swich a flour/From hym for whom she morneth nyght and day,/He myghte seyn he were a conquerour' (V 792–4).

The implications of traditional flower-imagery still surrounding the making of 'femininity' in our own culture are nicely displayed here. Plucked flowers do not speak, let alone answer back and walk away. They passively accept their place in the circuits of exchange and symbolism. In this model, the female is the spoils of male victory, the proof of masculinity in the community. As Monica McAlpine writes, 'the idea of competition between men for the possession of a woman is deeply engrained in the Greeks and the Trojans and in all their Western descendants'.[28] In fact, Diomede's desire is sharpened by seeing the woman as the possession of another man: through bringing her 'herte' into his 'net', through fixing her mouth onto his 'hook', he will, with one cast, be a double 'conquerour'.

It is true, as many readers feel, that Chaucer gives us good reasons to differentiate Troilus and Diomede quite sharply. But it is as true that Troilus and Pandarus themselves manifest the aggressive, sadistic dimensions of masculine love so plainly exhibited by the Greek magnate. For Pandarus, just like Diomede, Criseyde is an object whose existence is solely to gratify the desires of his friend, and so his own. By giving the most disturbingly aggressive aspect of Troilus's quest to Pandarus, Chaucer enables readers to think better of the young man than they otherwise might; yet Troilus depends on Pandarus in Books II and III, colluding with the most manipulative and unsettling plots against Criseyde.[29] The aggression in question can be illustrated briefly in characteristic instances like these:

> '. . . Refuse it noght', quod he, and hente hire faste,
> And in hire bosom the lettre down he thraste. . . .
> . . .
> Pandare, which that stood hire faste by,
> Felte iren hoot, and he bygan to smyte
>
> (II 1,154–5, 1,275–6)

Grabbing at her, smiting when the iron is hot, poking her (III 115–16), his approach is a committedly colonizing activity. It is well represented in lines where he likens Criseyde to an oak tree and the lover to a wood-chopper, reassuring Troilus that while it may seem, 'That though she bende, yeet she stant on roote':

> Thenk here-ayeins: whan that the stordy ook,
> On which men hakketh ofte, for the nones,
> Receyved hath the happy fallyng strook,
> The greete sweigh doth it come al at ones,
> As don thise rokkes or thise milnestones
>
> (II 1,378, 1,830–84)

This is a startling expression of the structures of feeling and dominion permeating masculine sexual love, all the more so for its utterly conventional components, to which Pandarus typically draws attention (II 1,390). Does not the pious Parson, quite as much as the practitioner of marital rape, Januarie, see marital sexuality in terms of 'a man' wielding 'his owene knyf'?[30] 'No wonder', reflects Pandarus, 'Though wommen dreden with us men to dele' (III 321–2).

Troilus mostly acts out his aggression through Pandarus, on the battlefield and in the conventional accusations that the woman is a sweet enemy, enmeshing, starving, and killing the male victim. But even in the book of sexual communion, one that contains a moving display of Criseyde's intelligence and generosity, we find the habitual male lying, aggressive manipulation, and a voyeurism which re-enacts in the private sphere the public male gaze analysed earlier; in all this Troilus's full collusion is made plain.[31] There is also some very curious material in the invocation he makes just before he goes to the room in which Criseyde is asleep:

> O Jove ek, for the love of faire Europe,
> The which in forme of bole awey thow fette,
> Now help! . . .
> . . .
> O Phebus, thynk whan Dane hireselven shette
> Under the bark, and laurer wax for drede,
> Yet for hire love, O help now at this nede!
> (III 722–4, 726–8)

These are fantasies of rape. Presumably such images take over Troilus's speech here because, like the sadistic language of Diomede and Pandarus, they represent a significant aspect of masculine 'love' (III 722, 728) in the prevailing culture. These images of rape are probably defused for many readers by being projected into fables about gods and by the poet's disclosure that they are a substitute for any action, let alone violent action. Pandarus points this out (III 736–42) and Troilus's later swoon besides Criseyde's bed confirms it (III 1,086–92). His fantasies are thus represented as the product of 'drede' (III 706–7), fear lest his masculine identity, so heavily dependent on performance in the sexual domain, might not, as it were, stand up. While Chaucer deals with all this in gamesome mockery, it does not seem wildly inappropriate to remember that 'drede' in human beings easily leads to violence against the person(s) seen as its cause, especially when that 'drede' involves what is taken as a threat to self-identity. Merely keeping in the fictional and domestic sphere, we can recall Othello.

It is in these contexts that I read Troilus's lines to Criseyde in bed, after she has forgiven him, resuscitated him, and astonished him with her trusting, generous affection.[32] Embracing her, he says: 'Now be ye kaught, now is ther but we tweyne!/Now yeldeth yow, for other bote is non!' (III 1,207–8). The language of catching, the imperative to yield, the claim of isolation, the denial of any choice to the caught person ('other bote is non'), all this links with Diomede's desires for conquest and, I think it is not too harsh to suggest, the strange fantasies of rape noted above.[33] The lines show how the knight's self-identity and love are bound up with the will to mastery, a will itself permeated by the 'drede' just considered. This threatens to control the intimate sphere so thoroughly that it will eradicate any individual and historical potentials it may have for nourishing pleasures and visions of human possibility denied in the daily world which is ruled by those who represent the current version of 'reality'. In this promising context too one feels the distressing resonances of the poet's decision to liken Troilus in bed to the hawk and Criseyde to the lark, 'Whan that the sperhauk hath it in his foot' (III 1,191–2). It is worth recalling the 'tiraunt' hawks in *The Parliament of Fowls*: one 'that doth pyne/To bryddes for his outrageous ravyne', or another that prays on larks (ll. 334–40). There the images unfold in an ironically playful political examination of the rhetoric of 'common profit' in a community composed of thoroughly self-interested and competitively assertive groups and individuals;[34] here the politics are sexual politics, the image once more evoking aggression and violence, only now of a male lover against the woman who has accepted him.

Yet Chaucer's vision of the potential of relations between male and female lovers is not as despairing and homogeneous as that of some of his moralizing readers, especially those Stephen Knight describes as 'a priestly caste of American professors'.[35] Nor does he collude with the habitual and often casual masculine denial of subjective existence to the woman, as I have argued at some length elsewhere.[36] So while Criseyde, trained to be a woman in a knights' community, characteristically accommodates to the language of the male, imported from the public sphere, she simultaneously draws on her own resources to resist its implications: 'Ne hadde I er now, my swete herte deere,/Ben yold, ywis, I were now nought heere!' (III 1,210–11). The resistance is in the deft way she takes responsibility for her own presence in bed with him. In doing so she reminds him that she is not here simply because she is 'kaught', but because she is a human agent who, whatever the gross pressures brought against her, had made decisions 'er now' without which, 'I were now nought heere'. Continually the poem works thus to negate man's traditional denial of subjectivity to women, brushing its culture and its own sources strongly against the grain, a mark of its idiosyncracy, lasting significance, and greatness.[37]

Criseyde's response encourages Troilus to make a move of recognition, even a move to abandon the will to mastery. Whether it is sustained is a question we shall consider, but on this move depends the mutual 'blisse' the poet now sets out to evoke in such memorable manner as the lovers float in the most intense joy they had felt 'syn that they were born'.[38] Only through such a move could Criseyde have any cause 'hym to triste' enabling the mutual delight figured in this memorable image:

> And as aboute a tree, with many a twiste,
> Bytrent and writh the swote wodebynde
> Gan ech of hem in armes other wynde.
> (III 1,230–2)

Together they are the entwining, twisting 'wodebynde', the honeysuckle. Unostentatiously but decisively this figure sets aside those common images which carefully reaffirm male dominion in emblems of interdependent love. For example, the image of the elm and the vine which 'twines' round it, where the elm is 'an emblem of firm masculine strength, the vine of fruitfulness and feminine softness, submission and sweetness'.[39] So in *Paradise Lost* Milton represents the unfallen Eve's hair, 'As the vine curls her tendrils which implied/Subjection' to the male, confirming his allegedly 'Absolute rule'.[40] But in *Troilus and Criseyde* the new moment of mutual recognition encourages a freedom from 'drede' in which the woman, 'Opned hire herte and tolde hym hire entente', a new context in which the recurrent word is *joy*, one that 'passeth al that herte may bythynke'.[41]

Troilus himself, we are told, is changed by this intimate experience of mutuality and joy. He himself claims, 'I feele a newe qualitee,/Yee al another than I dide er this', and much in the book supports the claim.[42] At this stage the poem may seem to invite the kind of reading so admirably made by Monica McAlpine: Troilus's commitment to a relationship with a specific woman develops into a love which corrects the earlier solipsism, the projective fantasies and narcissism which so dominate his presentation in Books I and II. 'Troilus is no longer the infatuated lover nor the courtly servant. He has become a true friend.'[43] In my view, however, the poem invites us to entertain this only as a possible direction, one that it did not take – for very good reasons. But before describing these reasons I wish briefly to follow the poem as it moves from the intimate sphere back to the public world under the rule of men locked in a war waged, as Troilus remarks, 'For ravysshyng of wommen' (IV 548).

This world is shown derisively rejecting Hector's insistence that, 'We usen here no wommen for to selle' (IV 182–96). The men in Parliament turn Criseyde into a commodity, perceiving women as mere objects in a system of exchange to be operated in what they take to be their own interest. Only men are subjects whose needs, fears, and aspirations should be considered. Unlike Hector or the narrator, Troilus unquestioningly accepts that in this parliamentary decision 'she is chaunged for the townes good' (IV 553). This reminds one how his identity remains profoundly bound up with the public values of the masculine world with which this chapter began, even when they threaten to destroy all potentials the intimate sphere has revealed and are, as the poem so often suggests, finally self-destroying. The crisis in Book IV brings out how precarious are individual transformations in the 'private' domain quite unsupported by simultaneous and congruent reconstruction of the 'public' realm. In reality, these spheres can never be autonomous. As Troilus rushes from the Parliament to his bedroom, 'allone', he experiences the truth of this statement from a perspective that is far from the theoretical (IV 218ff.).

He turns his rage at the public decision into violent self-abuse, hitting himself and banging his head against the wall (IV 243–5). While such displaced rage may well invite psychoanalytic attention, laughter, or both, it is the knight's orientation towards Criseyde that concerns me at the moment, encapsulated in lines such as these: 'O my Criseyde, O lady sovereigne/Of thilke woful soule that thus crieth,/Who shal now yeven comfort to my peyne?' (IV 316–19). She exists only as his healer. So unreal is her subjectivity to him that neither the dreadful fate decreed for her by Parliament nor her feelings come into his considerations. So far is her situation from his mind that he does not even wonder how she will learn of the parliamentary decision. Chaucer, however, does show us: not having any public existence, the woman learns of her fate by rumour and gossip, by 'tales' (IV 659–700). This sequence seems to me strong evidence that the poem does not take the line of interpretation Monica McAlpine pursues so persuasively, shows that it does not ask us to take the man's responses as a sign of 'true' friendship.[44] Pandarus's reaction is like Troilus's. He blocks out Criseyde's experience, painful fears, and needs, fixing her in the only role that the system envisages for women: healer of the male (IV 913–17). Forget your own grief, is his demand, 'And shapeth yow his sorwe for t'abregge' (IV 925). It is quite in line with all this that when Troilus comes to the woman who is to be sold to the enemy army he tells her that if she fails to escape to Troy in the agreed ten days, she will be 'unkynde' and he will never again have 'hele, honour, ne joye', for he will kill himself if she delays (IV 1,440–6; IV 1,328). This response may be masculine 'love' but it is hardly that of 'true friend'.

Chaucer highlights the specifically masculine nature of these responses by contrasting Criseyde's when she hears the men's decision about her life. Alone, in her bedroom:

> She seyde, 'How shal he don, and ich also?
> How sholde I lyve, if that I from hym twynne?
> O deere herte eke, that I love so,
> Who shal that sorwe slen that ye ben inne?
> (IV 757–60)

The poem juxtaposes masculine negation of female subjectivity with the woman's acknowledgement of both her own and the male's experience, their mutual vulnerability. She goes on to her own miserable prospect, exchanged to the Greeks, but asks how Troilus will manage 'in this sorwful cas', hoping he can somehow set her and his sorrow aside (IV 792–8). When Pandarus arrives she confirms what she has been thinking on her own: '"Grevous to me, God woot, is for to twynne,"/Quod she, "but yet it harder is to me/To sen that sorwe which that he is inne"' (IV 904–6).

These are rather underemphasized passages in critical commentaries, but they are important contributions to the poem's exploration of the horizons of masculine love and identity, in that culture at least. Here it might be worth remarking how irrelevant such contexts make the poem's closing and simple generalities about 'feynede loves' (V 1,848) and 'wrecched worldes appetites' (V 1,851). There is nothing 'feyned' nor wretchedly appetitive about Criseyde's affections. On the contrary, her form of loving is such that even while grieving in this calamity she fully acknowledges the man's subjective reality. As she has done before, she cares for him, loves him in an existence she unanxiously acknowledges as *other*. Unlike the male she sustains the mutuality achieved in Book III even in this crisis. One explanation of this sharp difference lies in the social making of 'masculine' and 'feminine' roles, ones that she, as much as Troilus, has internalized: her identity is bound up with being 'needed' by a male as his 'healer', with being a nurturer of men, one who accommodates to the male-governed world even when such accommodation seems against her own interests.[45] Another more speculative, but related, explanation may be that she has resources lacking in the male lover, and to this I shall turn in a moment. Whatever one decides about the appropriate explanation, the poem makes Criseyde a figure who breaks through received anti-feminist modes in her representation and helps us grasp some of the determinant features, not to say limitations, of masculine identity.

Book V sustains and deepens the contrasts we have just been following. It again juxtaposes Troilus's perspectives with Criseyde's, but now combines this with an extraordinary powerful representation of the situation into which Criseyde has been hurled by the Trojan men. Chaucer depicts her as a frighteningly isolated figure in the enemy's camp, miserably remembering and mourning her lover as she realizes the imposed separation cannot be circumvented by any of the plans she had so desperately suggested in Book IV. Rightly fearing rape if she seeks to 'stele awey by nyght', she emphasizes all the ways she was 'allone and hadde nede/Of frendes help'.[46] In doing so, the poem works against the idealizing mentality cultivated in the conventional discourses of love, just as it does against the desocialized and self-righteous moralism of the 'priestly caste' of scholars, ones who could do worse than ponder Monica McAlpine's view that 'Chaucer's readers may well hope that in a similarly complex situation, they would be able to rescue as much integrity as Criseyde does'.[47]

Troilus, however, cannot follow the imaginative acts of his maker into this domain, any more than the 'priestly caste' of critics seem able to. In Book V his horizons remain those just illustrated from Book IV. They are so similar that two examples will suffice. The first is his parting remark to Criseyde as she is led away by Greek soldiers: 'Now holde youre day, and do me nat to deye' (V 84). The attribution of untrammelled freedom to minister to his needs in these catastrophic circumstances is breathtaking.[48] It indicates the overwhelming difficulty he has in even beginning to imagine the woman's actual existence and the terrors she now faces, a difficulty amply displayed in the suicide threats he had attacked her with in Book IV (1,440–6). The second example is from the letter he writes to Criseyde later in the final book (V 1,317–421):

> With hele swich that, but ye yeven me
> The same hele, I shal non hele have.
> In yow lith, whan yow liste that it so be,
> The day in which me clothen shal my grave;
> In yow my lif, in yow myght for to save
> Me fro disese of alle peynes smerte;
> (V 1,415–20)

Whereas the poet has evoked Criseyde's agonizing and complicated feelings in the military camp, Troilus, in his own misery, does not begin to grasp them. He remains the conventional knightly lover for whom the woman is physician and only physician, a person whose sole existence is in relation to his own demands. She herself is assumed to be invulnerable, without needs of human solidarity or friendship; she is the endless fountain of male life. Or, as Troilus complains, she *should* be.

Nevertheless, in grasping the male's horizons the poem does not ask us to substitute an abstract set of individualizing moral judgements against Troilus for those traditionally thrown at Criseyde. As it began by evoking the cultural determinants in the man's constitution of 'woman', 'love', and 'beloved', treating Troilus as a paragon of his class and gender, so it continues to give us every reason to understand Troilus's role as representative. Just as in its making of Criseyde, the poem displays a profoundly social imagination and a profoundly cultural psychology in its making of Troilus.

It is within this perspective and the contrasts between Troilus and Criseyde that I now wish to consider the central place of *anxiety* in the form of love figured forth in Troilus. It is something very different to Criseyde's totally rational and always well-grounded fears.[49] Furthermore, as Elizabeth Hatcher has shown, this anxiety is itself conventional in the courtly traditions of love writing.[50] Nearly 200 years before Chaucer's poem, Andreas Capellanus observed, 'To be truthful, no-one can exhaust the catalogue of a single lover's fears', and that work made it plain that the anxieties in question were peculiarly male.[51] But just what is at stake for men formed in this tradition of love, just why should male love include such chronically anxious states?

In seeking some answers to the question it seems worth recapitulating certain lines developed in this chapter. If 'woman' is a focal point in the knight's social identity, if possession of woman is an essential component of his ability to be a 'man', to feel fully integrated in his community, to like himself, then it can hardly be surprising that loss of this object should have devastating consequences for him – unless that loss could be assimilated in mourning and the knight's identity be reaffirmed. In this perspective Troilus's anguished disintegration in Book V is fully intelligible – the transformation of the way in which he kills Greeks, the abandonment of the idealized courtly self-image with which he has so lovingly identified, and his frenzied pursuit of a new object of desire that proves more evasive than Criseyde, that is, the Greek man who 'un-manned' him by taking 'his' woman (V 792–4, 1,755–60).[52] For he cannot mourn, cannot accept Pandarus's suggestions about a suitable substitute for the lost woman (IV 400–76, V 1,695–701), and cannot any longer feel part of the public world which gave him his ideal self-image and the means to make a life embodying its patterns. It is not surprising that in this extreme social alienation he moves into a state of chronic melancholy from which suicide is the only escape: 'Myn owen deth in armes wol I seche' (V 1,718). These, in my view, are the factors the poem offers in answer to the question about what is at stake for the male in his anxiety and melancholy.

Yet it seems to me that the poem also allows, even encourages a more psychoanalytic explanation focusing on the especially intimate realm within the 'private' sphere evoked in Book III and addressed earlier in this chapter. In that context the woman becomes the bearer of rather different masculine projections, memories, and wishes than those we have just outlined, while the form anxiety takes is jealousy.[53]

Troilus actually displays considerable anxiety before he even speaks with the particular woman on whom he had cast his gaze. It pervades Book I:

> But thanne felte this Troilus swich wo,
> That he was wel neigh wood; for ay his drede
> Was this, that she som wight hadde loved so,

That nevere of hym she wolde han taken hede.
For which hym thoughte he felte his herte blede.
(I 498–502)

This 'drede' prefigures both the simulated jealousy in Book III and the obsessional form it takes in Book V. Grounded in the desperate need for exclusive loving it already generates misery and seems to lend support to Andreas's representation of masculine 'love' as enmeshed with 'fear' and 'jealousy' in its very generation.[54] This is certainly what Criseyde thinks about masculine forms of love (II 750–6) and what she attacks in Book III. There she challenges the tradition in which 'jalousie is love', suggesting instead that it is an aggressive move more like 'hate', one bound up with 'fantasie' (III 981–1,054). Reasonable as her arguments are, she makes one comment which points to the difficulty involved in attempting to cure such anxiety: jealousy, 'that wikked wyvere' can creep in 'causeles' (III 1,009–12). This is just what Emilia tells Desdemona in response to her lament that she never gave Othello 'cause' for his violent jealousy:

But jealous souls will not be answered so.
They are not ever jealous for the cause,
But jealous for they're jealous. It is a monster
Begot upon itself, born on itself.
(*Othello*, III 4, 155–9)

But if it is an obscure aspect of some male psychodrama in which women are unfortunately caught up, rational criticism is unlikely to make much impact and one is left asking where it comes from, why it exists. It is the seemingly 'causeles' nature of the anxiety that encourages some kind of psychoanalytic inquiry, however tentative and speculative it must remain.

One way into this is through the conventional language of courtly and romantic love in which the male presents himself as mortally sick, constituting the female as physician ('leche'), the male's magic healer. This scheme is tirelessly reiterated in *Troilus and Criseyde* as in countless other medieval and renaissance works, not to mention contemporary songs.[55] It carries implications that are equally prominent in the poem: since the woman has infinite life-giving powers, it must be her fault, her malevolent withholding of vital resources, if the male feels discomforted, vulnerable, and 'sick'. She becomes the 'cruel' enemy murdering a helpless victim.[56] As we have observed, we even meet this language in Book V, when the woman who has been sold to the enemy and thus locked up in a military camp, is perceived as the agent responsible for the Trojan knight's mental suffering, its 'cause' (V 427). In a passage quoted above (see p. 135) Troilus insists that unless the woman heals him he cannot live (V 1,415–20). The function of such idealization, for that is what we encounter in such claims, is plain enough at one level. It is a strategy for controlling the other person, defining her to fit one's own supposed needs: yet another strategy for outlawing female subjectivity independent of male fantasies.[57] But however basic this desire for controlling the other person is to idealization, reflection on the 'physician' image may suggest further dimensions. In seeking to describe these I have sought help from Melanie Klein's work, aware of the risks involved when the subject of study is a late medieval poem rather than a person living in the modern industrial societies within which Klein did her work, and when her methods involve an archaeology prioritizing infancy in a manner quite alien, I think, to any medieval forms of analysis. To me the risks seem worthwhile, for Klein's approach helps one focus on aspects of the poem addressed here, offering at least a plausible account of complex problems they raise. Furthermore, as the last chapter implied, however massive the transformations of economic organization and available ideologies between England in the later Middle Ages and in Klein's time, some fundamental features of gender arrangements and family formation survived, and probably still do.[58]

This is hardly the place or person to attempt a summary of Klein's work and it must suffice merely to outline the strands most relevant to my present concerns.[59] In Klein's work the relations between infant and 'mother', internal as well as external, predominate. The infant perceives the mother as an omnipotent godlike figure containing life resources essential to its survival. But the figure of the mother is necessarily ambivalent. Giver of all bliss and total gratification she is also the source of frustration, punishment, and threat. In response to this threat the child's own fears at losing the loved object (entailing the ego's own destruction) are combined with destructive aggression against what is seen as a persecuting force, the correlate of the ego's own internal aggression, the infant's sadistic impulse to harm and control the mother, aggression which in turn leads to guilt. If knowledge that the good and bad aspects of the mother are one is not assimilated, if the splitting of the object continues, then, in Klein's view, this will go along with a simultaneous splitting of the ego: 'I believe that the ego is incapable of splitting the object – internal and external – without a corresponding splitting taking place within the ego.' In this process the 'bad' parts are disowned, leading to severe psychological problems.[60] To fill out and apply this crude summary I shall quote a few of Klein's characteristic observations on idealization:

> Idealization is . . . bound up with . . . denial. Without partial and temporary denial of psychic reality the ego cannot bear the disaster by which it feels itself threatened . . . the idealized mother is the safeguard against . . . all bad objects, and therefore represents security and life itself.
>
> (Mitchell 1986: 152, 157–8)

For Klein idealization is bound up with splitting the loved object in a way which exaggerates its power and benevolence as a safeguard against fears of an aggressive, rejecting mother. It also 'springs from the power of instinctual desires which aim at unlimited gratification and therefore create the picture of the inexhaustible and always bountiful breast – an ideal breast' (Mitchell 1986: 181–2). Klein again writes of 'the infant's longing for an inexhaustible and always present breast – which would not only satisfy him but prevent destructive impulses and persecutory anxiety'. This longing, she remarks, 'cannot ever be fully satisfied' (Mitchell 1986: 212). In developing her account of idealization and the network of anxieties against which it is turned, she makes a connection which may, perhaps, illuminate the intensity of Troilus's anguish in Book V:

> There is a direct link between the envy experienced towards the mother's breast and the development of jealousy. . . . During the period characterized by the depressive position [pre-Oedipal in Klein's scheme] . . . he goes through states of mourning. . . . He also begins to understand more of the external world and realizes that he cannot keep his mother to himself as his exclusive possession.
>
> (Mitchell 1986: 218)

Klein's approach invites us to reflect on how much of the infant is still active in the adult, how infantile positions may actually be fostered and even institutionalized in adult gender arrangements and the discourses bound up with them, including that of 'love'. It seems to me that Klein's analysis describes the area in which we may find the sources of what puzzled Criseyde and Emilia, the sources of the profound anxieties Troilus displays before he has become Criseyde's lover which culminate in the obsessional jealousy Chaucer dramatizes in Book V, one that emerges even before Criseyde takes up with Diomede.[61]

Returning with these perspectives to Book III we can now observe a feature that has not, I think, seemed particularly noteworthy to many readers. The emotional warmth so strongly evoked, the images of a blissful, intimate paradise, suggest how in affectionate love-making the old griefs Klein unfolds, not to mention less ancient ones, may be repaired.[62] No wonder this oasis is so desperately sought. And yet there should be some wonder. For the *woman* neither shows herself obsessed with the need to possess Troilus nor unable to complete the processes of mourning when she is forced to live without him. While the poem continually shows Criseyde's joy and security in the sexual union with Troilus, shows her grieving and mourning at the loss of the man, it does not suggest she is consumed by generalized anxiety, the flames of jealousy, or chronic melancholy. Profoundly committed to a relationship she finds gratifying and pleasurable, the woman does not apparently invest her intimate sexual relation with the same function it serves in the male's psychodrama. Why? Could the answer be bound up with the way the female lover is represented as the nourishing, encompassing mother and physician, the adult male more as the nurtured, protected infant?

It is no coincidence that in Book III itself the male is explicitly called 'childish'; that he abnegates responsibility for his own action; that he relies on the woman to resurrect him in her encompassing physical affection; that he needs her reassurance that her forgiveness is unlimited. We understand why Criseyde sees the maternal role being activated: having reassured the trembling male she tells him, 'Now were it worthi that ye were ybete', 'And beth wel war ye do namore amys' (III 1,169, 1,180). These are all, unequivocally, images which signal a reactivation of the mother–infant relationship. We are in the realm conjured up in *The Chastising of God's Children*, where God is likened to a mother playing with her child, 'and suffreþ þe child to wepe and crie and besili to seke hir wiþ sobbynge and wepynge. But þanne comeþ þe modir sodeinli wiþ mery chier and lauȝhynge, biclippynge hir child and kissynge, and wipeþ awei þi teeris.' Or to: 'a louynge modir þat listeþ to pley wiþ hir sowkynge child, whiche modir in hir pley sumtyme hideþ hir, and comeþ aȝen to knowe bi þe countenaunce of þe child hou wele it loueþ þe modir'. One who educates the child, thus:

> she wiþdraweþ a litel and a litel þe mylke and oþer delicacies. . . . She wiþdraweþ hir glad chiere and sumtyme spekiþ sharpli, sumtyme þreteneþ him, and if þe childe wex wanton, she betiþ him, first wiþ a litel rodde, and þe strenger he wexiþ, þe sharper rodde she takeþ, and sharply leiþ on, sumtyme to kepe him ynne, whanne nedis he wolde oute . . . þe more she loueþ him, þe sharper she betiþ him to make him to bide at hom, and al is for loue, for looth she is to forgo hir child, which she derely loueþ.[63]

When Criseyde tells Troilus, 'Now were it worthi that ye were ybete', she has grasped the essential nature of the role in which the man has cast her and himself, accepting its terms just as she had already accepted her identification as the man's 'leche' (II 1,582; III 176–82). The Kleinian perspective thus seems even to have some surprisingly *explicit* analogies in Chaucer's poem, as it does in the tradition of European courtly poetry, where Herbert Moller long ago described the common construction of the female lover as a mother-image to the infantilized male. Among his illustrations to this theme, he shows 'Infantile identifications of love and food, of the lover's despair at the unfed infant's rage'. This is familiar material to readers of *Troilus and Criseyde* where the *woman* 'Made hym swich feste', and Pandarus demands that she should make Troilus 'moore feste,/So that his lif be saved', while the man so often claims, 'I sterve' (III 1,228; II 361–2, 1,530). Rarely, if ever, does this language seem reciprocated. We have also seen Criseyde image herself in a manner that belongs to the same traditions of 'love' in which 'Heinrich von Veldeke fears his beloved as a child the punishing mother: "I am afraid of the good one as a child of the birch".' Moller comments:

> many of these poets connect the relationship to their lady-love with memories of spanking. One minnesinger says: 'Her beautiful eyes were the birch by which she overpowered me

> from the first moment'; and another promises he will 'still faithfully serve the good one who thrashes me so severely without a birch'.[64]

Chaucer seems to be tactfully working rather common masculine fantasies into his own complex exploration of Troilus's 'lovynge' in its range of 'wo', 'wele', 'joie', and 'sorwe' (I 1–5).

Turning back to Book III and the problem of 'causeles' masculine anxiety which prompted these reflections, Chaucer shows such anxieties resurfacing even while Troilus and Criseyde are still in bed, suffused with the joy Book III, unlike some of its readers, celebrates. Dreading any separation, the knight asserts:

> Yit were it so that I wiste outrely
> That I, youre humble servant and youre knyght,
> Were in youre herte iset as fermely
> As ye in myn, the which thyng, trewely,
> Me levere were than thise worldes tweyne,
> Yet sholde I bet enduren al my peyne.
> (III 1,485–91)

The anxieties here seem peculiar when set against his experience of Criseyde and the present moment, with its mutual 'blisse' and trust. But the trouble is, not for the first time in the poem, Troilus wants to know utterly. He maintains that his survival of the forthcoming parting imposed by the dawn depends upon knowing 'outrely' the movements of her desires, her 'herte', as 'outrely' as he at least thinks he knows his own. But is such knowledge even possible? A few moments before, he had kissed the woman's eyes and claimed that they were her nets thus turning her into the fisher and himself into the victim, inverting Diomede's image considered earlier. He then observed of her disposition: 'God woot, the text ful hard is, soth to fynde' (III 1,352–8). In one sense, to represent the woman as a text for exegesis (or worse) by the male reader can be seen as simply another case of the male will to power. (Texts do not protest about the treatment they have received and walk out, at least literally.) Yet this is not how Troilus himself takes the image here. For he complains that he cannot control the text, cannot easily 'fynde' it. This is a major source of his anxiety and however great the reassurances that Criseyde shows him it cannot be alleviated for long. This is because the kind of knowledge he seeks is impossible;

the desire for it can only generate anxiety. In Langland's terms, the 'wil' of another can only be known, with the certainty Troilus seeks, by 'Piers þe Plowman, *Petrus id est Christus*' (XV 210–12). In Toril Moi's terms, commenting on Andreas Capellanus, 'the lady remains *other*: however hard he [the male lover] tries to master her by his discourse he will always suffer in the knowledge that her consciousness is not his'.[65] It seems impossible for the male to accept this without anxiety, to accept the woman as a centre of desire and will. Even here, in bed, it is likely to induce panic. If 'the lady remains *other*' then the resources of his life, his 'feast', remain outside his control and could be withdrawn. The 'other' is in the position of 'mother', and the man's desire to know 'outrely' and find total security in that knowledge, and its object, is a doomed project. It is the heritage of the infant in the adult, and fosters his inability to recognize the woman's subjectivity.

Criseyde is conspicuously free from any such project. For this striking difference the Kleinian tradition seems to offer at least part of a plausible answer. In Dorothy Dinnerstein's development of Klein's work along lines that pay more attention to cultural forces and the social construction of gender, we encounter an argument that is relevant to the difference in question. Analysing sex-role education in early childhood, with the identifications that emerge in this cultural process, she maintains that:

> The mother-raised woman is likely to feel, more deeply than the mother-raised man, that she carries within herself a source of the magic early parental richness. In this sense – even if not in others – she is more self-sufficient than the mother-raised man: what is inside oneself cannot be directly taken away by a rival.[66]

The pleasure of sexual love 'allows us to relive some of the original life-giving delight of infancy', and while this may be true for both male and female, she argues that differences in an earlier stage leave their traces here too:

> When the boy, as an adult, finds this delight in heterosexual lovemaking, he finds it outside himself, as before, in a female body. And if the inhabitant of this female body feels free to bestow its resources on a competitor, she is re-evoking for him the situation in which mother, unbearably, did not belong to baby.[67]

No wonder so many male critics have responded so angrily to Criseyde! No wonder that the male should have such difficulty in accepting the woman as a centre of subjectivity, of desire and will, potentially opposed or indifferent to his own. Nor can we then be too surprised to find Criseyde having to beg Troilus not to let venomous 'fantasie' creep from his anxieties to attack her (III 1,503–5, picking up III 1,009–12). The very intensity of pleasure in their sexual union immediately revives, for the male, old dependencies and with them old fears.[68]

This is at least one of the contexts in which we should understand Troilus's turn to Boethius. Immediately after a stanza describing his sexual delight, the poem has Troilus sing a hymn to 'love'. In it, 'Benigne Love' is the 'holy bond of thynges', intervening with 'grace' when Troilus had been likely 'to sterve' and setting him now 'in so heigh a place' (III 1,247–74). The hymn assimilates the woman and the couple's mutual joy to a metaphysical scheme in which Boethius's *Consolation of Philosophy* is one prominent component.[69] In doing so it negates the poem's own delicate account of the woman's decisive initiative in Book III, her existence as a subjective agent, as well as negating the tissue of pressures under which Criseyde has acted.[70] Transforming her into 'a place', however exalted, is conventional enough – the language in which Pandarus had praised the knight for projecting his erotic fantasies with proper decorum, into 'so good a place', 'in a worthy place' (I 909, 895). But why at this moment should the man feel moved to produce such negations, why in a moment of such intimate happiness should he transform the woman into a life-saving 'place' in a field of metaphysical forces? The answer to these questions seems clear when one sees that the man's hymn is a classic example of idealization. It attempts to secure the moment, to fix it into a timeless metaphysical scheme where the woman becomes a space existing solely in relation to his 'desir'. The transformations involve all the denials of social and psychic reality noted in Klein's account of idealization. Indeed, when Troilus turns his attention back to the woman in bed with him, he tells her that God so completely supports the courtly discourse of love that he wills her to be Troilus's guide or pilot, taking responsibility for his life or death: 'he wol ye be my steere,/To do me lyve, if that yow liste, or sterve' (III 1,285–302). This is as conventional as the image of 'physician' or magic 'leche', replete with the same range of meanings, and it has already been encountered in Troilus's song from Petrarch (I 414–20). The idealized and thus controlled woman will fend off the man's deepest fears, satisfying too his infantile longings for unlimited gratification and exclusive possession. At the same time the idealization is now itself seemingly guaranteed by a metaphysical system. Still, even this combination cannot convince the man that the old grief and risk has been conclusively exorcized. As dawn points and the knight prepares for another day he laments that the anguish of leaving breaks his heart 'a-two':

> For how sholde I my lif an houre save,
> Syn that with yow is al the lyf ich have?
> . . .
> And of my lif, God woot how that shal be,
> Syn that desir right now so biteth me,
> That I am ded anon, but I retourne.
> How sholde I longe, allas, fro yow sojourne?
> (III 1,471–84)

The knight's public identity, its 'manly' control, power, and invulnerability, is put at risk by the consummation of one of its own demands. In fulfilling the quest to 'possess' a courtly lady the male has opened himself to a long-forgotten but voracious sense of dependency on the woman. Metaphysical transformations and schemes are feeble consolation for the man confronted with these feelings of neediness, this panic that, 'I am ded anon, but I retourne'. It is immediately after this passage that the knight voices the wish to have entire knowledge of the woman's consciousness (III 1,485–91). This impossible demand, analysed above, is thus closely tied in with the reawakening of very primitive feelings of gratification, dependency, and panic-inducing anxieties about the loss of the male's sources of life.

Troilus again turns to Boethian metaphysics in the elegant hymn to love later in Book III (1,744–71). The knight's poetry seeks to assimilate his union with Criseyde to the metaphysical love which allegedly governs cosmos, 'erth and se', communities, couples, and individual hearts in harmonious order.[71] It is a celebration following the 'feste' he had made of Criseyde to Pandarus (III 1,737–42). Yet once again it dissolves the human particularity of his lover in a web of abstractions. This befits the idiom of a neo-platonizing song, of course, but such an observation gives no account of just why such a metaphysical move should seem attractive to the man, and why at this point. The answer to these questions, it seems to me, are precisely the same as in the case of his Boethianizing in bed we have already discussed. The attractions are those of idealization, the underlying anxieties no different. They emerge rather sharply in a peculiar feature, wryly described by Stephen Knight: 'Troilus hopes that the God of Love will make everybody, by force if necessary (III 1,765–9), into lovers.'[72] In fact the hymn begs the metaphysical 'Love' to *bynd* Troilus's union with Criseyde (III 1,750) before culminating in the lines Knight refers to:

> So wolde God, that auctour is of kynde,
> That with his bond Love of his vertu liste
> To cerclen hertes alle, and faste bynde,
> That from his bond no wight the wey out wiste;
> And hertes colde, hem wolde I that he twiste
> To make hem love.
>
> (III 1,765–70)

The stress on *binding*, the demand to be *bound*, bound so absolutely that one would not even know the way out, is remarkable. It contrasts sharply with the utopian vision at the opening of *The Franklin's Tale* in which it is said that both women and men 'desiren libertee,/And nat to been constreyned as a thral', relationships being built around the understanding that, 'Love is a thyng as any spirit free'.[73] It contrasts as sharply with Criseyde's reflections on the risks of loving:

> I am myn owene womman, wel at ese,
> I thank it God, as after myn estaat,
> Right yong, and stonde unteyd in lusty leese,
> Withouten jalousie or swich debat:
> Shal noon husbonde seyn to me 'chek mat!'
> For either they ben ful of jalousie
> Or maisterfull, or loven novelrie
>
> (II 750–6)

Nor is it just the sovereign institutional powers taken by men in marriage: 'Allas! syn I am free,/ Sholde I now love, and put in jupartie/My sikernesse, and thrallen libertee?' (II 771–3). Troilus does not have to play the woman's part of 'physician' and magic 'leche', does not run quite the same risk of having his subjectivity systematically denied, so it is understandable that he should not voice the same worries about freedom and the loss of liberty. Nevertheless, he could not even contemplate the vision in *The Franklin's Tale*, so compatible with Criseyde's thoughts, because it would activate the deep anxieties and panics we have been following. The 'force' Knight notes in Troilus's image of conversion to love is in fact pervasive. It is an inextricable aspect of the longing for bondage and its guarantee by a metaphysical seigneur. Through that bondage, which is the woman's bondage too, the masculine subject hopes to secure himself against the possible loss of the other who has become, once again, his source of life. The Boethianizing hymn is the needy song of the infant in the adult male, striving to stave off the great disaster he fears.

Yet it cannot be avoided, for the males who govern in Troy decide that Criseyde is an object which can be traded. As we saw, the consequences of this decision for Troilus are ruinous. His most deep-rooted fears and dependencies overwhelm him. Long before Criseyde's relationship with Diomede, he collapses into melancholy and moves towards suicide (IV 950–5, 1,081). He does try, however, to see whether the catastrophe can be displaced by the 'consolations' of metaphysical speculation (IV 956–1,082). In doing so he fails to repeat Philosophy's answers to Boethius, but those scholars who criticize the knight for this seem to miss the point – which is, as Boethius makes plain, 'consolation'. The *Consolation of Philosophy* itself does not tell us whether the condemned Boethius was actually consoled by Philosophy's metaphysics. Nor is it at all clear why anyone should think that answers to metaphysical questions about predestination and free will could afford 'consolation' to someone in Troilus's state, whether those answers are drawn from Boethius's Philosophy or Ockham's rather persuasive critique of her 'solutions'.[74] Reading the Boethianizing attempt in Book IV it is hard not to conclude that no form of thumb-sucking, however sophisticatedly abstract, could defend the knight against the anxieties that flood over him.

Book V elaborates what the previous book had made painfully clear: the man has not the resources to assimilate the loss his colleagues forced him to confront. As we see him 'sick' and crippled with 'malencolye',[75] Chaucer is still careful to prevent us from making the mistake of attributing the causes to Criseyde's turning to Diomede. It cannot be emphasized too strongly that the catastrophe for the man lies in his separation from the woman. Fear of this disaster underlies his form of love, its idealizations and its anxieties. Even the transformation of 'frenetik and madde' melancholy into 'woode jalousie' was prefigured in Book I.[76] As Troilus insists to the painfully isolated woman: 'In yow my lif, in yow myght for to save/Me fro disese of alle peynes smerte' (V 1,419–20). He cannot accept that the woman is not a magical life-source, but herself a vulnerable human in dire need: 'I in distresse'.[77] I recall Dorothy Dinnerstein's comment that if the female feels free to bestow her resources on a 'competitor', as Criseyde of course does, 'she is re-evoking for him the situation in which mother, unbearably, did not belong to baby'.[78] With this intimate support to his identity now removed, Troilus becomes so 'feble, that he walketh by potente [crutch]' (V 1,222). Unable to assimilate loss, unable 'To unloven yow a quarter of a day', his rage is displaced from the woman whom he sees as refusing to save him and turned against himself.[79] He withers away so that nobody recognizes him. His 'public' identity collapses and when he returns to battle it is not as the integrated paragon of his class's culture but as a man consumed with 'ire', cruelty, and 'hate' (V 1,751–64). To the end of the poem the 'public' and the 'private' realms are thus inextricably related, loss of the woman in the 'private' sphere undermining the knight's 'public' identity. He pursues death, and he finds it (V 1,718, 1,806). This is, indeed, the only absolute transcendence of the old loss and the dialectics of desire in which it played so powerful yet so ghostly a role.

Thus, in a rather literal sense, the subject of the present chapter comes to an end. Yet after reporting the death of Troilus (V 1,806–7), the poem contains a further sixty-two lines. These *post mortem* reflections are not strictly relevant to the explorations we have been following – the man is dead, his disembodied 'goost', removed from human culture, gone wherever 'Mercurye sorted hym to dwelle', the poetic dramatization of 'masculine identity in the courtly community' and the dialectics of 'love' now completed. But it might seem odd to offer no comment at all on these lines, given the bulk of conflicting commentary they have stimulated.[80] So I shall summarize my views about them.

These sixty-two lines are diversionary. They seek to divert readers' attention from the poem's long, complex explorations of human culture, gender, and psychology, to divert attention from the problems that have emerged in the making of masculine identity, indeed, to divert attention from the quite extraordinary and idiosyncratic achievements of the great poem we have been reading. Dismissing Troilus and Trojan culture in rhetorical incantations (V 1,828–34, 1,849–55), the lines select terms with little purchase on the poem's own subtle processes and the delicate analysis and discriminations these gradually unfold. The terms I have in mind are clichéd and unelaborated ones like 'worldly vanyte', 'wrecched worldes appetites', 'false worldes brotelnesse', and the irrelevant 'feynede loves' mentioned above (see p. 133). Such terms would not enable one to grasp crucial differences between the forms of loving we find in Criseyde and those that Troilus displays in all their contradictory and confusing force. They would not even distinguish a lover like Troilus or one like Criseyde from that accomplished master of courtly discourses and most predatory of lovers, Theseus (*The Legend of Good Women*, VI), probably not even from the courtly rapist, Tereus (*The Legend of Good Women*, VII). From a certain clerical perspective such discriminations may seem trivial, all simply 'worldly vanyte', and this is the pose struck in Chaucer's own retraction of *Troilus and Criseyde* as one of the 'enditynges of worldly vanitees, the whiche I revoke' (*The Canterbury Tales*, X 1,084). One can understand the pressures to talk like this in a culture where clerical accounts and iconography of purgatory and hell were so prominent, but it is not the perspective and language in which the poem was made. Chaucer does not, after all, 'revoke' what he calls 'bookes of legendes of seintes, and omelies, and moralitee, and devocioun' (X 1,087); he, unlike the 'priestly caste' of readers, saw the decisive differences between these and *Troilus and Criseyde*.

The closing sixty-two lines are also diversionary in the sense that they seek to avoid the problems posed by the historical community in which 'love' played an important role in the constitution of class, gender, and individual identity, a community without whose existence and traditions *Troilus and Criseyde* could never have been written, a community on which the poem's author depended for his own living. Yet the poet tells the 'fresshe folkes' of this community, in whom 'love up groweth': 'Repeyreth hom fro worldly vanyte'.[81] Vague as the demand remains, it poses certain questions. Does the poet envisage a transformation of current courtly communities and their ethos? The last thing the gamesome stoic and civil servant can be seen as is a social or religious reformer, and the answer has to be in the negative. Does he then demand that 'yonge, fresshe folkes', in whom 'love up groweth' as such communities fashion them, should simply set aside the discourses and forms of life that had given them their identities, even while they continue to compete and flourish in these untransformed communities? Commonplace as such contradictory moralistic exhortations are, they remain superficial: to demand a transformation of peoples' whole orientation (V 1,835–41) without even challenging the practices of the community which give them their self-images, their occupations, their codes, and their goals must remain an empty gesture, as Aristotle and a tradition of pre-enlightenment moralists recognized.[82] The fact is these few lines cannot possibly address such issues. Nor can they begin to suggest anything about the alternative forms in which these 'fresshe folkes' *should* 'love', reproducing themselves and their secular communities – is the clerical idea of marital sex, sampled in the last chapter, to replace the potential of 'joie' and 'wo' glimpsed in Book III? How would Chaucer have dramatized this? Would it be like the union of Griselda and Walter, or like the unconsummated one of Cecilie and Valerian in *The Second Nun's Tale*? The brief passage does not hold the faintest sketch of an answer. Perhaps the poet did want us to envisage something like *The Second Nun's Tale*? There, we recall, the courtly lady saint follows the demands of the ending we have been discussing, renounces all that conventional clerical teaching would classify as 'worldly vanyte' and casts her 'herte' to God. She tells her husband that if he touches her or loves her in a manner that includes their bodies, marital sexual love being 'vilenye', then the divine angel, 'right anon wol sle yow': 'And if that ye in clene love me gye,/He wol yow loven as me, for youre clennesse.'[83] But such clerical models are hardly compatible with the ethos and reproduction of courtly communities, together with the 'normal' masculine and feminine identities they fashioned. And, to reiterate, there is no grounds for seeing Chaucer as seeking to subvert and transform courtly communities or the class and gender arrangements bound up with them. One could go on worrying away at these lines, trying to unpack their implications and vacancies, but most of the issues have been amply debated in the critical literature on the poem's ending. Furthermore, such questioning can only, in the last resort, confirm that the lines are indeed diversionary, designed to make us turn our backs on the poem's preoccupations and resort to the consolations of clerical clichés. Many readers are not consoled by these and will not turn away from the still pressing issues the poem has explored with astonishing imaginative power and profound critical intelligence.

I will conclude with a very tentative question, irrelevant to the concerns of this chapter and the poem, but provoked by its last few lines. Would it actually make much existential difference were one to substitute tradition's God for human lovers such as Troilus and Criseyde? Does the choice of God, in Toril Moi's terms, 'put a final end to the discourse of desire'?[84] If the human subject makes the traditional God the object of desire, certain consequences seem to follow. God is love and by his own confession a very jealous lover, one demanding exclusive devotion and service from the human subjects exiled, as it were, in the Graecian camp – a thoroughly patriarchal place in which, as Criseyde found, there may be a father, a lover, and potential rapists but, alas, no mother, an absent mother. As the passages quoted above from *The Chastising of God's Children* show, and as Julian of Norwich also felt, God must be the lover's mother too, both playful and powerful, both threatening and the source of all nourishment.[85] Now the writings of God's medieval lovers, from St Bernard's commentary on the Song of Songs to Rolle and Julian of Norwich, suggest that their desire is grounded in suffering and lack, their love as much the love of a text they found obscure as was Troilus's, their joy bound up with anxiety, their life one of languishing 'love-longing', their discourse self-consciously that of the traditions deployed by the courtly knight and the Petrarch he translates. Their form of love and its existential agonizings is more similar to 'the dialectics of desire' than Moi implies. In both, lack and uncertainty are fundamental, in both, faith and need for the absent source of life drive the subject's desire. Of course, there is a *doctrinal* difference, as Chaucer's ending asserts: God is allegedly unwavering in his fidelity and will finally deliver the resources longed for by the desiring subject. I italicize 'doctrinal' to stress that existentially and textually the situations seem hardly distinguishable: for the mystics' writings return again and again to the fear of rejection, abandonment, loss, and loneliness. Nor should we forget that this heavenly mother/lover/father is also, as doctrine made so luridly clear on the walls of medieval churches and the pages of medieval manuscripts, the omnipotent figure who will finally reject in eternal torture the majority of the human species, condemned to his hell. The dogmatic 'fact' disturbed the benevolent

Margery Kempe so greatly that her divine lover punished her for her objections, but it also puzzled Julian of Norwich and Langland. That 'the dialectics of desire' would end in a plenitude of gratification rather than a prison house of torture would not be certain in this life, would not be the case for most Christians, let alone non-Christian seekers of God, and would only be credible to a faith as little based in 'reason' as the desire, demands, and longing of the masculine courtly lover. Can this be surprising when the lovers of God shared their discourse of desire with courtly male lovers and sought a hardly less absent and finally 'transcendental' other? Chaucer was certainly not prepared to pursue such questions in the last few lines of *Troilus and Criseyde*. Nor anywhere else, it should be noticed. They were, at most, utterly peripheral to his poetic works and their still wonderfully resonant achievements.

Chapter Four

'IN ARTHURUS DAY': COMMUNITY, VIRTUE, AND INDIVIDUAL IDENTITY IN *SIR GAWAIN AND THE GREEN KNIGHT*

Þe kyng comfortez þe knyȝt, and alle þe court als
Laȝen loude þerat and lufly acorden
Þat lordes and ledes þat longed of þe Table,
Vche burne of þe broþerhede, a bauderyk schulde haue,
A bende abelef hym aboute, of a bryȝt grene,
And þat, for sake of þat segge, in swete to were.
For þat watz acorded þe renoun of þe Rounde Table
And he honoured þat hit hade, euermore after
As hit is breued in þe best boke of romaunce.
(*Sir Gawain and the Green Knight*, 2,513–21)

This chapter concentrates on the relations between virtue and the community in which virtue is defined in *Sir Gawain and the Green Knight*, between the individual moral agent and the community which enables him to be such an agent. As in the previous chapter, we are considering a poem in which the imagined community is the court, the poem's people almost exclusively leading members of the landed class. Unlike *Troilus and Criseyde*, *Sir Gawain and the Green Knight* does not bracket Christianity, but it does set aside the economic, political, and military practices of the landowning class in the late fourteenth century, as it looks back to 'Arthurus day'.[1] Because this setting aside includes rather important areas of the dominant class's experience, and because it may help us understand some troubling silences at the poem's conclusion, it seems worth briefly recalling the kind of thing involved. Many of the features encountered in the first two chapters of this book are blocked out: for example, the struggles of those who 'welden þe welþe of þis worlde' (*Piers Plowman*, X 24) to maintain their incomes through a whole battery of weapons (labour legislation, rents, fines, services, judicial powers, etc.) in a time when demographic and economic forces brought sharp pressures to bear on their customary forms of life; the diversified resistance of peasants and labourers; the urban class and community to which Margery Kempe belonged, together with the role of markets in land, food, luxuries, and manufactured commodities.[2] Also blocked out are the conflicts within the ruling class, including armed struggle between magnates and king, culminating in the deposition and murder of the king whose connections with the region in whose language the poem is written were so extraordinarily close.[3] Furthermore, there are no signs of 'the political rise of the gentry' in the later Middle Ages, which Edward Miller and John Hatcher associate with 'the changing character of knighthood' and the transformation of English feudalism as 'the growing complications of tenurial relationships made the old feudalism unworkable and drained the feudal connection of real meaning'.[4] Nor is it remotely plausible to assert that the poem shows an 'obvious concern with commerce and economics', such that even Sir Gawain is turned into 'a merchant' and 'a commodity'.[5] On the contrary, there are no signs, 'obvious' or obscure, of the way in which for well over two centuries before the poem English military organization had depended on money: as early as Rufus and Henry I one finds kings who were 'great hirers of mercenaries' and the fourteenth-century nobility fought:

> not as leaders of feudal contingents but . . . as military entrepreneurs recruiting companies of horse and foot under contract to the king in return for carefully defined cash considerations. In these companies knights also played an essential part, but they too served under contract and for wages and not as an incident of tenure. . . . Everywhere, in fact, the nexus between lord and vassal was assuming a monetary form.[6]

In this context the knight was becoming the lord of a fee which was 'verging upon property' in a community where the gentry were bound together in networks of kinship, local government, common economic and social concerns, as well as in the cohesiveness of a common culture.[7] This cultural factor was no mere 'superstructural' element in the later Middle Ages but, according to Miller and Hatcher, more a crucial 'cement' which countered economic and other potentially antagonistic divisions within 'landowning society'.[8] In summing up the role of a common knightly culture in the changed circumstances of the fourteenth century, Miller and Hatcher offer observations which may be of considerable relevance in grasping how a subtle late medieval poem written in the milieu described so well by Michael Bennett, should see fit to reinvent 'Arthurus day' as a golden age for the knightly ethos:

> the coherence of what is sometimes called 'bastard feudalism' owed a good deal to traditional assumptions about the relationships of lords and their men. Perhaps it can be said that the survival of feudal ways of thought and of a feudal distribution of the basic sources of wealth . . . did much to modify the impact on society and politics of the medieval rise of the gentry.[9]

It seems to me that at least *part* of *Sir Gawain and the Green Knight*'s commitment is to the celebration of the 'cement' of 'traditional assumptions' in changed circumstances.

An important aspect of the 'survival' Miller and Hatcher discuss was the version of virtue and the self-image in which magnates, knights, and leading gentry formed a chivalric community committed to individual and collective goals of honour. In this project English romances were produced, received, and taken as offering 'imitable and useful models' as Susan Crane has recently argued, showing the links between literature, knightly imitations, and literary representations of those practices. For example:

> The great 1358 festival of the Knights of the Garter was said to be 'invisa a tempore regis Arthuri,' of a kind unseen since the reign of Arthur. A combat of 1351, arranged between thirty knights on the English side and thirty on the French during a truce in the general hostilities, was celebrated in verse and prose as 'ung moult merveilleux fait d'armes que on ne doibt pas oublier' [a most wonderful feat of arms that should not be forgotten]. Far from breaking off the encounter when one of the participants was killed, the knights 'se maintinrent noblement d'une part et d'aultre aussy bien que tous fussent Rolant ou Olivier' [carried on as nobly on both sides as if they had all been Roland or Oliver]. As the Chandos Herald asserts in his *Life of the Black Prince*, of such lives as these 'homme en purroit faire un livre/Bien auxi grant come d'Artus,/D'Alisandre ou de

> Clarus' [one could make a book as long as that of Arthur, Alexander, or Clarus].[10]

There is no question of critical or ironic perspectives in such representations and practices, no question of invoking scholastic analysis of the vices and pious sermons against pride, tournaments, and luxury. One may thus see the typicality of the Chandos Herald when he celebrates the behaviour of the English knightly class after the victory of Poitiers as Arthurian: 'Dauncier et chacier et voler,/ Faire grantz festes et juster,/Faisoit [com] en regne d'Artus/L'espace de quatre ans ou plus' ('for four years or more they danced and hunted and hawked, held great feasts and jousted, as in the reign of Arthur').[11] Into this upper-class community Christianity was assimilated, making perfectly understandable the existence of men such as Bishop Despenser or William Cloune, the hunting abbot of Leicester lauded by Knighton, or abbot Thomas Pype of Stoneleigh who, 'like so many monks of the later Middle Ages', came from a local gentry family, kept a 'concubine', and alienated abbey land to his eldest son and other offspring.[12] As Nicholas Orme shows in his study of upper-class education in the Middle Ages, great ecclesiastical households 'were aristocratic in status . . . almost equally involved in affairs of the world', and trained knights, squires, and servants in 'a life-style similar in many ways to that of the lay nobility'. Even between the magnates' household and the monastery or nunnery there was 'no great gulf'.[13] To this context, as Crane demonstrates, religion is accommodated by even 'pious' romances.[14] It becomes intelligible that a devout magnate should commission a Book of Hours in which the painter has to overwhelm his work with the lord's family emblems and devices – cluttering up such places as the tent in which Christ crowns the Virgin Mary or the cope of St Augustine – and in which he depicts an angel as a personal page carrying the great man's helmet.[15] To invoke preacherly criticism of such practices is not going to contribute anything to one's understanding of the mentality and community which produced them as signs of both piety and self-affirmation. To the general domain of such ruling-class communities *Sir Gawain and the Green Knight* belongs, a domain which also explains the setting aside with which this chapter began its discussion. But in this poem, the setting aside goes with a subtle representation of the culture of honour which includes a disclosure of emerging contradictions which could prove extremely troublesome to honourmen, in 'Arthurus day' or in the poet's which made and received that legendary epoch.

Sir Gawain and the Green Knight begins with a statement that Britain is the product of brave, heroic males who loved fighting, that the noblest ('þe hendest') of its kings was Arthur and that the poem itself is part of this heroic tradition (1–36).[16] It is a story about the knightly élite in its golden age (54–9), and readers are to perceive within the traditional paradigms of the ruling class – a courtly community, it turns out, where the heroic ethos is in a refined home. As its members celebrate Christmas, 'a great feast', as John Bossy writes, 'more a season than a day',[17] the court is introduced with superlatives (36–84). In loving detail the poetry evokes a plenitude of material comforts and social power – unimaginable as an object of pleasurable participation in works like *Piers Plowman*. From diverse games, dancing, music, revelry, and noise so 'glorious to here', to the embroidered canopy set with 'þe best gemmes', to the abundance of elegantly presented food, we are overwhelmed by a veritable cornucopia. It is the very image of 'Arthurian' celebrations the Chandos Herald described after Poitiers, an upper class at ease with itself – 'With all þe wele of þe worlde þay woned þer samen' (50; see also 37–84, 116–29). And here too Christianity is unproblematically assimilated.

The King, knight, and ladies move easily from mass to games and feasting in hall, from public sacred space to public secular space with both areas legitimized by 'clerkeȝ' who, like the poet himself, join in the lay peoples' celebrations (60–5). This integration of Christianity is what we find later at Hautdesert, where masses punctuate but never impede or question courtly life with its enormous material privilege and pleasures. Such religious punctuation is actually a powerful sanctification of upper-class life; the eucharist an affirmation of the current class hierarchy, distribution of power, and resources. It is appropriate that a Bishop feasts at high table in honour (109–15), a just figuration of the relations between leading ecclesiastics and lay ruling class, between landowning Church and landowning gentry. Whatever the virtues articulated in the discourses of scholastic theologians or evangelical teachers following St Francis, the specificity of upper-class virtues, forms of life, and religion must be acknowledged. Here the virtues involved the competitive and aggressive cult of honour in a collective bound together in that pursuit.[18] As both A. C. Spearing and

J. Nicholls shown, the poem's vision includes as unironic a celebration of 'the courtly culture of fourteenth century England' as ones provided by the ideal models in courtesy books or writings such as those by the Chandos Herald.[19]

Into this celebration the poet introduces one of romances' most conventional motifs, 'the discourteous challenge'.[20] In challenging the rules of courtesy this figure challenges the very identity of the courtly community, its virtues, and goals, all of which could be reaffirmed through the encounter. The Green Knight comes to test the court's 'renoun', its great 'los [fame]' produced by the fact that its 'burnes best ar holden,/Stifest vnder stel-gere on stedes to ryde', the 'wyȝtest and þe worþyest of þe worldes kynde', the community as famous for its 'cortaysye' as for its heroic practices (231, 258–72). If the knights do *not* prove so reckless ('brayn') that they are prepared to 'stifly strike a strok' without any cause other than a challenge to do so, then the community's identity, its virtue, and its *telos* collapses (285–319). In such a community failure is not constituted by defeat in itself. Heroic works produced in 'Christian' cultures witness to this view as plainly as the *Iliad* – for example, the *Chanson de Roland*, the *Battle of Maldon*, Malory's 'Arthuriad'. Such works suggest that individual and collective defeat is known to be inevitable, like death, so that one must accept the hidden will of the gods, fate, or, to use Gawain's own terms, 'destiné', 'þe wyrde' (1,752, 2,134). Similarly, victory won by strategies such as Mellyagaunce's ambush using mercenaries, a perfectly realistic one in the later Middle Ages, cannot contribute to honour. It may actually be worse than the most decisive defeat for those upholding the identity of heroic communities.[21] For in these, virtue is the correct fulfilment of the given social role, in the actions and language required by that role, while failure to do this is villainy, dishonour.[22] The code in question is a *public* one, emphatically not a matter of private judgements arrived at through inward conscience alone with God or his human surrogate, whether confessor or psychiatrist.

In this context Arthur's first two responses are a perfectly appropriate fusion of courtesy and heroic assertiveness.[23] Just so, the challenger's mockery at the court's silence selects the key terms under scrutiny (309–15):

> 'What, is þis Arþures hous,' quoþ þe haþel þenne,
> 'Þat al þe rous rennes of þurȝ ryalmes so mony?

Wher is now your sourquydrye and your conquestes,
Your gryndellayk and your greme and your grete wordes?
Now is þe reuel and þe renoun of þe Rounde Table
Ouerwalt wyth a worde of on wyȝes speche,
For al dares for drede withoute dynt schewed!'

Both challenger and challenged understand that fame, pride, ferocity, wrath, renown, and heroic language are essential virtues in this community's project and self-image. To fail here is to fail decisively, to lose identity: 'What, is þis Arþures hous'? It is in this particular culture of discourse, not in some penitential manual, clerical homily, or morality play that Arthur's third response returns scorn for scorn (316–28).[24] In doing so he reaffirms his own heroic 'kynde' (320), his court's, and a major characteristic of the honour ethos as it was assimilated to the culture of late medieval knightly classes. In this, Mervyn James has shown how 'the mentality defined by the concept of honour',

> emerging out of a long-established military and chivalric tradition is characterized above all by a stress on competitive assertiveness; it assumes a state of affairs in which resort to violence is natural and justifiable; the recurrence of personal and political situations in which conflict cannot be otherwise resolved than violently. Honour could both legitimize and produce moral reinforcement for a politics of violence.

James shows how 'aggressivity' was always latent in relationships of men of honour: 'From honour's self-assertion there also followed its competitiveness and aggressivity.' The Green Knight's challenge with Arthur's response are part of *this* system, one in which, according to James, courtesy played an important but limited containing role (as it did in *Troilus and Criseyde*): 'The competitiveness of honour was veiled by the routines of good manners and courtesy, which helped to contain the latent violence within acceptable limits.' Yet, 'even courtesy did no more than demarcate the battlefield'.[25] In the Green Knight's encounter with Arthur and his court we see wilful violence fused with elaborate forms of courtesy, as elaborate as the syntax of Gawain's speech to Arthur; ruthless aggression fused with the restraints imposed by the very code that demands the aggressive assertiveness; complex and gamesome courtly mediations of a reckless violence in which killing is a matter of little consequence providing correct forms are honoured. Just as the devout Henry of Lancaster was prepared to play games in which he was quite likely to kill or be killed, as he in fact killed Sir Alex Ramsey in a joust, so *before* the Green Knight's entry the King looks forward to a mortal game in which knights will set 'lif for lyf' as 'fortune' will decide.[26] It is most appropriate that the pious paragon of courtesy, the 'fyn fader of nurture', should move through the most intricate courtly rhetoric and rituals, through an appeal to the heroic collective, through assertion of his own magisterial pre-eminence in courtly language, including its forms of modesty, through invocation of blood and lineage (so important in the class's self-identity), to a most violent and death-dealing act (338–429, 919). It is also most fitting that the 'couenaunt' Gawain makes with the Green Knight appeals to the honourman's promise, his 'trauþe', his *public* word embodied in his social role and community (378–409, 448–56). The penalty of failure is the loss of heroic identity for both individual and the community he represents, without which neither he nor heroic virtue would be conceivable. Come, says the challenger, 'oþer recreaunt be calde þe behoues' (456).[27] Confronting that threat, Gawain confronts a fate, in the honourman's culture worse than death.

The seasonal and liturgical year passes within the courtly community and we move to All Saints' day on which Arthur makes a special celebration for Gawain (538–42):

> With muche reuel and ryche of þe Rounde Table.
> Knyȝtez ful cortays and comlych ladies
> Al for luf of þat lede in longynge þay were;
> Bot neuer þe lese ne þe later þay neuened bot merþe.
> Mony joylez for þat jentyle japez þer maden.

This represents well the assimilation of Christianity to the worldly orientations of the social élite. Once more religious festivals become reaffirmations of the community, its glorious nobility ('muche reuel and ryche'), its social exclusiveness ('Knyȝtez ful cortays and comlych ladies'), and its own forms of consoling solidarity which are rather far removed from the homiletic material so frequently invoked by the 'priestly caste' of professors.[28] Nor is such incorporation of religious festival in the affirmations of a particular class's self-image and identity peculiar to the knightly élite, as the organization of urban Corpus Christi processions and plays, with the conflicts surrounding them, witnesses clearly enough.[29] To emphasize the community's outstanding virtue the poet chooses this moment to present a list of knights, 'þe best of þe burȝ' (550–7). Gawain's response to this 'compayny of court' as it counsels him about his apparently doomed journey is one of heroic nonchalance and stoical acceptance of fate, a stance in no way criticized by poet or court clerics (562–5). In this context Gawain is armed for his task on the next day, All Hallows (566–665).

This passage includes the description of Gawain's pentangle. It has been thoroughly discussed by Burrow and Spearing, both of whom draw attention to the poet's emphatic union of sacred and profane values, ones that belong to an exclusive class and serve as a marker for membership.[30] Religion and poem remain immanent to the élite's culture as once more we find it relishing the objects signifying power and material abundance (568–91). The pentangle itself includes a reassuring sacralization of the court's values, practices, and language. Even the Blessed Virgin Mary herself apparently stimulates Gawain's heroic toughness, his 'forsnes' as he fights 'in melly', for which he has her painted inside his shield, 'þat quen he blusched þerto his belde [courage] neuer payred' (644–50). There is no hint of irony here. Nor is there any in these lines being introduced by an account of how 'alle his afyaunce' was in the five wounds that Christ received on his horrid cross, wounds representing an act of non-violent self-sacrifice preceded by explicit rejection of violence as the solution to human problems. And given the behaviour of English Christian knights and soldiers in the long war in France, one which involved massacres of civilians and destruction of the peasantry's resources, why should there be any irony here for one identified with that class?

As Gawain takes up his lance and spurs off on his war-horse the court allows utterance to the grief so carefully controlled (666–86). In tears at his loss (684–6), they blame their leader for risking a hero's life to met the terms of a Christmas game, in this moment of misery judging it as 'angardez pryde' (681). Some readers see this passage as anti-chivalric, even 'bourgeois' or cynical, but such judgements seem oddly closed to the grief and loss in which the words are uttered.[31] Neither mourners nor poet develop an alternative system of virtues, whether 'bourgeois' or cynical, nor is there any need to invent one for them. No more than the poignant moments in the *Iliad* where a great hero weeps, or laments, or flees in fear, does such an incident in such a context displace the heroic system. The poet is acknowledging the way a primordial love of life and grief at loss will pressure any system of virtues. Gawain, however, maintains an unwavering commitment to his heroic and suicidal task, now 'alone' (693, 749) as he endures freezing conditions and fights his way towards the axe of his community's challenger (687–762). He reaches Hautdesert, his rest after an arduous journey and his springboard to the 'destiné' that would 'dele hym his wyrde' (1,752).

In making Hautdesert the poem continues to display its immanence to court culture. This is evident in many ways, for example in its appreciation of contemporary architecture of the ruling class (778–810), its reverence for 'honour' (830), its celebration of luxury, even in small particulars like furnishings of the 'bryȝt boure' where Gawain is lodged or the clothes he is given (852–74), and its relish of courtly gamesomeness, dancing, music, 'clene cortays carp', drinking, and feasting. The poet fully accepts the complete integration of Christianity in court culture, precisely reflecting Camelot's, and, most elaborately of all, he pays joyful attention to the energies, rituals, and specialized language of that exclusive class-marker, hunting, something that was treated as an 'educational institution' by gentry and magnates, despite the criticism of some clerical moralists. The fusion of courtly and heroic traditions found at Camelot is reaffirmed. As Gawain 'cortaysly' names 'þe court' to which he belongs, its leader, and only then his individual name (903–6), the host community responds in language that reiterates the virtues with which Camelot and the poet so closely identify: 'prowes . . . pured þewes . . . his mensk is þe most [note the competitive dimension] . . . þe teccheles termes of talkyng noble . . . þat fyn fader of nurture . . . manerez mere . . . luf-talkyng' (910–27).[32]

Within the network of the massive continuities between Gawain's home community and the Hautdesert which receives him as an ideal model stepping out of a courtesy book, certain discontinuities emerge. On these I now wish to focus. They are not in themselves presented as matter for lamentation, for celebration, or for moralistic censoriousness. But they do provide crucial elements of the plot and their significance is resonant as their consequences pervade the poem's ending. What their cultural and historical significance may be, we shall also consider. The discontinuities I have in mind can be characterized as the privatization or domestication of space, together with what that enables, and the privatization or interiorization of consciousness. Both of these are realized by some shift in poetic mode.

The privatization of space is one aspect of a complex social history.[33] At Hautdesert solitude is not just the effect of heroic mission in wild country but as much a potential of life within the castle as it was for Troilus in his community and palace. We are now shown Gawain alone, lying contentedly in bed, 'Vnder couertour ful clere, cortyned about' while daylight shines on the walls (1,178–81; see also 1,469–71, 1,731–2). In the public world and its heroic word a domestic sphere has suddenly been opened out or, depending on one's perspectives, closed in. The poet did not make space or time at Camelot in which the knight could be described like this, or in which he could be found getting dressed alone or seeking a place to hide a gift (1,871–5). Given his grasp of the consequences such private spaces contained, the need to moralize about them would have been understandable – one may recall Langland's anger at the privatization of upper-class eating habits (*Piers Plowman*, X 97–103). But he never does. While this accords with the poem's avoidance of the prophetic and judgemental registers of *Piers Plowman* or *Cleanness*, perhaps the poet's immanence to court culture meant that even when looking back to Arthur's day he saw no point in already belated attempts simply to close the stable door with moralization, attempts such as Langland's. He did, however, dramatize the way such spaces could encourage interactions which would affect honourmen even in their public relations and roles.

One especially impressive example of this process will suffice here. It comes after Gawain has safely negotiated the difficulties presented to him by the lady's second visit to his bedroom. He is enjoying a typical courtly evening of 'al þe manerly merþe þat mon may of telle' (1,648–57), a characteristic celebration of the collective, the means and ends of heroic virtue. Customary decorum is maintained and the most honoured guest, 'oure luflych knyȝt' sits beside the lady (1,657). Suddenly the poet shifts the narrative's mode and focus (1,658–63):

> Such semblaunt to þat segge semly ho made,
> Wyth stille stollen countenaunce, þat stalworth to plese,
> Þat al forwondered watz þe wyȝe and wroþ with hymseluen,

Bot he nolde not for his nurture nurne hir aȝaynez
Bot dalt with hir al in dayntė, how-se-euer þe dede turned
Towrast.

On this passage A. C. Spearing comments that 'we are not left merely as observers of the behaviour of the Lady and Gawain, but are taken into Gawain's consciousness and given a most detailed and subtle account of the eddying conflict in his feelings'.[34] Privatization of space and interiorization of consciousness has disturbing implications. As with Troilus, Gawain's gender and class identity is bound up with a 'nurture' which includes 'dayntė' and 'luf-talkyng' (927). What happens now is that the public identification-marks of an honourman become sources of serious difficulty, forcing the knight to direct his baffled anger against himself rather than the woman with whose 'stille stollen countenaunce' he colludes, and must collude. Gawain's public 'nurture' and the identity it guarantees has exposed him to forces in the private, domestic spaces which in turn bring distressing pressures to bear on him in the public domain itself. A troublesome private space is opened up within the collective and within the knight. The coherent, integrated heroic figure is thrown into unfamiliar self-division. The poet highlights the subtle and painful dialectic involved here by having Gawain's disturbance take place in the most public and symbolically central area of collective life, the great hall. It is here, before the leader's inner group withdraws to the 'chambre', that Gawain determines to pursue the contradictions now opening out in his 'nurture' and the identity it gives him, 'how-se-euer þe dede turned/Towrast'. In this desperate resolution we should not underestimate the man's baffled rage at finding how mastery of courtly discourses, a mastery that represents control of his world, including relations with females, now appears as a form which simultaneously enslaves him, 'how-se-euer þe dede turned/Towrast'.[35] In these new interactions between private and public, mastery becomes bondage and collective solidarities come under confusing pressures they themselves seem to sponsor. The knight's sense of contradiction, of self-division, potentially poses grave problems to the culture whose idealized self-image he represents.

This brilliant and resonant passage must stand here for the poem's increasing concern with Gawain's consciousness. The concern, by no means consistently sustained, is to evoke an identity in a mode which includes introspective activity and the possibility of sharp self-division. Other episodes, like the third temptation, display the features we have been analysing.[36] But rather than reiterate and reapply the kind of argument developed above, it will suffice to note that the pressures brought to bear on the heroic virtues lead to slippages in their language. In the private sphere Gawain ruminates how if the woman's girdle were to save his life 'þe sleȝt were noble' (1,855–9). In the public domain of the community to which Gawain belongs it would be impossible to categorize an action or a 'sleȝt' as 'noble' simply because it might enable an individual to live longer. The knight's terms represent an increasingly troublesome split between private and public, inner and outer. They probably account for a puzzling aspect of the third temptation: namely, why Gawain never mentions his public agreement with the woman's lord, his host, and why the poet never hints that 'hit come to his hert' (1,855). His motives for ignoring it when he hears the girdle might save his life are hardly obscure, but the case is different earlier in the scene. There he *is* attempting to extricate himself from the woman's 'luf' without showing any marks of being a 'craþayn' (a villein, a churl) lacking 'cortaysye' (1,772–3); there he *is* attempting to reject the ring (both literal and sexually symbolic). Why should he ignore an agreement which would allow him to disentangle himself from the woman's web, retain 'cortaysye' with mastery over discourse and woman, and simultaneously affirm the masculine bond between honourmen as well as his public identity? It seems that the splits between the private and the public have become such that the public game (whatever its legal terminology it remains a holiday game) seems so infinitely remote from the intimacy of the private sphere that it simply does not 'come to his hert' in any form, neither when it could help his purposes nor when it would impede them as a guilty thought. The split in domains and spaces has generated a split in forms of consciousness, a split in 'obligations', and, as we have outlined, divisions in the knight's identity.[37]

It is a consequence of just such splits that the hero can be represented as making what he assumes to be his final confession and returning to fulfil his social role with heroic gaiety, apparently now free from any introspective agonizings. One can see why scholars of the 'priestly caste' should turn to clerical texts on confession, trying to sort out whether Gawain's confession was 'consciously or unconsciously incomplete' and assessing his theological guilt. Perhaps the privatizations of space and consciousness at Hautdesert might seem to justify such a familiarly prying, inquisitorial anatomization, inviting readers to become confessor to this straying sheep, this 'learner' penitent.[38] But only 'might seem' to do so. For the poet makes the contrasts between different forms of representation quite sharp enough for us to respect them, and here one must respect the absence of introspective tremors such as those shown by Gawain as he sat next to the lady at dinner. When a community complete with court clerics, Bishop, and daily ecclesiastical service produces a pious knight who represents its idealized self-image, and when this paragon fails to classify an act as 'sin', fails apparently even to wonder whether it might be so classifiable, then it is quite irrelevant to categorize that failure as 'sin', whatever scholastic *Summae* or counter-reformation Catholic dogmatics might maintain. If the poet ever considered making such a judgement, something we cannot know, he certainly decided not to do so. Instead he keeps his imaginative attention on how habitual dispositions shaped by a network of cultural practices, including knightly Christianity, respond as they come under unfamiliar pressures in changed circumstances – new spaces, new splittings. It seems to me that here the poem figures forth aspects of a long historical change within the class which produced honourmen, a change which would, according to Mervyn James's study *English Politics and the Concept of Honour*, not be completed until the resilient and adaptable honour culture was superseded in the seventeenth century with the emergence of a ruling class whose composition, contexts, and dominant ideology was significantly different from its predecessors'.[39] Part of this history was the lay appropriation and cultivation of forms of privacy and inwardness stimulated for their own reasons by the scholastic élite (based especially in the universities).[40] It would, however, be a mistake to think that it is appropriate to fill in silences or seeming inconsistencies in a poem produced for a distinctly ruling class community living within and *making* this very historical process.

The poem's final section opens with a description of a wild winter dawn listened to by a sleepless Gawain (1,998–2,002). With the exception of one assistant he arms himself alone.[41] He then goes to take leave of his host community, reaffirming the virtues and vocabulary of Christian honourmen (2,052–68). He does so again on the way to the Green Chapel when the servant seeks to open up another private sphere within the public world of 'menske', promising Gawain a path to survival. Gawain confirms his heroic identity, the collectively endowed role which constituted him in the poem's first part. Becoming 'a knyȝt kowarde', seeking to avoid 'chaunce' and fate ('þe Wyrde') in flight would be worse than death (2,089–155). The context and the very mode of Gawain's assertion here blocks out the possibility of private spaces and self-divisions opened up at Hautdesert. When the servant seeks to conjure up ambiguity around 'lelly' (echoing the lady) Gawain is totally unimpressed (2,124, 1,863). Speculations about his 'private' state in opposition to his 'exterior' or 'public manner' in this encounter are thus unwarranted, for in the mode and the heroic virtue it represents there is no such split.[42] When Gawain reaches the Green Chapel the poet certainly does evoke Gawain's perspectives in this desolate place (2,178–211). But if, as Spearing writes, 'we enter into Gawain's very mind', it is a mind directed outwards, one seeking to grasp the feel of the place and its significance.[43] There is no sign of a mind turned 'inwards', reflecting on its own movements, seeking to anatomize its religious state or experiencing any kind of split between inward and outward performance.

Under the axe itself the heroic virtues are displayed, Gawain's identity as their bearer tested in the most fearful way and confirmed. The poet mentions the bare white flesh of the knight's neck to evoke the human vulnerability with which heroic traditions contend. In this test Gawain is not only being required to face death, but to turn himself voluntarily into a passive object, as one inanimate, already dead. That he only shrank a little with his shoulders, and only once, is a sign of the monumental self-discipline he has achieved within the ethos of his community (2,251–67). Still, it is enough for the Green Knight to taunt him (as the lady had done) with the most exacting demands of his social identity (2,270–3):

> 'Þou art not Gawayn,' quoth þe gome, 'þat is so goud halden,
> Þat neuer arȝed for no here by hylle ne be vale,
> And now þou fles for ferde er þou fele harmez!
> Such cowardise of þat knyȝt cowþe I neuer here.'

This vocabulary neither seeks nor allows splits between public and private, inner and outer in its version of virtue, and the challenger goes on to claim that he has won the competition for honour which defines such communities as Gawain represents (2,274–7).[44] The knight fully accepts the challenger's terms, only pointing out that they compete under rather different conditions (2,280–3). As he stands absolutely still, rock-like, under the second stroke he shows total mastery over the fear of death, won in and through his total identification with the heroic ethos (2,291–3). The same identification is plain both in his challenge to the Green Knight after the latter has withheld his hand and in his reaction on surviving the third stroke (2,299–301, 2,314–30). It is just this that the Green Knight so appreciates as he admires Gawain's physical vitality and courage (2,331–5),[45] challenger and challenged bound together in a common culture the poet shares. What remains is for the Green Knight to unpack aspects of Gawain's trials that are still hidden from him, and for Gawain to return to his own community.

This unpacking proves extremely complex because it reactivates the split we have considered in discussing Gawain's time at Hautdesert, splits that the final journey to the Chapel and the encounter with the Green Knight had seemed to transcend so decisively. This is certainly not the Green Knight's purpose. His praise of Gawain is unambiguous and immense, finding him, 'On þe fautlest freke þat euer on fote ȝede', a pearl among 'oþer gay knyȝtez' (2,362–5). The lord of Hautdesert, Sir Bertilak, is as immanent to the ethos of the heroic virtues and the honour community as Arthur or Gawain. For him it is Gawain's commitment to *this* ethos that has been tested (2,345–68), one in which his retention of the girdle was only 'a lyttel' failing, based in an understandable love of life for which, 'þe lasse I yow blame' (2,368). This seems the authentic voice of that social élite with whom the poem is identified, the dominant groups in Michael Bennett's study of the poet's homeland or in Mervyn James's study of those bearing the concept of honour in English political practices.[46]

For 'a gret whyle' Gawain stands silent as he takes in the stunning information that what were private transactions in a private space are now brought into the public domain. The Green Knight's assurance that the failure was only 'a lyttel' matters less to him than its categorization as a failure in 'lewté' (2,366) and its exhibition in a domain that to Gawain seems public, at least in contrast with the apparently private encounters with his host's wife. His anguish is painful (2,370–2):

> So agreued for greme he gryed withinne;
> Alle þe blode of his brest blende in his face,
> Þat al he schrank for schome þat þe schalk talked.

Gawain responds as a chivalric hero for whom virtue is very much a matter of 'reputation' and the avoidance of any 'public sense of shame': 'it is not until Gawain realizes that he has been found out that he starts to feel guilty.'[47] Spearing's observations are correct and could apply with equal precision to the English men of honour described by Mervyn James, a fact which emphasizes Gawain's representative and normative status even here.[48] When his 'schome' allows him to speak it is to curse cowardice and covetousness, aligning 'vice' with 'vylany', a moral term which encapsulates the class perspective of his community's ethos and a specific social history (2,374–5). Once he has unfastened the girdle and fiercely ('broþely') flung it to Sir Bertilak (2,376–7), he turns against himself:

> For care of þy knokke, cowardyse me taȝt
> To acorde me with couetyse, my kynde to forsake:
> Þat is larges and lewté, þat longez to knyȝtez.

In these words Gawain affirms the heroic virtues, the knightly honourman's code. His 'kynde' *is* his social identity, private and public seem so fused that the very distinction becomes irrelevant. Confronted with his transgression being classified as a lack of 'lewté', albeit a 'lyttel' lack, the knight feels his identity dissolving, his being disintegrating. He feels he has negated the code which gave him his goals, his projects, his very existence (2,381–6). It is in terms of *this* code that Gawain's confession must be read, including his self-accusation of 'couetyse'. This code, it should be plain enough by now, is not that of a scholastic *Summa theologiae*, a penitential manual, or assorted homilies. So nothing could be more irrelevant than using such material to give one the 'real' meaning of Gawain's language, to assure us that it shows how Gawain is 'acknowledging not only his material theft but his turning away from God to an object valued for itself rather than from love of God . . . and his rejection – conscious or unconscious – of sacramental grace'.[49] As for Gawain's use of the term 'couetyse' alongside terms such as 'cowardyse', 'larges and lewté', 'trecherye and vntrawþe', it functions here as a generalized and self-punitive acknowledgement of possessiveness, inspired by what Gawain brands as 'cowardyse' but what Sir Bertilak sees as a mitigating and inevitable love of life. Both during the third temptation and now, it is made perfectly clear why Gawain took the girdle: 'Myȝt he haf slypped to be vnslayn þe sleȝt were noble', a view whose problems we discussed earlier (see above, p. 165) and which return to torment him.[50] Neither the anguished Gawain nor his poet ask the way to the nearest scholastic specialist in the analysis of vice and the distinctly clerical remedies of penitential discipline.

On the contrary, Sir Bertilak laughingly accepts the role of confessor into which Gawain's anguished request to know his challenger's 'wylle' has placed him (2,384–406). And he does so as an appreciative fellow honourman. He reassures the knight of his great virtue, insisting that he himself considers Gawain as pure as if he had never transgressed since he was born (2,389–94). This admiring language certainly echoes the description of Gawain's confession before a priest at Hautdesert (1,883–4), but it does not call for investigation into scholastic theology concerning the rights of lately bewitched and green laymen to hear confession and issue absolution. The informing code and the writer's attention simply do not send any responsible reader in that direction. Instead we are shown the knight's 'lufly', laughing declaration as a ringing affirmation of the relative autonomy and sufficience of the heroic fraternity and its values, of its own system of sanctions and reconciliations – both 'in Arthurus day' and, the poet hopes, long after.[51] Sir Bertilak hands back the girdle to Sir Gawain as 'a pure token' of the adventure of the Green Chapel. This is now explicitly classified, in a dialogue between two honourmen, as a chivalric contest to be celebrated as such when Gawain is amongst 'prynces of prys' and 'cheualrous knyȝtez' (2,394–9). With that he invites Gawain back to a trap-free Hautdesert where 'we schyn reuel þe remnaunt of þis ryche fest/Ful bene'.[52]

Gawain's 'schome', however, is so overwhelming that he cannot respond with the easy 'larges' that would be his habitual disposition. He does thank his host for the invitation, manages a less than forgiving greeting 'to þat cortays, your comlych fere' and then bursts into a self-pitying anti-feminist rant (2,406–28). The wounded male ego displaces responsibility for its own decisions and unhappiness onto 'wymmen' and their 'wyles'. Even the lustful and murderous King David is relieved of responsibility for his vicious actions and turned into one who was 'blended' by the woman who, according to the Biblical narrative, was a powerless victim (2,418–19: 2 Kings [Samuel] 11. 1–12, 19). That such displacements are as commonplace in our own culture as in the Middle Ages suggests, once again, decisive continuities in gender arrangements and ideologies across massive transformations in the forces and modes of material production. While it is true that forms of knightly decorum and 'love' covered over the most unambiguously aggressive aspects of conventional misogyny, anti-feminism pervaded these forms too and there is nothing especially 'clerical' about Gawain's outburst.[53] He would have found men aplenty in his own 'broþerhede', as in all social groups, to share the views that emerge here. Indeed it seems that masculine solidarity may actually be strengthened, perhaps even enabled, by making woman the scapegoat. After all, Sir Bertilak had already told Gawain that normal patriarchal relations were in operation since he himself had 'wroȝt' his wife's 'wowyng' (2,361). Responsibility here is directly acknowledged, and it would seem more cogent for Gawain to turn his anger against the lord rather than against his obedient pawn, more a veritable Griselda than that other archetype of masculine fantasy, the powerful and voracious demon-lover. But to do this would disrupt the male bonding essential to the 'broþerhede' of honourmen. So it makes good sense to invoke common masculine views on womanly 'wyles', appealing to his former competitor and fellow-knight in an act calling for male collusion, 'Me þink me burde be excused' (2,438). Critics have censured this, laughed at it and, most bizarre of all, found it cause for congratulating Gawain.[54] But the heart of Gawain's appeal is for male solidarity in the face of the common enemy, the one who is, as we observed in the previous chapter, an essential element in the making of masculine identity and the one secretly feared by even the best honourmen. This perspective is, of course, open to both comic treatment and the kind of tragic treatment perhaps most resonantly achieved in Shakespeare's *Othello*, the tragedy of a later honourman who might have survived better 'in Arthurus day' than in commercial Venice.

It is in these contexts that we should consider the role of Morgan la Fay. Until she is brought in, the final responsibility for a pretty treacherous way of competing with one's guests rests with the idealized image of upper-class masculinity, the lord of Hautdesert. But this is displaced onto Morgan. Sir Bertilak invokes her 'myȝt'. He recollects her magic, her 'koyntyse' in learning, and her legendary sexual power. So powerful is she that she is called, 'Morgne þe goddes' and can 'tame' anyone, including Sir Bertilak. One may recall Gawain's, 'Me þink me burde be excused' and reflect on the way the northern knight's speech carries the same burden – the Chaucerian pun on this word seems rather appropriate here.[55] In this way the archetypally dangerous woman is made the final cause of all that is 'other', disturbing, and potentially destructive of the heroic community centred on 'þe broþerhede'. Furthermore, it is acknowledged that while she is 'other' she is also *within* the community she threatens. She lives at Hautdesert, engages in competition for 'renoun' (by male proxies) and runs, in a striking sense, within the royal blood of the hero himself – 'Ho is euen þyn aunt'.[56] Nevertheless, her invocation at least *allows* the reassertion of male solidarity, bonded in competition for honour and the pursuit of heroic virtue with an appropriately shaped and legitimating religion.

We are never given any indication of Gawain's response to this version of his aunt and the dangers she represents to knightly communities, one of those silences which mark the boundaries of the poet's sporadic making of Gawain's inwardness. What is not left in silence, however, is Gawain's rejection of the meaning given to the girdle by Sir Bertilak. Instead of an emblem of chivalric achievement by 'On þe fautlest freke þat euer on fote ȝede' (2,363), Gawain insists it should be read as a badge of disastrous failure, of *dishonour*, a reminder of 'þe fayntyse of þe flesche crabbed,/How tender hit is to entyse teches of fylþe' (2,433–6). Here the 'priestly caste' of scholars may seem, at last, to be summoned by a knight in the process of religious conversion, perhaps like Sir Launcelot at the end of Malory's work. In that catastrophe, the great hero, 'the mekest man and the jentyllest that ever ete in halle emonge ladyes . . . the sternest knyght to thy mortal foo that ever put spere in the reeste', retires from the pursuit of heroic virtue to the specialized community and ethos of the professional religious.[57] But there is no summons, for even in his sharpest rhetorical self-flagellation, Gawain sees himself still very much part of the heroic, competitive community: 'When I ride in renoun . . . quen pryde schal me pryk for prowes of armes' (2,434, 2,437). The pursuit of prowess and honour, decisive markers of the lay élite, will continue to constitute his life. No alternative form of life is imagined. He does not even consider that path which sought to combine the cult of honourmen with the penitential pursuit of salvation – the holy war, the crusades on which Launcelot's own brotherhood die in Malory's work, just as did Chaucer's friend Sir John Clanvowe at about the time this poem was written. In fact Gawain's response to Sir Bertilak displays the continuation of an honourman's 'intense and sensitive concern for reputation', while there is not even the most basic consideration of crucial theological categories such as 'grace' and 'charity', nor of fundamental ecclesiastical teaching on the sacramental economy of Christian regeneration.[58]

The heroic community welcomes Gawain back, a knight, so the poet tells us in a resounding phrase, 'al in sounde' (2,489–94). In response to questions about how he had fared Gawain tells his story. The poet begins the account of Gawain's report with the word 'Biknoweȝ', the verb of confession that Gawain had used earlier to the Green Knight, or Sir Bertilak (2,385, 2,495). This is juxtaposed to the poet's comment in the previous line that Gawain, 'ferlyly he telles', a phrase which 'suggests a story of wonders'.[59] Every system of virtue has its favoured narrative forms and the shift from 'ferlyly' to 'Biknoweȝ' suggests that the knight may perhaps be about to shift the literary form in which his identity is made, courtly romance, to exemplary homily or even penitential manual. Does he manage this shift with more conviction and consistency than he had done at the Green Chapel? Once again he shapes his narrative into a confession of 'vnleuté', of 'couardise and couetyse', of 'vntrauþe', denying that he has succeeded in the pursuit of honour (2,495–510). But Spearing's comment brings out some of the contradictions in Gawain's performance here:

> When Gawain rides back to Camelot wearing the green girdle as a baldric, he still has in mind his reputation . . . he will punish himself openly in his reputation by wearing something that will call other people's attention as well as his own to his imperfection . . . without judging him unsympathetically, may we not feel that there are still traces of pride in the feeling that one's own imperfection deserves such ostentatious treatment?[60]

The appropriate response to this question seems to be that 'pride' is at the core of the honourman's identity and Gawain, however ashamed, is very much still an honourman, his oration not part of scholastic or conversion discourses. His conclusion does nothing to upset this view (2,511–12):

> For mon may hyden his harme bot vnhap ne may hit,
> For þer hit onez is tachched twynne wil hit neuer.

These lines have understandably disturbed the more scrupulous among the 'priestly caste' of scholars, eliciting fears about Gawain's immortal soul, contributory evidence that he is sunk in 'spiritual treason' and deserving 'eternal punishment' unless redemption is sought through the correct priestly channels.[61] But such interpretations simply dissolve the specificity of knightly communities, their virtues, their language, and their form of religion. It was perfectly possible in fact and fiction to cross from such communities to ones controlled by clerics (of the same class), especially when the honourman's active days were over, as Sir John Fastolf told Scrope, or in the kind of disaster that Malory's Launcelot confronted.[62] Gawain, as we have seen, made no such move and his final two lines confirm that his basic perspectives remain those of honourman.

As such the court embraces him, responding to his shame without the slightest sign of dismay or religious anxiety – no one sends for Bishop Baldwin, for an evangelical parson or an expert confessor. There is not the slightest indication that anything is amiss with the community, its ethos, its form of life, or its blushing, groaning hero (2,513–21):

> Þe kyng comfortez þe knyȝt, and alle þe court als
> Laȝen loude þerat and lufly acorden
> Þat lordes and ledes þat longed to þe Table,
> Vche burne of þe broþerhede, a bauderyk schulde haue,
> A bende abelef hym aboute, of a bryȝt grene,
> And þat, for sake of þat segge, in swete to were.
> For þat watz acorded þe renoun of þe Rounde Table
> And he honoured þat hit hade, euermore after
> As hit is breued in þe best boke of romaunce.

For some scholars the court's language recalls 'the superficiality and moral inadequacy of Camelot in the face of the Green Knight's challenge . . . social tact covering moral indecision and duplicity', while the poet's aim here is 'the ironic undermining of the conventional close of Arthurian romance'.[63] What purpose would such an aim serve – to undermine the ethos of the community for which *Sir Gawain* was produced and to convert northern men like Sir John Stanley or Sir Robert Knowles? To convert them to what? To abandon their habitual dispositions, their 'virtue', and practices, to follow some form of life more easily recognized as 'religious' by modern neo-Christian scholars? Yet the poem completely fails to indicate what would constitute such a religious form of life, let alone substantialize it. It is most implausible that a poem whose representations of the lay élite's forms of life are so immanent to their culture should seek to pull up its own roots without some explicit annunciation, such as a retraction, or a malediction on the bad old days of Arthur, when courts were not committed to reproducing the virtues of scholastic *Summae theologiae* and of manuals like *Handlynge Synne* or *Jacob's Well*. But the poet does nothing remotely approaching this. The lines just quoted offer a model of collective solidarity and unity, the kind Sir Thomas Malory so yearned for and admired. The celebration is of a very different fraternity to any that inspired the imagination of Langland, St Francis, or St Benedict. But it is nonetheless 'þe broþerhede', the idealized representation of the gentry's élite in a literary mode and language appropriate to the class in whose life and fantasy this work so intimately belongs. As it was to Gawain's northern admirer, the lord of Hautdesert, to these honourmen the girdle is a sign of the basic virtue of honour, of the 'renoun' which the Green Knight had challenged. So unequivocal is the assertion of such continuities that the emblem will now honour the most outstanding participants in the courtly virtues – 'And he honoured þat hit hade, euermore after'. As observed earlier, the community contains its own fully integrated priests blessing its forms of life and it is perfectly understandable that its members should feel no need for standards from without against which these should be questioned. The exuberant and fraternal honouring of Gawain is simultaneously an affirmation of the solidarity in the upper-class community, its ceremonies, its virtue, and its goals, an affirmation confidently projected into a future ('euermore after') which includes the poet's present.[64]

Does Gawain himself participate in this celebratory affirmation, is he 'reincorporated into his society', as some readers maintain?[65] As we noted, Gawain still sees himself as part of the heroic, competitive community in which he will continue to 'ride in renoun', committed to 'prowes of armes' (2,434, 2,437), free from any thoughts about alternative forms of life and the communities which might be able to sustain them. Nevertheless, the poem simply does not show Gawain being 'reincorporated' at its conclusion: it gives us no indication of his responses to the court's reassurances that the fraternity includes him and that he is just like its other members. Commenting on this feature, Wilson decides that once Gawain's 'sense of identity dissolves' it is replaced by a 'new identity', a 'new self-definition' which leaves him both isolated 'from the author's ethos' and 'from the comprehension of his "honour group", the Round Table'.[66] While his persuasive reading takes seriously the poet's refusal to show us that Gawain is 'reincorporated' into his community, it encounters problems which call for some qualification.

These problems are not only caused by Gawain's continuing commitment to 'ride in renoun' and in the 'prowes of armes'. Perhaps more important still is the fact that the poet has given us so little on which to build any notion of Gawain's 'new self-definition', that 'new identity' which allegedly separates him from his 'honour group'. Margery Kempe's book shows that at least some people in this period were engaged in something that can legitimately be described as a struggle for a 'new identity', one that often involved the sense of singularity that so disturbed Langland.[67] While it may be tempting to set Gawain amongst such contemporaries of the poet the grounds for doing so are not given in any detail or depth. About such struggles the poet has nothing to say. Nor does he evoke Gawain's feelings and thoughts as he has done on more than one occasion in his poem. What he did not do we need not try to do for him. Instead, we might do better to make his silence, his brevity, a topic for interpretation. We can ask why he does not convey any of the processes involved in struggling to make a 'new identity' and in sustaining one. The answer seems bound up with the poem's immanence to the courtly community, the class it represents and its virtue. Gawain, as I have emphasized, imagines no alternative form of life to the culture figured by Camelot. Nor does the poem.[68] It is not concerned with a 'new' individual and collective identity, let alone with the struggles in which they might be fashioned.

The poet's brevity does, however, involve an abandonment of troublesome issues his poem has introduced. Its ending could represent a collective whose unity is now threatened by conflicting judgements about what constitutes virtue and the community's *telos*. After all, there can be no doubt that hero and community interpret the girdle and the experience it betokens in sharply conflicting ways. The signs of a split between individual and community are as marked as Wilson maintains, however much one has to qualify his claims about the knight's 'new identity'. But once the collective project becomes a topic for debate, once it ceases to be the unquestioned framework giving the members their version of virtue, the dispositions to be cultivated, and the goals to pursue, then the traditional heroic community, with its politics of honour and its bonds of 'cortaysye', is in danger of disintegration. This is a surprisingly substantial difficulty to leave unexplored at the end of so accomplished a poem. If we recognize, with the historians Miller and Hatcher, that chivalric culture and a neo-feudal way of thought was no merely superstructural decoration but a crucial 'cement' in countering potentially dangerous divisions in 'landowning society' during the fourteenth century, then the implications of the difficulties in question can be seen in their full significance.[69] One sympathizes with readers' reluctance to accept that the poet abandoned such profound issues in courtly laughter and his own non-judgemental silence. Still, this is what he did, leaving the issues not only unresolved but unexamined. Furthermore, his ending sharpens our discomfort with this move by reactivating the split between the public and the private to which this chapter has paid considerable attention. It now emerges in a particularly disconcerting form. Gawain will pursue the public goals of 'renoun' and 'prowes of armes' but apparently this public identity will coexist with a shadowy private self bearing judgements and language which contradict public identity and public world. Refusing to write a 'new identity' for Gawain, something that would have entailed imagining a 'new' community in which this could be lived, the poet just leaves us with this disjunction. In it the public world ceases to be the realm forming relatively integrated individual identity and promises to become a mere setting for the private and inner individual consciousness, a mere space now devoid of intrinsic meaning in the face of a rather disembodied ego. No longer does the public, collective world provide the decisive paradigms of all standard and self-understanding. When analysing the private and inner spaces opened out at Hautdesert I noted the dangers they posed to heroic virtue and the honourman's identity. They are taken up in this final disjunction, one that both prefigures and contributes to the supersession of the knight's community and its culture. The long process this involved generated complex tensions across those historical transitions described with such acuteness by Mervyn James.[70] To this process, the ending seems to confirm, *Sir Gawain and the Green Knight* belongs. Belonging to this process, immanent to the honourman's community, the poem could not transcend it, had no access to some godlike perspective from which to escape its own historical horizons. It is perfectly possible that the substantial questions about the consequence of the disjunctions with which the poet leaves us were never formulated as *explananda*, not even in the poet's uncollected notebooks. It is also possible that the disturbing contemporary forces the romance chose to repress, with which we began the chapter, may have returned to discourage the poet from seeking to work through the problems posed by the disjunction. The only alternative to the difficulties emerging 'in Arthurus day' might have seemed the still more tricky features of the poet's present he had sought to bracket and which his poem now threatened to figure forth in a manner that might prove thoroughly disrupting. While the repressed returns, as it tends to do, the poet exercised his privilege against the intractable. He closed his poem and walked away, leaving it to the history it could not control.

NOTES

Full title, publisher, and date at first reference within chapter section; thereafter short title.

INTRODUCTION

1 Translated from Public Records Office documents in the indispensable collection by R. B. Dobson (1970) *The Peasants' Revolt of 1381*, London: Macmillan, revised edition (1986), pp. xxviii–ix.

2 See the *De regimine principum* of Aquinas edited and translated in A. P. D'Entrèves (ed.) (1965) *Aquinas: Selected Political Writings*, Oxford: Blackwell, pp. 3, 5, 7, 67; also passages from his *Summa*, in *Aquinas*, pp. 109, 161 and from his commentary on Aristotle's ethics, in *Aquinas*, p. 191. For Aristotle see, for example, *The Politics*, Harmondsworth: Penguin, 1981, section 1,253. For some helpful observations on the usage of the term 'community' and its problems, see Alan Macfarlane, S. Harrison, and C. Jardine (1977) *Reconstructing Historical Communities*, Cambridge: Cambridge University Press, chapter 1.

3 A. MacIntyre (1985) *After Virtue: a Study in Moral Theory*, London: Duckworth, pp. 172–3, chapters 13–15. The whole book is of great interest to people concerned with the issues addressed in my own book.

4 The work is published under the name of V. N. Volosinov, but seems to have been by M. Bakhtin, *Marxism and the Philosophy of Language*, London: Seminar Press 1973; Cambridge, Mass.: Harvard University Press 1986, p. 86, author's italics. On the issues here see Gunther Kress and Bob Hodge (1979) *Language as Ideology*, London: Routledge & Kegan Paul, and Gunther Kress (1985) *Linguistic Processes in Sociocultural Practice*, Victoria, Australia: Deakin University Press. My debts to Gunther Kress are immense and go back many years, to our collaborative work at the University of East Anglia in the 1970s.

5 *Marxism and Philosophy of Language*, pp. 86, 87. On the writer, see Katerina Clark and Michael Holquist (1984) *Mikhail Bakhtin*, Cambridge, Mass.: Harvard University Press.

6 M. Bakhtin (1981) *The Dialogic Imagination*, Austin: University of Texas Press, p. 417.

7 M. Sahlins (1985) *Islands of History*, Chicago: Chicago University Press, see chapters 1, 4, 5.

8 *Islands of History*, p. 145.

9 *Islands of History*, p. 149.

10 P. Anderson (1984) *In the Tracks of Historical Materialism*, London: Verso, chapter 2. The output of poststructuralist writings and the diverse critiques they have elicited is immense and still growing. The grounds for my own rejection of what I take to be the distinctive premises and methods of poststructuralist theory are most lucidly presented in the following: Sean Sayers (1985) *Reality and Reason: Dialectic and the Theory of Knowledge*, Oxford: Blackwell; Kate Soper (1986) *Humanism and Anti-Humanism*, London: Hutchinson, especially chapters 5–7; T. Eagleton (1983) *Literary Theory*, Oxford: Blackwell, chapter 4; Frank Lentricchia (1980) *After the New Criticism*, London: Methuen, 1983, chapters 5 and 8, and his (1983) *Criticism and Social Change*, Chicago: Chicago University Press. For two extremely important critiques of Foucault's work, see Charles Taylor, 'Foucault on freedom and truth', and Michael Walzer, 'The politics of Michael Foucault', reprinted in David C. Hoy (ed.) (1986) *Foucault: A Critical Reader*, Oxford: Blackwell, pp. 52–102. For a lively attempt to bring together traditions that to me still seem profoundly incompatible, see Michael Ryan (1982) *Marxism and Deconstruction*, Baltimore: Johns Hopkins University Press.

11 *Islands of History*, pp. 154–5, 156; the Hirst quote is not Sahlins's and comes from (1976) 'Althusser and the theory of ideology', *Economy and Society* 5: 385–412, here p. 104.

12 D. W. Robertson (1963) *Preface to Chaucer*, Oxford: Oxford University Press, p. 51.

13 Thomas of Wimbledon's 1388 Paul's Cross sermon quoted from the edition by N. H. Owen (1966) in *Medieval Studies* 28: 176–97, here pp. 178–9 (accepting editorial interventions). On the tradition of this model, see G. Duby (1978) *Les Trois ordres ou l'imaginaire du féodalisme*, Paris: Gallimard; Chicago: Chicago University Press, 1980. Also relevant: Ruth Mohl (1933) *The Three Estates in Medieval and Renaissance Literature*, New York: Ungar, 1962; Jill Mann (1973) *Chaucer and Medieval Estates Satire*, Cambridge: Cambridge University Press; Rodney Hilton (1985) 'Ideology and social order in late medieval England', in his *Class Conflict and the Crisis of Feudalism*, London: Hambledon. For a characteristically commonplace contemporary version, see John Lydgate (1934) *Minor Poems* vol. 2, Oxford: *Early English Text Society* 776–80, o.s., and John Gower, *Vox Clamantis*, translated in Eric Stockton (1962) *The Major Latin Works of John Gower*, Washington: University of Washington Press.

14 S. Weil (1949) *The Need for Roots*, London: Routlege & Kegan Paul, 1952, pp. 214–15; J. Goodie (1983) *The Development of the Family and Marriage in Europe*, Cambridge: Cambridge University Press, pp. 183, 185.

15 J. L. Bolton (1980) *The Medieval English Economy 1150–1500*, London: Dent, pp. 9–10. For outstanding examples of the kind of work that still tends to be ignored by literary specialists: J. Toussaert (1963) *Le Sentiment religieux en Flandre à la fin du Moyen Age*, Paris: Plon; K. Thomas (1973) *Religion and the Decline of Magic*, Harmondsworth: Penguin, especially chapters 2, 3; J. Delumeau (1971)'La légende du Moyen Age Chrétien' in his *Le Catholicisme entre Luther et Voltaire* part 3, Paris: Presses Universitaires; Christine Larner (1982) *The Thinking Peasant*, Glasgow: Pressgang, pp. 27–31, 52–4, 86–7; P. Burke (1978) *Popular Culture in Early Modern Europe*, New York: Harper & Row, pp. 22–47; E. le Roy Ladurie, *Montaillou*, London: Scolar Press 1978 (abridged English trans.); Anthony Gash, 'Carnival against Lent: the ambivalence of medieval drama', in David Aers (ed.) (1986) *Medieval Literature: Criticism, Ideology and History*, Brighton: Harvester.

16 I quote from the shrewd essay on Althusser by Susan James, in Q. Skinner (ed.) (1986) *The Return of Grand Theory*, Cambridge: Cambridge University Press, p. 155.

17 The coy medievalization suggests the place for medieval literature in the influential report's vision of literary criticism as 'a bond of union between classes' and a battle against 'opinions' which related culture and class, a sign of 'a morbid condition' in 'the body politic': (1921) *The Teaching of English in England*, London: HMSO pp. 22, 252–4. On the 'correction' in this vision I refer to Derek Pearsall's wise observations in 'Chaucer's poetry and its modern commentators: the necessity of history', in David Aers (ed.) (1986) *Medieval Literature: Criticism, Ideology and History*, Brighton: Harvester.

18 For the use of *Piers Plowman* in 1381, see the documents in R. B. Dobson, *The Peasants' Revolt*, pp. 380–3. See the comments on the need to consider the great differences in social experience and belief between different groups in medieval England when describing medieval religious culture, in Miri Rubin (1987) *Charity and Community in Medieval Cambridge*, Cambridge: Cambridge University Press, pp. 54–5, 98.

19 Rodney Hilton (1985) *Class Conflict and the Crisis of Feudalism*, London: Hambledon, p. 153.

20 Mervyn James (1983) 'Ritual, drama and the social body in the late medieval English town', *Past and Present* 98: 3–29.

21 R. B. Dobson, *The Peasants' Revolt*, p. xxxvii.

22 On the first three towns in 1380–1 see R. B. Dobson, 'The risings in York, Beverley and Scarborough', in R. Hilton and T. Aston (eds) (1984) *The English Rising in 1381*, Cambridge: Cambridge University Press. On the others: J. L. Bolton, *The Medieval English Economy*, pp. 259–67; Ruth Bird (1949) *The Turbulent London of Richard II*, London: Longman; Rodney Hilton (1973) *Bond Men Made Free*, London: Temple Smith, pp. 198–206 on Bury St Edmunds, St Albans, and Cambridge; Robert S. Gottfried (1982) *Bury St. Edmunds*, Princeton: Princeton University Press, pp. 220–36.

23 Edward Miller and John Hatcher (1978) *Medieval England: Rural Society and Economic Change 1086–1348*, London: Longman, p. 147.

24 J. L. Bolton, *The Medieval English Economy*, pp. 39, 36, 117–18.
25 The statement comes from the illuminating essay by Z. Razi (1981) 'Family, land and village community in later medieval England', *Past and Present* 93: 3–36, p. 15. See also note 26.
26 Z. Razi (1980) *Life, Marriage and Death in a Medieval Parish Economy: Society and Demography in Halesowen 1270–1400*, Cambridge: Cambridge University Press. The quote is from p. 36. See also Z. Razi, 'The struggles between the abbots of Halesowen and their tenants in the thirteenth and fourteenth centuries', in T. H. Aston (ed.) (1983) *Social Relations and Ideas*, Cambridge: Cambridge University Press. See also Eleanor Searle (1974) *Lordship and Community*, Toronto: Pontifical Institute, pp. 162–4, 344–5, 396.
27 Henry T. Riley (ed.) (1869) *St. Albans Monastery* vol. 3, London: Rolls series, Longman, Green, & Co., pp. 285–372; this should now be read alongside Rosamond Faith's commentary in 'The class struggle in fourteenth century England', in R. Samuel (ed.) (1981) *People's History and Socialist Theory*, London: Routledge & Kegan Paul, pp. 50–66.
28 Rosamond Faith, 'Berkshire: fourteenth and fifteenth centuries', in P. D. A. Harvey (ed.) (1984) *The Peasant Land Market in Medieval England*, Oxford: Oxford University Press, chapter 3, here p. 164.
29 D. G. Watts (1983) 'Peasant discontent on the manors of Titchfield Abbey, 1245–1405', *Proceedings of the Hampshire Field Club and Archaeological Society* 39: 121–35.
30 M. J. Bennett (1983) *Community, Class and Careerism: Cheshire and Lancashire Society in the Age of Sir Gawain and the Green Knight*, Cambridge: Cambridge University Press; some of the fruits of the Norwich group's work are edited by Barbara Cornford (1984) *The Rising of 1381 in Norfolk*, Gorleston, Norfolk: Huggins; Hilton's comment is in *Bond Men Made Free*, p. 234. See also Rodney Hilton (1975) *The English Peasantry in the Later Middle Ages*, Oxford: Oxford University Press, pp. 58, 60–9, and his *Class Conflicts*, chapter 9; and J. H. Hilton (1974) 'Peasant unrest in the England of Richard II: some evidence from royal records', *Historical Studies*, 16: 1–16.
31 J. L. Bolton, *The Medieval English Economy*, p. 181; see J. R. Maddicott (1975) *The English Peasantry and the Demands of the Crown, 1294–1341*, Oxford: Past and Present Supplement.
32 M. M. Postan (1972) *The Medieval Economy and Society*, London: Pelican, 1986, pp. 193–4.
33 A. C. Spearing (1985) *From Medieval to Renaissance in English Poetry*, Cambridge: Cambridge University Press, pp. 20–1; Derek Pearsall, 'Chaucer's poetry', pp. 137–40. Also very relevant here are Frank Lentricchia's comments on Curtius, Eliot, and tradition in *Criticism and Social Change*, pp. 126–32.
34 Nothing could be more commonplace than variations on the theme that 'Chaucer's medieval society was almost entirely a status society' in which the 'chief executive is a status-creating God', a 'wiser' vision than those in modern individualistic 'contract society': J. B. Allen (1982) *The Ethical Poetics of the Later Middle Ages*, Toronto: Toronto

University Press, pp. 305, 306, 304. There is similar emphasis on markets to mine in Alan Macfarlane (1978) *The Origins of English Individualism*, Oxford: Blackwell, pp. 127–8, 151–5, but see note 46 below.

35 See J. L. Bolton, *The Medieval English Economy*, chapters 4, 5, 9, and the following works: J. B. Blake (1967) 'The medieval coal trade of North East England', *Northern History* 2; Edward Miller and John Hatcher, *Medieval England*, pp. 70–9, 247–50; E. M. Veale (1966) *The English Fur Trade in the Later Middle Ages*, Oxford: Oxford University Press; M. K. James (1971) *Studies in the Medieval Wine Trade*, Oxford: Oxford University Press; T. H. Lloyd (1977) *The English Wool Trade in the Middle Ages*, Cambridge: Cambridge University Press; J. Hatcher (1973) *English Tin Production and Trade before 1550*, Oxford: Oxford University Press; M. M. Postan, *Economy and Society*, chapter 12.

36 J. L. Bolton, *The Medieval English Economy*, p. 137.

37 See Sylvia Thrupp (1948) *The Merchant Class of Medieval London*, Chicago: Chicago University Press; Colin Platt (1973) *Medieval Southampton*, London: Routledge & Kegan Paul; E. Gillett and K. A. MacMahon (1980) *A History of Hull*, Oxford: Oxford University Press, chapter 2; Charles Phythian-Adams (1979) *Desolation of a City: Coventry and the Urban Crisis of the Late Middle Ages*, Cambridge: Cambridge University Press; Jennifer Kermode, 'The merchants of three northern English towns', in Cecil H. Clough (ed.) (1982) *Profession, Vocation and Culture in Late Medieval England*, Liverpool: Liverpool University Press.

38 Miller and Hatcher, *Medieval England*, chapter 3, especially pp. 76–9; Postan, *Economy and Society*, chapters 11–12.

39 Miller and Hatcher, *Medieval England*, pp. 228, 229, and chapter 8; Hilton, *Class Conflict*, chapter 15.

40 Miller and Hatcher, *Medieval England*, p. 83; similarly, Postan, *Economy and Society*, pp. 221–6.

41 Hilton, *Class Conflict*, p. 218; see also his *English Peasantry*, chapter 3.

42 Postan, *Economy and Society*, p. 226; Miller and Hatcher, *Medieval England*, pp. 162–4; R. Hilton, *English Peasantry*, chapter 3.

43 R. Hilton, *Class Conflict*, p. 195: see chapters 13–15 and *English Peasantry*, chapter 5.

44 'Wife of Bath's Prologue' in F. N. Robinson (ed.) (1979) *The Works of Geoffrey Chaucer*, Oxford: Oxford University Press, p. 80, line 414. On Robertson's new turn to social history see Pearsall's just observations in 'Chaucer's poetry', p. 139. On the relations of sex–gender systems and economic systems in late medieval urban economies see the outstanding work by Martha C. Howell (1986) *Women, Production and Patriarchy in Late Medieval Cities*, Chicago: Chicago University Press. Unfortunately this only came to me after I had completed my own writing.

45 Marjorie K. McIntosh (1986) *Autonomy and Community: The Royal Manor of Havering 1200–1500*, Cambridge: Cambridge University Press, pp. 136, 138, 152–8, 159, 160–6.

46 McIntosh, *Autonomy and Community*, pp. 136–7. Like McIntosh's, my own account of 'individualism' and community in this book differs from Alan Macfarlane's *Origins of English Individualism*. For Macfarlane, 'English' individualism seems to run happily and painlessly from Germanic tribes through to Mrs Thatcher, like capitalism, while classes and the culture and the collective class struggles of peasant communities against lords are dissolved. See the intelligent review article by S. D. White and R. T. Vann (1983) 'The invention of English individualism: Alan Macfarlane and the modernization of pre-modern England', *Social History* 8: 345–63; Lawrence Stone (1979) 'Goodbye to nearly all that', *New York Review of Books* 26, 6, offers another extremely weighty range of criticisms, from its methods and evidence to its version of England from about 1500 to 1800, to its 'myopia' in the treatment of peasant communities; R. Hilton's review is extremely sharp (1980) *New Left Review* 120: 109–11. For Macfarlane's responses, see his (1987) *Culture of Capitalism*, Oxford: Blackwell, pp. 191–222.

47 McIntosh, *Autonomy and Community*, pp. 176, 177.

48 P. H. Barnum (ed.) (1976, 1980) *Dives and Pauper* 2 vols, Oxford: *Early English Text Society* 275, 280, here vol. I, p. 357.

49 G. Kane and E. T. Donaldson (eds) (1975) *Piers Plowman: the B Version*, London: Athlone, XIII 282, 284.

50 R. Williams (1976) *Keywords: a Vocabulary of Culture and Society*, London: Fontana, p. 134.

51 Representative of the work I have in mind: Francis Barker (1984) *The Tremulous Private Body*, London: Methuen, for example the bizarre claims about the absence of 'subjectivity' in 'pre-bourgeois' societies, equated with pre-seventeenth-century England, pp. 31, 41, 63; Catherine Belsey (1985) *The Subject of Tragedy: Identity and Difference in Renaissance Drama*, London: Methuen, pp. 33, 40; Terry Eagleton (1986) *William Shakespeare*, Oxford: Blackwell, denying the existence of commodity production as he seeks to teach us what is novel in society and individual identity in Shakespeare's time, pp. 98, 100.

52 Quotation from Judith Bennett discussing the overlap of gender arrangements and ideology between élites and peasantry (1986) *Women in the Medieval English Countryside*, Oxford: Oxford University Press, p. 45, see also p. 47; Martha Howell's brilliant study (1986) *Women, Production and Patriarchy in Late Medieval Cities*, Chicago: Chicago University Press; David Nicholas (1985) *The Domestic Life of a Medieval City: Women, Children and the Family in Fourteenth-Century Ghent*, Lincoln, NE: Nebraska University Press; David Herlihy (1985) *Medieval Households*, Cambridge, Mass.: Harvard University Press, chapters 4–6; Rodney Hilton, 'Women traders in medieval England', in his *Class Conflict* and 'Women in the village', in his *English Peasantry* (though against that account set Judith M. Bennett, *Women in the Medieval English Countryside*); Keith Wrightson (1978) 'Medieval villagers in perspective', *Peasant Studies* 7: 203–17, especially pp. 213–15, with its astute use of and comments on M. Sheehan

(1971) 'The formation and stability of marriage in fourteenth century England', *Medieval Studies* 33: 228–63; Barbara Hanawalt (ed.) (1986) *Women and Work in Preindustrial Europe*, Bloomington: Indiana University Press; J. Goodie (1983) *The Development of the Family and Marriage in Europe*, Cambridge: Cambridge University Press; Alan Macfarlane, *Origins of English Individualism*, pp. 138–40.

53 Frank Lentricchia, *After the New Criticism*, p. 207.

54 Max Horkheimer and Theodor Adorno (1972) *Dialectic of Enlightenment*, New York: Herder & Herder, p. 230, revised translation and elaboration in Herbert Marcuse (1979) *The Aesthetic Dimension*, London: Macmillan, p. 73; see also Frank Lentricchia, *Criticism and Social Change*, part 4.

CHAPTER 1 *PIERS PLOWMAN*: POVERTY, WORK, AND COMMUNITY

1 An earlier, shorter version of this chapter was written for the Elizabeth Salter Memorial Volume which comprised *Leeds Studies in English* 14 (1983). For demography, economy, subsistence, and levels of exploitation in the long thirteenth century see E. Miller and J. Hatcher (1978) *Medieval England: Rural Society and Economic Change*, London: Longman; J. L. Bolton (1980) *The Medieval English Economy 1150–1500*, London: Dent, chapters 2–6; there is an excellent summary of trends in Miri Rubin (1987) *Charity and Community in Medieval Cambridge*, Cambridge: Cambridge University Press, pp. 15–33, 49–53.

2 A hundred years earlier Aquinas had stated, 'Workmen who hire out their labour are poor, they seek their daily bread by their exertion', quoted by Rubin, *Charity and Community*, p. 8.

3 On poverty in the period of the demographic and economic expansion, see: Rubin, *Charity and Community*, pp. 15–33, 49–53; Miller and Hatcher, *Medieval England*, pp. 147–9, 151, 154–6; M. M. Postan (1972) *The Medieval Economy and Society*, London: Pelican, 1986, pp. 142–50, 157–8; M. Mollat (1978) *Les pauvres au Moyen Age*, Paris: Hachette, part 3, English translation (1986) *The Poor in the Middle Ages*, Connecticut: Yale University Press, hereafter reference to English translation as Mollat, *Poor*.

4 Mollat, *Poor*, chapters 4–6.

5 Mark 10.25: quotations in this chapter from Douai-Rheims translation of vulgate (Burns & Oates, 1964).

6 Mollat, *Poor*, 106; P. H. Barnum (ed.) (1976, 1980) *Dives and Pauper* 2 vols, Oxford: *Early English Text Society* 275, 280, vol. II, p. 283.

7 Mollat, *Poor*, p. 121.

8 Translated in L. D. Sherley-Price (1959) *St Francis of Assisi: His Life and Writings*, Oxford: Mowbray, p. 212; see M. D. Lambert (1961) *Franciscan Poverty*, London: Society for Promoting Christian Knowledge, pp. 122–3.

9 See M. A. Moisa, 'Fourteenth-century preachers' views of the poor', in R. Samuel and G. S. Jones (eds) (1983) *Culture, Ideology and Politics*, London: Routledge & Kegan Paul, here pp. 165–7.

10 'The Rich Man's Salvation' in G. W. Butterworth (ed.) (1968) *Clement of Alexandria*, Cambridge, Mass.: Harvard University Press, pp. 260–367, here p. 341.
11 Richard of Maidstone's work (1958) is printed in *Carmelus* 5: 132–80: here see pp. 139–44, 167–8, 178–9; warnings against prying discrimination, pp. 141–3.
12 *Dives and Pauper*, vol. II, pp. 284–94: quotes from pp. 286, 288, 291. On the use of St John Chrysostom in canon law, Brian Tierney (1959) *Medieval Poor Law*, Berkeley and Los Angeles: University of California Press, pp. 54–7.
13 Tierney, *Medieval Poor Law*; Mollat, *Poor*, p. 134; Rubin, *Charity and Community*, pp. 71–2 and his references in notes 111–17.
14 I. H. Sbaralea and C. Eubel (eds) (1898) *Bullarium Franciscanum* vol. 5, Rome: on the pre-lapsarian state and God's creation of private property after the fall, see pp. 422–4, 439–41 (*Quia vir reprobus*); quoted here from pp. 422, 421; on Christ, see pp. 441–3; see also, on Christ and apostles, *Quia quorumdam mentis*, pp. 244–5, 275–9.
15 G. Leff (1967) *Heresy in the Later Middle Ages* 2 vols, Manchester: Manchester University Press, vol. I, pp. 247, 249, chapter 2, and see Lambert, *Franciscan Poverty*, chapter 10.
16 R. Tuck (1977) *Natural Rights Theories*, Cambridge: Cambridge University Press, p. 22.
17 Rubin, *Charity and Community*, p. 71.
18 Rubin, *Charity and Community*, p. 72.
19 I use the English translation of FitzRalph's *Defensio Curatorum* in A. J. Perry (ed.) (1925) *Dialogus*, Oxford: *Early English Text Society* 167, o.s., pp. 83–5, 31, 80. The attraction of FitzRalph for the Lollards in *these* contexts needs further investigation ('St Richard' to some Lollards – A. Hudson (1972) *Journal of Theological Studies* 23: 73). On FitzRalph, Katharine Walsh (1981) *A Fourteenth Century Scholar and Primate*, Oxford: Oxford University Press, especially chapter 5 on 'The mendicant controversy'.
20 FitzRalph in *Dialogus*, p. 71; c.f. G. R. Owst (1966) *Literature and Pulpit*, Oxford: Blackwell, pp. 555–7.
21 See Mollat, *Poor*; J.-C. Schmitt (1978) *Mort d'une hérésie*, Paris: Mouton, *passim*, but especially pp. 152–7, 162–73, 182–91; on economic change and impoverishment, see note 1 above, and C. Lis and H. Soly (1979) *Poverty and Capitalism in Pre-Industrial Europe*, Brighton: Harvester, chapters 1, 2: there are obvious problems in establishing significant regional variations – C. C. Dyer (1980) *Lords and Peasants in a Changing Society*, Cambridge: Cambridge University Press, pp. 349–54, 110–12.
22 Walsh, *Scholar and Primate*, pp. 410–16.
23 On the mortality rate, see Miller and Hatcher, *Medieval England*, p. 29; Postan, *Economy and Society*, pp. 41–2.
24 See note 3 above.
25 See, for example, references in R. H. Britnell (1986) *Growth and Decline in Colchester*, Cambridge: Cambridge University Press, p. 148.

26 See Miller and Hatcher, *Medieval England*, pp. 171–9, 191–2; Postan, *Economy and Society*, p. 195; R. Hilton (1973) *Bond Men Made Free*, London: Temple Smith, p. 154.

27 Quotations and translations of the statutes and petitions are from R. B. Dobson (1970) *The Peasants' Revolt of 1381*, London: Macmillan, p. 64: references hereafter in text. Where the original word is added in brackets, this has been done by me, not Dobson.

28 Bertha H. Putnam (1908) *The Enforcement of the Statutes of Labourers*, New York: Columbia University Press, p. 55; Dobson, *The Peasants' Revolt*, p. 69; L. R. Poos (1983) 'The social context of Statute of Labourers enforcement', *Law and History Review*, 1: 27–52. On resistance see R. Hilton (1985) *Class Conflict and the Crisis of Feudalism*, London: Hambledon, pp. 135–8, 156–7, 159, 163, 203, 219, and Barbara Hanawalt, ' "Peasant resistance" ', in F. X. Newman (ed.) (1986) *Social Unrest in the Late Middle Ages*, Binghamton, NY: Center for Medieval and Renaissance Texts and Studies, State University of New York, pp. 38–40.

29 My translation and selection from documents printed in Bertha H. Putnam (ed.) (1938) *Proceedings before the Justices of the Peace in the Fourteenth and Fifteenth Centuries*, London: Spottiswoode, Ballantyne, & Co., pp. 342, 346, 356, 358. Besides this invaluable collection see examples for Essex in Nora Kenyon (1934) *EcHR* 4: 429–51, and for Wiltshire in E. M. Thompson (1903–4) *Wiltshire and Natural History Magazine* 33: 384–409.

30 Putnam, *Enforcement*, p. 91.

31 Putnam, *Proceedings*, p. cxxv.

32 See Bertha H. Putnam (1915–16) 'Maximum wage-laws for priests after the Black Death, 1348–1381', *American Hist. Rev.* 21: 12–32, here p. 25; see also *Rotuli Parliamentorum* (1783) London, 6 vols, II, pp. 268–75, especially p. 271.

33 See M. A. Moisa, 'Fourteenth-century preachers' views of the poor'.

34 R. M. Jordan (1967) *Chaucer and the Shape of Creation*, Cambridge, Mass.: Harvard University Press, and S. Medcalf (1981) *The Later Middle Ages*, London: Methuen, p. 57; the comments of Pearsall and Spearing cited in note 33 to the Introduction are again relevant.

35 See note 10 to the Introduction for comments on dominant poststructuralist methods and their incompatibility with my own concerns.

36 Lis and Soly, *Poverty*, p. 50; Mollat, *Poor*, pp. 200–3, 292; Postan, *Economy and Society*, chapter 8.

37 See Rubin's table on prices and wages, *Charity and Community*, p. 26.

38 Postan, *Economy and Society*, pp. 170, 158.

39 For praise of Gower's civilized art, the produce of 'a poet perfectly well bred' (the phrase is without intentional ironies), see John Burrow (agreeing with C. S. Lewis) (1982) *Medieval Writers and their Work: Middle English Literature and its Background*, Oxford: Oxford University Press, p. 30. For a more alert response to Gower, see Janet Coleman (1981) *English Literature in History 1350–1400*, London: Hutchinson, pp. 138–56.

40 In *The Major Latin Works of John Gower*, trans. Eric W. Stockton, Washington: University of Washington Press, 1962; quotations from Book V, 9 and 10, pp. 208–10.
41 Quotations from Book I, written after Book V, which preceded the rising, pp. 58, 70, 78, 94–5.
42 Thomas of Wimbledon's Paul's Cross sermon of 1388, quoted from the edition by N. H. Owen (1966) in *Medieval Studies* 28: 176–97, p. 179.
43 Lis and Soly, *Poverty*, p. 51; see also Mollat, *Poor*, pp. 251–8, 290–300; on the secularization of charity, pp. 272–90.
44 Rubin, *Charity and Community*, p. 293.
45 FitzRalph in *Dialogus*, p. 83.
46 FitzRalph in *Dialogus*, p. 88.
47 FitzRalph in *Dialogus*, p. 91.
48 The history of this model and its accommodation to shifts and different interests within the ruling classes is traced by G. Duby (1978) *Les Trois ordres ou l'imaginaire du féodalisme*, Paris: Gallimard; Chicago: Chicago University Press, 1980.
49 David Aers (1980) *Chaucer, Langland and the Creative Imagination*, London: Routledge & Kegan Paul, chapters 1, 2.
50 All references to Langland's poem are to G. Kane and E. T. Donaldson (eds) *Piers Plowman: the B Version*, London: Athlone; when the C-version is referred to the text is D. A. Pearsall (ed.) (1978) *Piers Plowman*, London: Arnold. On beggars in *Piers Plowman*, see E. T. Donaldson (1949) *Piers Plowman*, Connecticut: Yale University Press, pp. 130–6; also relevant M. Day (1932) 'Piers Plowman and the poor relief', *RES* 8: 445–6, responding to N. Coghill's essay in the same volume, and the extraordinarily moving chapter by Geoffrey Shepherd, 'Poverty in *Piers Plowman*' in T. H. Aston, P. R. Coss, C. Dyer, and J. Thirsk (1983) *Social Relations and Ideas*, Cambridge: Cambridge University Press. The essay by R. Adams (1978) 'The nature of need in *Piers Plowman*', *Traditio* 34: 273–301, argues that 'Langland never shifts his basic principles on the issues associated with poverty' from those of FitzRalph and William of St Amour. My own views, as will emerge, are very different.
51 This practical autonomy is evidenced in most studies of medieval peasant communities, as plain in the conflicts at Halesowen described by Razi (see notes 25 and 26 to the Introduction) as in the accounts of the way peasant communities functioned in the works of J. A. Raftis and the Toronto school or in the general descriptions by M. M. Postan, *Economy and Society*, chapters 7–8, or by Miller and Hatcher, *Medieval England*, chapters 4–6. Indeed, in her study (1979) *Crime and Conflict in English Communities 1300–1348*, Cambridge, Mass.: Harvard University Press, Barbara Hanawalt sees the lords' so-called 'protection' as like that offered by a protection racket, such as one run by the Mafia (p. 143). The study of Battle Abbey and its Banlieu by Eleanor Searle (1974) *Lordship and Community*, Toronto: Pontifical Institute, p. 164, includes some nice examples of this (as do Hanawalt

and Razi in their studies). The greatest threat to the well-being of peasant communities was the gentry, not only through incidents of direct violence recorded by Hanawalt, Razi, Searle, and others, but through the heavy extractions of peasant labour and produce in rents, fines, taxes, and services.

52 On these encounters, see Dobson, *The Peasants' Revolt*, pp. 259–61, 237–8, 311–12; see also p. 314, Knighton's account of Tresilion's activities.

53 Hilton, *Class Conflict*, p. 155; see pp. 154–64.

54 For the relevant history see Lis and Soly, *Poverty*, chapters 3, 5; on the sixteenth and seventeenth centuries, see C. Hill (1958) 'William Perkins and the poor', in *Puritanism and Revolution*, St Albans: Panther, 1968, and (1964) 'The poor and the parish', in *Society and Puritanism*, St Albans: Panther, 1969; P. A. Slack (1974) 'Vagrants and vagrancy in England 1598–1664', *EcHR* 27: 360–97; A. L. Beier (1974) 'Vagrants and the social order in Elizabethan England', *Past and Present*, 64: 8–29. On the complex later period see the way offered by John Barrell (1986) *The Dark Side of the Landscape*, Cambridge: Cambridge University Press, and E. P. Thompson (1963) *The Making of the English Working Class*, London: Gollancz, pp. 262–8, 302–3.

55 I quote from a letter responding to an earlier draft of this chapter, one to which I am extremely grateful. See also the references in note 28 above.

56 Aers, *Chaucer, Langland*, chapters 1, 2. My sentence recalls K. Marx (1970) *Capital* I, London: Lawrence & Wishart, p. 85.

57 Marjorie K. McIntosh (1986) *Autonomy and Community: The Royal Manor of Havering 1200–1500*, Cambridge: Cambridge University Press, p. 257.

58 P. H. Barnum (ed.) (1976, 1980) *Dives and Pauper* 2 vols, Oxford: *Early English Text Society* 275, 280, vol. I, pp. 199, 189, 357 (see also 358 on rebellion).

59 Lis and Soly, *Poverty*, pp. 188–202; D. V. Erdman (1969) *Blake: Prophet Against Empire*, Princeton: Princeton University Press, pp. 273–4; E. P. Thompson, *Making of the English Working Class*.

60 Perhaps Bakhtin's account of carnival, the body, and popular culture, in (1968) *Rabelais and His World*, Cambridge, MA: MIT Press, might be relevant here – despite the unexamined assumptions about the maleness of the body in Bakhtin's work.

61 R. Hilton, 'Women traders in medieval England', in *Class Conflict*, here p. 215.

62 V 376–7, 395–6, 402, 404; I refer to N. P. Tanner (ed.) (1977) *Norwich Heresy Trials*, London: Royal Historical Society, Camden 4th series vol. 20.

63 See the references in notes 25–32 to chapter 1, above.

64 On this breakdown, see Aers, *Chaucer, Langland*, chapter 1.

65 Z. Razi (1981) 'Family, land and village community', *Past and Present* 93: 15.

66 On peasants both as wage-labourers and employers of labour see, for example: Miller and Hatcher, *Medieval England*, pp. 49–53, 219–24;

Postan, *Economy and Society*, pp. 147–50, 257–8; R. Hilton (1973) *Bond Men Made Free*, pp. 154–6, 171–5, 235; McIntosh, *Autonomy and Community*, pp. 149–50, 157, 160–6; Poos, 'The social context'.

67 Dobson, *The Peasants' Revolt*, p. 74. As B. Tierney notes, the foundations of the sixteenth-century poor and settlement laws were in place already: *Medieval Poor Law*, pp. 128–9.

68 Dobson, *The Peasants' Revolt*, p. 65.

69 Piers is unequivocally a layman – see, for example, V 17–32, 91–3, 546–8.

70 See V 483–505.

71 See Kane and Donaldson, *Piers Plowman*, p. 361, critical apparatus to VI 223: the manuscripts they have chosen to alter here make the shift very explicit by advising Piers to help out not only the needy but the 'nouȝty' with his 'goodes'. It is unjustifiable to use the C-version to tell us what the poet's earlier version or versions must have been, since this only short-circuits the processes of the poet's struggles to find his way through complex moral and social issues. For a different view of work and wasters (in A-version, VIII) see Guy Bourquin (1978) *Piers Plowman* 2 vols, Lille: University of Lille, p. 714.

72 C VIII 232ff. and see Pearsall's commentary pp. 154–5 on C VIII 210, useful despite its stance being uncritically a gentry/clerical one which blurs the cultural shifts and conflicts. This last comment applies with far greater force to some recent books on *Piers Plowman*: J. M. Bowers (1986) *The Crisis of Will in Piers Plowman*, Washington, DC: Catholic University of America Press, pp. 105–6 (including an unwary but typical enough homogenization of 'the nation' under the interests of gentry); A. Baldwin, with her unquestioning assumption of gentry interests in her version of 'fair' and 'honest', in (1981) *The Theme of Government in Piers Plowman*, Cambridge: Boydell & Brewer Press; M. Stokes with her ranting about 'the Marxist rhetoric of the down-trodden proletariat' and 'the authentic note of self-righteous whining against the "bosses" ' in Passus VI, is perhaps the most striking case (1984) *Justice and Mercy in Piers Plowman*, London: Croom Helm, pp. 210–12.

73 C VIII 242 even *latinizes* the addition, giving it 'real' authority.

74 Matthew 25.14–30: see Pearsall's astute comments on C VIII 247, p. 157.

75 See the examples of FitzRalph's exegesis in section one of this chapter, and the story told in L. K. Little (1978) *Religious Poverty and the Profit Economy*, St Albans: Elek, as well as in Mollat, *Poor*, Schmitt, *Mort d'une hérésie* and, for a later period, R. H. Tawney (1926) *Religion and the Rise of Capitalism*, Harmondsworth: Penguin.

76 The precarious existence on the very margins of survival led by so many European people in the long thirteenth century (amply documented in Miller and Hatcher, *Medieval England*, Postan, *Economy and Society*, Mollat, *Poor*, and others) makes the approach of literary scholars such as Stokes (see note 72 above) rather foolish in its equation of justice and fairness with the employers' efforts to force

working people to remain in that miserable state under changed circumstances, to make the poorer people of the community pay for the (relative) economic problems of the more affluent.

77 Hilton, *Bond Men Made Free*, p. 184.

78 A commonplace, illustrated plainly in Gower's *Vox Clamantis*, trans. Stockton, e.g., pp. 58, 70, 72, 75, 80, 90, 94–5, or Walsingham's celebration of the suppression of the 1381 rising, Dobson, *The Peasants' Revolt*, pp. 310–13. The similarity between the outlook of Gower or Walsingham and modern literary scholars like Stokes (see note 72 above) is marked – it hardly represents the objective historical criticism it purports to be!

79 Hilton, *Bond Men Made Free*, p. 235: this should be read with his essays 'Feudalism and the origins of capitalism' and 'Capitalism – what's in a name?' reprinted in *Class Conflict*, especially here pp. 2,290–1; also relevant here, chapters 13–16.

80 Quoting Lis and Soly, *Poverty*, pp. 50–1.

81 On the pardon, see Donaldson, *Piers Plowman*, pp. 130–6, Aers, *Chaucer, Langland*, pp. 20–3, but the literature on this passage is substantial and conflicting.

82 On contemporary lawyers here see, for example, Bertha Putnam (1943–4) 'Chief Justice Shareshull and the economic and legal codes of 1351–1352', *University of Toronto Law Journal* 5: 251–81; Alan Harding, 'The revolt against the justices', in R. H. Hilton and T. H. Aston (eds) (1984) *The English Rising of 1381*, Cambridge: Cambridge University Press.

83 Rubin, *Charity and Community*, p. 32.

84 See especially the works by Putnam and Poos cited in notes 28 and 29 above.

85 The literature on the late medieval and early modern nuclear family and gender-systems is increasing rapidly in number and depth: see note 52 to the Introduction.

86 Quoting Hans Medick from 'The proto-industrial family economy', in P. Kriedte, H. Medick, and J. Schlumbohm (1981) *Industrialization before Industrialization: Rural Industry in the Genesis of Capitalism*, Cambridge: Cambridge University Press, p. 56. Passus IX returns to problems posed by the market to Langland's ideal model of family relations.

87 R. Adams (1978) 'The nature of need in *Piers Plowman*'; for a different view, and in my opinion more relevant to *Piers Plowman*, M. W. Bloomfield (1961) *Piers Plowman as a Fourteenth-Century Apocalypse*, New Brunswick, NJ: Rutgers University Press, especially p. 72.

88 In line 123 Kane and Donaldson substitute 'bilyue' for 'bely ioye': 'bilyue', meaning livelihood as in XIX 235, makes good sense but I cannot see any good reason for overruling the weight of manuscripts here; see critical apparatus p. 377 and compare VII 130 where the editors change to 'bely ioye'.

89 While the C-version could well delete this passage as a fearful response to radical uses of the poem in 1381 (Dobson, *The Peasants'*

Revolt, pp. 380–3), C IX adds an equally powerful version of a neo-Franciscan ethos equally antithetical to the work ethos (IX 105ff.).

90 See the sermon quoted, in a different context, by E. J. Douglass (1966) *Justification in Medieval Preaching*, Leiden: Brill, pp. 144–5; also on Geiler, see Schmitt, *Morte d'une hérésie*, pp. 185–7.

91 I have not the space to quote some customarily moving comments of Simone Weil strikingly relevant to this theme, ones still, sadly, pertinent today: 'Reflections concerning the causes of liberty and social oppression', in (1958) *Oppression and Liberty*, London: Routledge & Kegan Paul, see the passages reprinted in S. Miles (ed.) (1986) *Simone Weil: An Anthology*, London: Virago, pp. 151–64.

92 See IX 159ff., as Pearsall notes, a common complaint (note to C X 25, p. 191).

93 See Aers, *Chaucer, Langland*, chapters 1, 2.

94 Here see X 13–87: on the rents, X 15 and XIV 230–1.

95 An example of Will's understandable resistance is in the response to Scripture, X 377, and the way he turns the dialogue to another aspect of theology proving exceptionally troublesome to contemporaries concerned with such matters in such an idiom: see Janet Coleman (1981) *Piers Plowman and the Moderni*, Rome: Edizioni di Storia e Lettaratura. This turn leads to the collapse into 'þe lond of longynge' (XI 8), a yielding up of moral questions in despair. On Langland and despair, see Bowers, *Crisis of Will.*

96 See XI 259–69 and 199–204; on 'kynde', kindness and unkindness, salvation and damnation, XVII 206–98, XVIII 371–6, 397–8. See too the values in XI 271–8.

97 See XIII 224–70: c.f. VI 231–4, and an explicit identification with the early Piers, XIII 235–7: VII 5–8.

98 For a more extensive discussion of Haukyn, see Aers, *Chaucer, Langland*, pp. 27–9.

99 For example: XIII 375–8, 355, 390; indeed, 354–98 all relevant. See too V 200ff., and for changes in moral theory, Little, *Religious Poverty*.

100 See XIII 391–8, 301–10: on the figure of the poet, Bowers, *Crisis of Will*, pp. 204–5; on minstrels and the poet, see Donaldson, *Piers Plowman*, pp. 136–55 and, on the poet, chapter 7.

101 See XIII 281–6: it could as well be *herself.*

102 See XIV 190–259, 280–321; on XIV 313–15 J. T. Noonan's study of doctrine concerning usury is essential: (1957) *The Scholastic Analysis of Usury*, Cambridge, Mass.: Harvard University Press, part 1. Compare Haukyn at XIII 375–6, 390–8 and the *sale* of time.

103 Also in Passus XIV, see lines 109–25, 160–80, 213–15; and X 59–66, 83–9, 205–7, 361–7; XI 176–91, 243–5; XIII 438–43; XV 244–8, 342–3; and the C-version addition, IX 70–97.

104 Some classic statements of late sixteenth- and early seventeenth-century applications are provided by the immensely popular Dodd and Cleaver, on 'rungates', able-bodied vagrants, and Hildersam, while the 1590 quarter session records for Middlesex

alone showed 'vagrants were being whipped and branded . . . at the rate of one a day', C. Hill, *Society and Puritanism*, pp. 274–7.

105 Quoted in section one, translated in Lambert, *Franciscan Poverty*, p. 59.

106 Bourquin, *Piers Plowman*, pp. 328, 722; also A. V. Schmidt (ed.) (1978) *The Vision of Piers Plowman*, London: Dent, p. 343.

107 I write 'no sustained return' to acknowledge that there may be, perhaps, signs of some slight wavering, some small hesitations. For example, XII 146–7, Jesus born 'in a Burgeises place, of Bethlem þe beste'. But Imaginitif does not sustain this line, treats possessions as 'combraunce', and supports the critique of the rich in Passus X and XIV (XII 45, 151–4, 238–68). Overall then, Passus XII offers no challenge to the identification of Christ and contemporary poor, to the claim that 'he bereþ þe signe of pouerte/And in þat secte oure saueour saued al mankynde' (XIV 258–9). Another possible example may, perhaps, be in Passus XV. Logically, lines 195–212 should support the abandonment of discriminatory and judgemental alms-giving (only Piers, figuring forth Christ, can know the real state of a human being), yet Anima turns them against beggars, both vagrant and static (XV 213–15, 227). Yet it seems to me that in this brief turn the primary object of the poet's perception is himself, as figured in his poem at least, a pseudo-hermit, a vagrant, one who seems 'an ydel man' and a beggar, as the C addition stresses (V 26–31: c.f. C XVI 334–5, 349, and Donaldson, *Piers Plowman*, pp. 135–6), corroborating much in the B-version, including XV 4–9. Passus XV *also* affirms the traditional ideal of 'parcel mele' charity (244–8), the line supported earlier by St Gregory.

108 The literature on this figure is surveyed in Adams, 'The nature of need'.

109 The C-version makes the distinction between 'beggares with bagges' and those that 'bereth none bagges ne boteles' a decisive one: see C IX 98–101, 109–20, 139–40, 153–61; also Luke 9.3 and 22.5 conflated in IX 120. Pearsall's note to V 52 stresses the importance of this distinction in the C-version.

110 On such rights, see for example, Thomas Aquinas, *ST*, II–II, pp. 66–7: note the careful qualifications at lines 11–16, 18–20, 22 which are overlooked by Adams, 'The nature of need'.

111 Similar to Holy Church at I 17–22. Geoffrey Shepherd's comments on 'temperance' in the poem's closing stages, and his criticism of Bloomfield, are very shrewd: 'Poverty in *Piers Plowman*', pp. 187–8 (note 35 on Bloomfield) in T. H. Aston *et al.*, *Social Relations and Ideas*.

112 *Dives and Pauper*, II 141.

113 M-M Dufeil (1972) *Guillaume de Saint Amour*, Picard, pp. 295–324, 352; also, Jill Mann (1973) *Chaucer and Medieval Estates Satire*, Cambridge: Cambridge University Press, pp. 37–54, 226–33.

114 W. W. Skeat (ed.) (1886) *Piers the Plowman* 2 vols, Oxford: Oxford University Press, 1968, II 212.

115 On the friars in Passus XX, lines 230–384 *passim*, and note Little's account of their accommodation to urban and market economy in *Religious Poverty*, chapters 9, 12.
116 With the account of the work ethos in Passus V–VII and XIV, and in section one of the chapter, here see Little, *Religious Poverty*, chapters 9–12.
117 Aers, *Chaucer, Langland*, chapter 2.
118 Aers, *Chaucer, Langland*, pp. 28–31.
119 Quoting from XVII 374–5, XVIII 376–7, 397–8: see XVII 252–305 and XVIII 375–403. On Langland and the salvation of the heathen, G. H. Russell (1966) *JWCI* 29: 101–16.
120 Piers's assumptions at VI 45 are totally congenial to the conservative poet's. On the final processes of serfdom, R. Hilton (1969) *The Decline of Serfdom in Medieval England*, London: Macmillan, and Postan, *Economy and Society*, pp. 169–73.
121 Dobson, *The Peasants' Revolt*, p. 371.
122 Dobson, *The Peasants' Revolt*, pp. 374–5: on Ball, see Hilton, *Bond Men Made Free*, pp. 221–4, 227–8, with chapter 9 on the aims of the rising.
123 Dobson, *The Peasants' Revolt*, pp. 380–3: literary scholars still seem to overlook the significance of such reception for our understanding of medieval culture (its heterogeneity) and of the difficulties in knowing how texts were received, what they meant to different groups of medieval people.
124 On fraternities in late medieval England and Europe see Rubin and her references, *Charity and Community*, pp. 250–9 and M. James (1983) 'Ritual, drama and social body in the late medieval English town', *Past and Present* 98: 3–29.
125 The fascinating study by J. Chiffoleau (1980) *La comptabilité de l'au-delà: les hommes, la mort et la religion dans la région d'Avignon à la fin du moyen-âge*, Rome: L'Ecole Française de Rome, includes speculations about this: it would be good to know how relevant they are to English people of this era.
126 James, *Past and Present* 98: 8.
127 I have in mind Sartre's comments on fraternity/terror in (1982) *Critique of Dialectical Reason*, London: New Left Books, Verso, pp. 428–44, 468–70.
128 Hilton, *Class Conflict*, pp. 203–4.
129 This figure, almost as controversial as Need, seems only 'lewed' in the way any critic of the powerful is, including the poet: immediately after this, the poem recapitulates the critique of the leading classes made in Passus X: XIX 459–76. No hope of reform here.
130 The most recent attempts to analyse the figure 'I' or 'Will' is Bowers, *The Crisis of Will*.
131 Chiffoleau's book, *La comptabilité de l'au-delà*, has haunting comments on literal and spiritual orphanage in the post-plague period around Avignon, as well as on the cult of purgatory and fraternities as a response to this catastrophic mortality. Langland eschewed both

these comforts. It will be extremely helpful if English historians can take up some of the great themes in Chiffoleau's book and see how they relate to English experience – and if they do not, why not.

CHAPTER 2 THE MAKING OF MARGERY KEMPE: INDIVIDUAL AND COMMUNITY

1 All quotations from Margery Kempe are to S. B. Meech and H. E. Allen (eds) (1961) *The Book of Margery Kempe*, Oxford: *Early English Text Society*, o.s., 212. References to this edition now in the text. Sarah Beckwith, 'A very material mysticism: the medieval mysticism of Margery Kempe', in David Aers (1986) *Medieval Literature: Criticism, Ideology and History*, Brighton: Harvester, here p. 37. For Margery's life, see Clara Atkinson (1983) *Mystic*, Cornell: Cornell University Press.

2 Atkinson, *Mystic*, chapter 7, quotations from pp. 197, 200, 210; Beckwith, 'Material mysticism', pp. 37–40.

3 S. Medcalf (1981) *The Later Middle Ages*, London: Methuen, p. 115; and D. E. Hinderer (1982) 'On rehabilitating Margery Kempe', *Studia Mystica* 5: 27–43, quoted in Kieckhefer (cited in note 4 below), p. 196. On 'hysteria' see Luce Irigaray's reflections in 'Plato's hysteria' in (1985) *Speculum of the Other Woman*, trans. G. C. Gill, Cornell: Cornell University Press; Ilza Veith (1965) *Hysteria: The History of a Disease*, Chicago: Chicago University Press; and Alan Krohn (1978) *Hysteria*, New York: International Universities Press.

4 Atkinson, *Mystic*, p. 201; here I quote Beckwith, 'Material mysticism', pp. 39–40; her comments on the monk's wishes, pp. 38–9, and the quotation from Knowles on p. 39 should be savoured. On Margery Kempe's place in tradition, Atkinson's invaluable work is well supplemented by R. Kieckhefer (1984) *Unquiet Souls: Fourteenth-century Saints and their Religious Milieu*, Chicago: Chicago University Press.

5 Sheila Delany (1975) 'Sexual economics, Chaucer's Wife of Bath and *The Book of Margery Kempe*', *Minnesota Review* 5, reprinted in her collection (1983) *Writing Woman*, New York: Schocken, to which references here are made, pp. 80–1.

6 Atkinson, *Mystic*, pp. 67–80, 86–101: also relevant, unavailable to Atkinson, D. Owen (ed.) (1984) *The Making of King's Lynn*, Oxford: British Academy, Oxford University Press.

7 On pre-capitalist market economies and society see my Introduction, with relevant references. For studies cited there of special relevance to the culture of Margery Kempe's class see the works by Thrupp, Kermode, and Howell in notes 37 and 44 to the Introduction.

8 Delany, 'Sexual economics', p. 86.

9 Similarly, Atkinson, *Mystic*, pp. 78–9, 101.

10 On display in the merchant class, see Sylvia Thrupp (1948) *The Merchant Class of Medieval London*, Chicago: Chicago University Press, 1962, pp. 130–54, 234–56, 317–18; Elspeth M. Veale includes a relevant discussion of sumptuary legislation in chapter 1 of (1966)

The English Fur Trade in the Later Middle Ages, Oxford: Oxford University Press; relevant to these aspects of her milieu is M. James (1983) 'Ritual, drama and social body in the late medieval English town', *Past and Present* 98: 3–29, and R. B. Dobson, 'The risings in York, Beverley and Scarborough, 1380–1381', in R. H. Hilton and T. H. Aston (eds) (1984) *The English Rising of 1381*, Cambridge: Cambridge University Press.

11 On women in the urban economy, see Martha C. Howell (1986) *Women, Production and Patriarchy in Late Medieval Cities*, Chicago: Chicago University Press; David Nicholas (1985) *The Domestic Life of a Medieval City: Women, Children and the Family in Fourteenth-Century Ghent*, Lincoln, NE: Nebraska University Press; on brewing and Rose the regrator, see R. H. Hilton (1985) *Class Conflict and the Crisis of Feudalism*, London: Hambledon, pp. 203–4. What was the relation between Margery's brewing and John's (*Book of Margery Kempe*, p. 364)?

12 See Jean Delumeau (1971) *Le Catholicisme entre Luther et Voltaire*, Paris: Presses Universitaires, part 3, chapter 3, 'La legende du Moyen Age Chrétien', especially pp. 234–7; Jacques Toussaert (1963) *Le Sentiment religieux en Flandre à la fin du Moyen Age*, Paris: Plon; Keith Thomas (1973) *Religion and the Decline of Magic*, Harmondsworth: Penguin, chapters 2, 3, 6, 9; Ronald Finucane (1977) *Miracles and Pilgrims*, London: Dent. Grave reservations, which I fully share, are offered concerning J. Bossy (1985) *Christianity in the West*, Oxford: Oxford University Press, by R. W. Scribner (1986) in *English HR*, 100: 683–6.

13 The tricks and relativity in any notion of autonomy, whether of individuals, 'elements', 'levels', or whatever is made clear in most theoretical traditions, including marxist, Hegelian, psychoanalytic, structuralist and poststructuralist.

14 R. Hilton (1973) *Bond Men Made Free*, London: Temple Smith, p. 174, see pp. 171–95, 154–6: most studies of peasant communities reveal the market's role in increasing polarization in post-plague England, whether the studies are done from within the Toronto school paradigm (e.g., E. B. Dewindt (1972) *Land and People in Holywell-cum-Needingworth*, Toronto: Pontifical Institute), or a neo-marxist one (e.g., Z. Razi (1980) *Life, Marriage and Death in a Medieval Parish*, Cambridge: Cambridge University Press), or neither (Marjorie K. McIntosh (1986) *Autonomy and Community*, Cambridge: Cambridge University Press, chapter 3 and pp. 226–8).

15 Atkinson, *Mystic*, p. 60; similarly Delany, 'Sexual economics', pp. 86–7.

16 On the upper-class economy of purgatory, see J. T. Rosenthal (1972) *The Purchase of Paradise*, London: Routledge & Kegan Paul; the most culturally resonant study known to me on this subject is Jacques Chiffoleau's haunting study (1980) *La comptabilité de l'au-delà: les hommes, la mort et la religion dans la région d'Avignon à la fin du Moyen Age*, Rome: L'Ecole Française de Rome. Note also: M. Mollat, *The Poor in the Middle Ages*, Connecticut: Yale University Press, pp. 259, 263–5; M. Rubin (1987) *Charity and Community*, Cambridge: Cambridge

University Press, pp. 259, 279, 280, 281. Despite warnings such as those in *Dives and Pauper* (I 186), the Church's accommodation to these extensions of the market economy seems to have been as total as Langland feared.

17 F. N. Robinson (ed.) (1979) *The Works of Geoffrey Chaucer*, Oxford: Oxford University Press, all quotes to this edition, here *Pardoner's Prologue and Tale*, 11. 927–40. On the details of this dialectic, see T. N. Tentler (1977) *Sin and Confession on the Eve of the Reformation*, Princeton: Princeton University Press. There are examples of compulsive and anxious daily and more than daily confession among Margery Kempe's fourteenth-century antecedents studied by Kieckhefer, *Unquiet Souls*, pp. 127–35. Also see the comments on such practice by Jennifer Kermode, 'The merchants of three northern English towns', in C. H. Clough (ed.) (1982) *Profession, Vocation and Culture in Late Medieval England*, Liverpool: Liverpool University Press, pp. 23–4.

18 G. Kane and E. T. Donaldson (eds) (1975) *Piers Plowman: B version*, London: Athlone, VII 24–33; on this aspect see Thrupp, *Merchant Class*, pp. 174–80, 188–90, 311–12, and the Norwich wills around which N. P. Tanner builds his study (1984) *The Church in Late Medieval Norwich*, Toronto: Pontifical Institute, chapter 3 and appendix 14.

19 *The Book of Margery Kempe*, p. 298.

20 R. W. Southern (1970) *Western Society and the Church in the Middle Ages*, Harmondsworth: Penguin, pp. 136–43, quoting from pp. 137–8, 139.

21 She gets there on Lammas Day, 'þe principal day of pardon' (p. 246): there is a classic list of pardons printed in George J. Aungier (1840) *The History and Antiquities of Syon Monastery*, London: J. B. Nichols, pp. 424–5; for example: 'in the fest of Sent Peter, whiche is callid Lammas or Advincula, shall have . . . playne remission in all casis reserued and unreserued, thre owte take, that is, the voo of chastite, beheste to Sent James, and violently smytyng and killing a preste, this except shall haue playne remission, and the thirde parte of pennans enyoyned and relesid, with a thousant yere of pardoune, CCCCCCC daies and fifte.'

22 Any printed collection of wills shows this readily enough: for example, R. R. Sharpe (ed.) (1889–90) *Calendar of Wills Proved and Enrolled in the Court of the Hustings, 1258–1688* 2 vols, London: Francis, vol. 2 for later Middle Ages, e.g., p. 109 (John Hiltoft for 1,000 masses immediately after death), p. 152 (John de Ellerton), p. 178 (Edelena Atte Legh, money for 3,000 masses within month of death), pp. 185–6 (Roger Longe, rich vintner), pp. 216–17 (John Orleaux, 20 shillings for two trentals on death).

23 As N. P. Tanner observes, lay testators 'came disproportionately from the upper ranks of urban society', for obvious reasons: *The Church*, pp. 115 and 100. Recall that in the later fourteenth century labourers were being fined and punished for asking 2*d*. or 3*d*. a day – as excessive wage claims: for many examples, see Bertha H. Putnam (ed.) (1938) *Proceedings before the Justices of the Peace*, London: Spottiswoode, Ballantyne, & Co., as p. 346 (75 and 77), p. 347 (91), p. 348 (95), p. 367 (500).

24 Tanner prints Setman's will in *The Church*, pp. 242–4, and comments p. 102; quoting here from p. 105.
25 Tanner, *The Church*, pp. 62, 85; for other examples, see R. S. Gottfried (1982) *Bury St. Edmunds*, Princeton: Princeton University Press, pp. 185–6 and many in Sharpe's collection, *Calendar of Wills*.
26 Tanner, *The Church*, p. 102.
27 D. M. Owen (1971) *Church and Society in Medieval Lincolnshire*, Lincoln: History of Lincolnshire Committee, p. 90. Margery Kempe herself accepts money to pray for people, including the substantial sum of 7 marks from a Lynn woman: pp. 27, 30, 106.
28 Consult documentation in *The Book of Margery Kempe*, pp. 372–4. Atkinson's account seems to exaggerate Margery's role in the conflict – even in Margery's own account it was only her scribe–priest who 'consulted' her; that the episode is 'a rygth notabyl matere of þe creaturys felyng' is a statement that Margery's 'felyng' was vindicated, not that her role 'attracted considerable attention' (*Mystic*, pp. 113–14). The point I make is that even Atkinson underestimates the marginalization of women in the community's politics, including its ecclesiastic politics, even if the woman was a mayor's daughter and a possibly prophetic figure. The comments of Judith M. Bennett on the absence of women's public/political status and its consequences applies in towns as well as countryside: (1986) *Women in the Medieval English Countryside*, Oxford: Oxford University Press, pp. 22–32: this perspective is far more alert to the effects of male public power than D. Nicholas, *Domestic Life*, as is the one informing Howell, *Women, Production and Patriarchy*.
29 David Aers (1980) *Chaucer, Langland and the Creative Imagination*, London: Routledge & Kegan Paul, chapter 2.
30 See Atkinson, *Mystic*, pp. 151–5.
31 Lawrence F. Powell (ed.) (1908) *The Mirrour of the Blessed Lyf of Jesu Christ*, Oxford: Oxford University Press, see pp. 25, 28, 121–2. Love is totally explicit about the battle against Lollardy and adds an anti-Lollard treatise on the sacrament to his translation (pp. 301–24). On Love here, see Elizabeth Satter (1974) *Nicholas Love's Myrrour of the Blessed Lyf of Jesu Christ*, Salzburg: Analecta Cartusiana, University of Salzburg, pp. 2, 14, 26–7, 47–8.
32 On the criteria of a 'good' confession, see T. N. Tentler, *Sin and Confession*, pp. 104–33.
33 For celebration of the 'decentred' subject, no longer self-identity, see, for example, Luce Irigaray, *Speculum*, pp. 191–202; or Jonathan Dollimore (1984) *Radical Tragedy*, Brighton: Harvester, pp. 181, 269–71; or J. Kristeva (1981) *Desire in Language*, Oxford: Blackwell, pp. 133–5; or H. Cixous (1985) 'The laugh of Medusa', in E. Marks and I. de Courtivron (eds) (1985) *New French Feminisms*, Brighton: Harvester, pp. 255–64.
34 Susan Dickman takes this encounter with Jesus as signifying that Margery 'heard her problematic desire for autonomy divinely rather than infernally sanctioned', in M. Glascoe (ed.) (1980) *The Medieval*

Mystical Tradition in England, Exeter: University of Exeter. Yet the scene also side-steps these terms: the desire is for *acceptance*, for delivery from guilt induced by the institution of confession, while the issue of 'autonomy', what it could even mean in this milieu, is not confronted at this point, although Jesus is indeed implying that he has not judged her as some of his officials have led her to believe.

35 Delany, 'Sexual economics', p. 88; Atkinson, *Mystic*, pp. 86–8, 98–101.

36 Thrupp, *Merchant Class*, pp. 169–74; but on 'lower'-class women see the important study by Bennett, *Women in the Medieval English Countryside*, a powerful rejoinder to the more optimistic accounts she addresses in her opening pages. We obviously need many more studies like this before we will be able to make adequate comparisons between women's experiences in different classes.

37 *Dives and Pauper*, II 328.

38 For example, Christopher Hill, 'The spiritualization of the household', in (1969) *Society and Puritanism*, St Albans: Panther, quoting p. 432.

39 (1928) *The Goodman of Paris*, trans. E. Power, London: Routledge & Kegan Paul, pp. 107–8, similarly pp.110–12, 138, 140, 149; the class peculiarities of the household formation and women's function in this text are emphasized by Howell, *Women, Production and Patriarchy* pp. 18–19.

40 Delany, 'Sexual economics', p. 88.

41 For example, *Wife of Bath's Prologue*, 693–710. Delany notes how Margery's work helps one see some of the gendered horizons of Chaucer's work, 'Sexual economics', p. 79.

42 *Parson's Tale*, pp. 938–9; on Christian dogma concerning marital sex the following are especially important: J. T. Noonan (1966) *Contraception: A History of its Treatment by the Catholic Theologians and Canonists*, Cambridge, Mass.: Harvard University Press; T. N. Tentler, *Sin and Confession*, pp. 162–232.

43 Noonan, *Contraception*, pp. 256–7, and pp. 36–49, 126, 129, 151, 193–9, 248–54; H. A. Kelly (1975) *Love and Marriage in the Age of Chaucer*, Cornell: Cornell University Press, pp. 247–61, 316, 322–3.

44 Tentler, *Sin and Confession*, pp. 165, 168.

45 Tentler, *Sin and Confession*, pp. 176, 184.

46 Foresti, 'Confessionale', in Tentler, *Sin and Confession*, p. 176.

47 Quoted in Tentler, *Sin and Confession*, p. 177.

48 Tentler, *Sin and Confession*, pp. 230–1. Similar attitudes in J. Bazire and E. College (eds) (1957) *Chastising of God's Children*, Oxford: Blackwell, pp. 212–14, but the most commonplace of clerical norms.

49 Bokenham (1938) *Legendys of Hooly Wommen*, Oxford: *Early English Text Society*, o.s., 206, 1971, pp. 201–25. Saints' legends deserve more sustained psychoanalytic and cultural study than they seem to have received: Atkinson rightly notes 'pornographic' dimensions (*Mystic*, p. 190) and Simone de Beauvoir provides stunning examples of holy sadism/masochism in (1983) *The Second Sex*, Harmondsworth: Penguin, pp. 679–86; although short on analysis Kieckhefer, *Unquiet Souls*, contains some relevant material.

50 Quoted in Kieckhefer, *Unquiet Souls*, p. 179.
51 Her miserable experience of pregnancy and childbirth could have been sufficient cause for rejecting sexuality (*Book of Margery Kempe*, pp. 6–8): both Delany and Atkinson mention 'post partum psychosis' ('Sexual economics', p. 84; *Mystic*, p. 209). This would be compatible with the account offered above though it would address neither the categories Margery herself deploys nor their cultural meanings and sources.
52 Delany, 'Sexual economics', pp. 85, 89.
53 On the pervasive anti-feminism through which female opposition was mediated, see *Wife of Bath's Prologue*, 693–6, 707–10.
54 On women in Lollardy, see Claire Cross, 'Great reasoners in scripture', in D. Baker (ed.) (1978) *Medieval Women*, Oxford: Blackwell, and Margaret Aston (1984) *Lollards and Reformers*, London: Hambledon, pp. 49–70. The 1428–31 Norfolk abjurations edited by Norman P. Tanner (ed.) (1977) *Norwich Heresy Trials*, London: Royal Historical Society, Camden 4th series vol. 20, contain eloquent testimony to the role of women in the form of Margery Baxter and Hawisia Mone. Quotation here from (1970) *Hoccleve's Works: The Minor Poems*, Oxford: *Early English Text Society*, o.s., 61 and 73, p. 13.
55 Dorothy Dinnerstein (1976) *The Rocking of the Cradle, and the Ruling of the World*, London: Souvenir Press, is a fascinating exploration of this.
56 For a powerful study which illustrates such collective projections and their ghastly consequences, see Richard Slotkin (1973) *Regeneration through Violence*, Middletown, Conn.: Wesleyan University Press; for a haunting medieval example, see Lester K. Little, 'The Jews in Christian Europe', in (1978) *Religious Poverty and the Profit Economy*, St Albans: Elek.
57 Dickman, 'Margery Kempe', p. 171.
58 The places are Canterbury (p. 28), Lincoln (p. 33), London (p. 36), Leicester (pp. 111ff.), York (pp. 124ff.), Hessle (p. 129), and Beverley (p. 133). On Leicestershire Lollardy, see James Crompton (1968–9) *Transactions of the Leicestershire Archaeological Society* 44: 11–44; and Charles Kightly (1975) 'The early Lollards', unpublished D. Phil, University of York, chapter 2.
59 'Men's feeling that we are not really human originates in their infancy', writes Dinnerstein, *Rocking of the Cradle*, p. 91.
60 Dinnerstein, *Rocking of the Cradle*, p. 112.
61 A. C. Cawley (ed.) (1958) *The Wakefield Pageants in the Towneley Cycle*, Manchester: Manchester University Press, p. 24.
62 Criseyde's observations in *Troilus and Criseyde*, II 750–6, are never really refuted in Chaucer's writing and tally well with the Wife of Bath's made in such a different genre.
63 Chaucer's *Wife of Bath's Prologue* and *Troilus and Criseyde*, Spenser's construction of Radigund (*Faerie Queene* V 4.21 to V 7) and Shakespeare's *Othello* are examples of this anxiety being worked over in different literary forms and contexts. I have found the work of Melanie Klein, especially (1977) *Love, Guilt and Reparation*, New York:

Delta, and the essays in Juliet Mitchell (ed.) (1986) *The Selected Melanie Klein*, Harmondsworth: Penguin, Dinnerstein, *Rocking of the Cradle*, and Carol Gilligan (1982) *In a Different Voice*, Cambridge, Mass.: Harvard University Press, more illuminating to my own concerns in this and the next chapter than the French feminisms mentioned in note 33 above. See the all too brief critical remarks by Toril Moi (1985) *Sexual/Textual Politics*, London: Methuen, pp. 167–72, and Sarah Beckwith in 'Material mysticism', pp. 35–6, 41, 47–8.

64 On this, see Nikki Stiller (1980) *Eve's Orphans*, Westport, Conn.: Greenwood. Contrast the violent female aggression against Margery at pp. 129 (lines 29–31) and 36 (lines 14–16): does Margery represent feelings they have but must deny – a threat to gender arrangements on which they seem to themselves to be as dependent as the men they service?

65 Chiffoleau's book, *La comptabilité de l'au-delà*, seeks to fuse historical research and psychoanalysis in his study of developments in representations of the Holy Family, community, and the Virgin Mary.

66 The representative nature of Margery's piety needs stressing – Atkinson, *Mystic*, chapters 5, 6.

67 See also Matthew 19.29 and 23.9. A revealing contrast is between Luke 2.42–51 (the 12-year-old child abandoning distraught parents) and its treatment in Nicholas Love, *Myrrour*, pp. 75–7: Love shifts the Gospel to emphasize the 'grete compassioun of the grete angwische' we should have for the mother's suffering: when the mother finds the son 'he wente to her', quite unlike the account in Luke; the kissing and hugging is also Love's transforming invention.

68 Besides the guilt already examined, her burning desire for white clothes, the mark of virginal 'purity', displays the same orientation, one affirmed by Jesus's traditional ecclesiastic view (p. 49).

69 On this 'maternal authority', see Dinnerstein, *Rocking of the Cradle*, chapter 8: in the Middle Ages it was also *women* who were responsible for infant care in all social classes.

70 For examples of 'homly', see pp. 3, 44, 79, 90, 210, 218.

71 See pp. 86–91: on dates, see pp. 298–9 (note to 79/25–6) and p. 301 (note to 86/10).

72 St Bernard's commentary on the Song of Songs, J.-P. Migne (ed.) (1844 *et seq.*) *Patrologia, Series Latina*, vols 183, 184, Paris: Garnier; on this allegorical tradition, chapter 4 in David Aers (ed.) (1986) *Medieval Literature: Criticism, Ideology and History*, Brighton: Harvester.

73 Atkinson, *Mystic*, p. 120.

74 Atkinson, *Mystic*, chapter 4; A. Goodman, 'The piety of John Brunham's daughter, of Lynn', in Derek Baker (ed.) (1978) *Medieval Women*, Oxford: Blackwell, pp. 347–58, here p. 356; for 'case history', see D. R. Howard (1980) *Writers and Pilgrims*, Berkeley and Los Angeles: California University Press, pp. 34–5.

75 For examples of the former, see pp. 39–41, 44–5, 63–4, 167, and for the relations with Master Aleyn of Lynn, see pp. 168–9; for examples of the latter, pp. 165, 167, 44, 67, 61, 84–5.

76 For Thorpe's examination, see S. R. Cattley (ed.) (1837) *The Acts and Monuments of John Foxe* vol. 3, London: Seeley & Burnside, pp. 249–82; on the text, see Anne Hudson (1978) *Selections from English Wycliffite Writings*, Cambridge: Cambridge University Press, pp. 155–6.

77 It is no coincidence that the examination in the Minster Chapterhouse also began with a question about her status as a woman (p. 122).

78 Note John Gerson, her illustrious contemporary: 'the female sex is forbidden on apostolic authority to teach in public, that is either by word or by writing. . . . All women's teaching . . . is to be held suspect unless it has been diligently examined, and much more fully than men's. The reason [*sic*!] is clear: common law – and not any kind of common law, but that which comes from on high – forbids them. And why? Because they are easily seduced, and determined seducers; and because it is not proved that they are witnesses to (*cognitrices*) divine grace' (from 'De examinatione doctrinarum', trans. E. College and J. Walsh in (1978) *A Book of Showings to the Anchoress Julian of Norwich* vol. I, Toronto: Pontifical Institute, p. 151.

79 On Lollard versions of the priesthood of all believers, see characteristic examples in Tanner, *Norwich Heresy Trials*, pp. 49, 57, 60–1, 67, 140, 142, 147.

80 Goodman, 'The piety', pp. 354–5.

81 Qualifying and adding to Goodman, 'The piety'.

82 *The Book of Margery Kempe*, p. 349; A. C. Spearing has developed similar arguments in (1985) *From Medieval to Renaissance in English Poetry*, Cambridge: Cambridge University Press, pp. 89–92, and this line of research needs sustained elaboration.

83 See pp. 66–7, for similar lay outlook.

84 Printed as appendix to Love's *Myrrour*, pp. 301–24, here see pp. 308–18, 320–1, 305–6. For similarly very material spirituality, and utterly commonplace, see Chiffoleau, *La comptabilité de l'au-delà*, pp. 98–9, around the Plague, and the miracles in Peter Idley's work, Charlotte D'Evelyn (ed.) (1935) *Instructions to his Son*, Oxford: Oxford University Press, II 894–940 (pp. 122–3).

85 Love, *Myrrour*, p. 208. Representative examples of Lollard views on the eucharist are given in Tanner, *Norwich Heresy Trials*, references given under 'eucharist' in his index, p. 225.

86 *Contra* Medcalf on 'Misplaced concreteness' in *Later Middle Ages*; Atkinson, *Mystic*, notes that in the contexts of affective piety Margery's 'seems neither aberrant nor even very unusual' (p. 155).

87 Atkinson, *Mystic*, chapter 5.

88 Toussaert, *Le Sentiment religieux*: one should note Jean Delumeau's response to persuasive criticism of the quantitative aspects of Toussaert's argument, in *Le Catholicisme*, p. 234, and his own evidence for the argument that, 'à la veille de la Reforme l'Occidental moyen n'aurait été que superficiellement christianisé', p. 237 – at least from the counter-reformation Catholic perspective of the historian! It is

better to acknowledge the extraordinary diversity of forms of Christianity found in different cultural and economic contexts.

89 Margery Baxter, in Tanner, *Norwich Heresy Trials*, pp. 41–51, 72.

90 Readily accessible in Tanner, *Norwich Heresy Trials*, in Hudson's *Selections* or in L. M. Swinburn (ed.) (1917) *The Lanterne of Liȝt*, Oxford: *Early English Text Society*, 151.

CHAPTER 3 MASCULINE IDENTITY IN THE COURTLY COMMUNITY: THE SELF LOVING IN *TROILUS AND CRISEYDE*

1 Susan Crane (1986) *Insular Romance: Politics, Faith and Culture in Anglo-Norman and Middle English Literature*, Berkeley and Los Angeles: California University Press, pp. 177, 178, 181, 4.

2 The literature on the poem is immense and this is not the place to offer a bibliography. Particularly prolific is the group that has been called 'a priestly caste of American professors' which 'has baptized the text in a shower of footnotes and pronounced it devout Christian allegory' by Stephen Knight (1986) *Chaucer*, Oxford: Blackwell, p. 32. Its basic framework was established by D. W. Robertson (1952) 'Chaucerian tragedy', *ELH* 19: 1–37 and (1962) *Preface to Chaucer*, Oxford: Oxford University Press, 1963, and its assumptions pervade many approaches which eschew the master's allegorism, even when using structuralist vocabulary as in chapter 9 of E. Vance (1986) *Marvelous Signals: Poetics and Sign Theory in the Middle Ages*, Lincoln, NE: Nebraska University Press, e.g., pp. 286–7, 289, 292–3, 296, 297, 298, 301. The opposition to such readings has been extremely diverse and includes the most intelligent and sensitive work on the poem. Particularly memorable are the following: Elizabeth Salter, '*Troilus and Criseyde*: a reconsideration', in J. Lawlor (ed.) (1966) *Patterns of Love and Courtesy*, London: Arnold, pp. 86–106; Monica E. McAlpine (1978) *The Genre of Troilus and Criseyde*, Cornell: Cornell University Press; A. C. Spearing (1976) *Chaucer: Troilus and Criseyde*, London: Arnold; and Stephen Knight, *Chaucer*, chapter 2. All quotations of *Troilus and Criseyde* are from F. N. Robinson (ed.) (1957) *The Works of Geoffrey Chaucer*, 2nd edn, Oxford: Oxford University Press.

3 David Aers, 'Chaucer's Criseyde', in (1980) *Chaucer, Langland and the Creative Imagination*, London: Routledge & Kegan Paul.

4 Knight, *Chaucer*, pp. 35, 36, 65.

5 Knight, *Chaucer*, pp. 33, 34–5, 37. My parenthetic remarks about 'allegedly wicked' lovers refers to the tradition represented by Robertson, 'Chaucerian tragedy', and Vance, *Marvelous Signals*.

6 Mervyn James (1983) 'Ritual, drama and social body in the late medieval English town', *Past and Present* 98: 3–29.

7 Knight, *Chaucer*, p. 41.

8 R. Coward (1984) *Female Desire*, St Albans: Paladin, p. 75; similar is Apius's gaze at Virginia, 'Physician's Tale', in F. N. Robinson (ed.) (1979) *Complete Works of Chaucer*, Oxford: Oxford University Press, p. 146. I am not saying *all* looks in *all* contexts have the same

meaning as the male gaze discussed here. For example, the meaning of the reciprocal gaze between baby and mother is very different – see the revision of Lacan's mirror-stage by D. W. Winnicott (1971) *Playing and Reality*, New York: Basic Books, pp. 111–18; or the adoring gaze of the multitude at huge, fattened, and oiled Hawaiian chiefs described in M. Sahlins (1985) *Islands of History*, Chicago: Chicago University Press, p. 17.

9 Susanne Kappeler (1986) *The Pornography of Representation*, Oxford: Polity, pp. 57–8.

10 *Book of the Duchess*, 862–70.

11 The critics I have in mind here are Knight's 'priestly caste', ones who scatter their text with terms like 'fornication' to describe the love between Criseyde and Troilus – for a recent example, see Vance, *Marvelous Signals*, p. 298.

12 The relations of language, desire, and class have been finely analysed in Toril Moi's important essay, 'Desire in language: Andreas Capellanus and the controversy of courtly love', in David Aers (ed.) (1986) *Medieval Literature, Criticism, Ideology and History*, Brighton: Harvester, here p. 24. Also relevant, Daniel Poirion (1965) *Le poète et le prince*, Paris: Presses Universitaires, p. 131 and L. D. Benson, 'Courtly love and chivalry in the later Middle Ages', in R. F. Yeager (ed.) (1984) *Fifteenth Century Studies*, Hamden: Archon, pp. 237–57.

13 For 'percede' and 'smot', discussed above, see I 272–3.

14 For his reading of this passage, and Book I, see Stephen Knight, *Chaucer*, pp. 42–4.

15 Monica McAlpine, *The Genre*, p. 127: chapters 5 and 6 seem to me outstandingly sensitive and responsive reading.

16 P. G. Walsh (1982) *Andreas Capellanus On Love*, London: Duckworth, p. 223. While the work is immensely controversial (see Moi, 'Desire in language') these views are not.

17 Ovid, *Metamorphosis*, III 463–6. For some medieval traditions, see Frederick Goldin 1967 *The Mirror of Narcissus in the Courtly Love Lyric*, Cornell: Cornell University Press, chapters 1, 2; for a very different approach, see Julie Kristeva (1983) *Histoires d'amour*, Paris: Denöel, 1983, chapters 1, 3, 4, here p. 38.

18 Knight, *Chaucer*, p. 36.

19 See, for example, IV 1,471–98, V 141–54, 859–63, 918–24.

20 Mervyn James (1978) *English Politics and the Concept of Honour, 1485–1642*, Past and Present Society, pp. 1, 5. Also relevant, Stephen Knight (1983) *Arthurian Literature and Society*, London: Macmillan.

21 James, *Honour*, pp. 5–6.

22 *Wife of Bath's Prologue*, 813 and her spurs in *General Prologue*, 473. My reading of the *Wife of Bath's Prologue* is outlined in *Chaucer, Langland*, pp. 83–9, 146–52.

23 Throughout this chapter my references to Criseyde assume the reading I argued for in *Chaucer, Langland*, chapter 5.

24 Knight, *Chaucer*, p. 84.

25 On Emily, see Knight, *Chaucer*, p. 84; Troilus's awareness is expressed in IV 1,485–91.
26 The consequences of these for Criseyde are discussed both by McAlpine in *The Genre*, chapter 6 and Aers in *Chaucer, Langland*, chapter 5.
27 See Walsh, *Capellanus On Love*, p. 37 and Moi's comments on this passage, 'Desire in language', pp. 22–3.
28 McAlpine, *The Genre*, p. 174.
29 Relevant here is Melvin W. Askew (1965) 'Courtly love: neurosis as institution', *Psychoanalytic Review* 52: 19–29.
30 *Parson's Tale*, 858–9: *Merchant's Tale*, 1,839–40.
31 Troilus is fully involved in the manipulation and lying, see III 1,158. For male voyeurism, see III 596–602.
32 III 1,116–17, 1,128–34, 1,177–84.
33 For a careful introduction to the appalling subject of rape relevant to the contexts of this essay, see Ray Wyre (1986) *Women, Men and Rape*, Oxford: Perry Publications.
34 Knight, *Chaucer*, pp. 23–31; David Aers (1981) '*The Parliament of Fowls*', *Chaucer Review* 16: 1–17.
35 Knight, *Chaucer*, p. 32.
36 Aers, *Chaucer, Langland*, chapter 5.
37 On the denial of subjectivity to women, the literature from a multitude of ideological perspectives is immense: a strikingly fine statement is made by Luce Irigaray (1985) *Speculum of the Other Woman*, Cornell: Cornell University Press, p. 133.
38 See III 1,212–414, quoting III 1,221–2.
39 Quoting from *Paradise Lost*, V 216, the tradition is summarized in A. Fowler's note on *Paradise Lost* V 215–19, pp. 687–8 of J. Carey and A. Fowler (eds) (1968) *The Poems of John Milton*, London: Longman.
40 *Paradise Lost*, IV 304–8, 295–301, 742–7: also relevant 492–502 and 738–74: relevant reflections by David Aers and Bob Hodge in, ' "Rational burning": Milton on sex and marriage', in David Aers, Bob Hodge, and Gunther Kress (1981) *Literature, Language and Society in England 1580–1680*, London: Gill & Macmillan.
41 See III 1,226–351, 1,394–414, 1,671–715; quoting III 1,239 and 1,694. Vance is wrong to assert that 'there can be no "joy" in "Troy" ', *Marvelous Signals*, p. 278: the poem has a very different idea of 'joy' and of complexity and contradiction in human experience than Vance or the 'priestly caste' of critics have.
42 III 1,654–5, 1,685–94; also III 1,349–51.
43 McAlpine, *The Genre*, chapters 5, 6, quoting from p. 162.
44 McAlpine, *The Genre*, pp. 165–6 for her explanation of Troilus's behaviour.
45 On Criseyde's internalization of patriarchal views, see Aers, *Chaucer, Langland*, pp. 132–5; McAlpine, *The Genre*, p. 202.
46 See, for example, V 687–765, 1,023–36; see McAlpine, *The Genre*, pp. 165–6, 173, 201–4, 216, and Aers, *Chaucer, Langland*, pp. 135–8.
47 McAlpine, *The Genre*, p. 216.

48 Compare McAlpine's rather different perspectives here, *The Genre*, pp. 165–6.
49 Besides McAlpine, *The Genre*, chapter 6, see M. Fries on Criseyde in A. Diamond and L. R. Edwards (eds) (1977) *The Authority of Experience*, Amherst: Massachusetts University Press, pp. 45–59.
50 E. Hatcher (1973) 'Chaucer and the psychology of fear: Troilus in Book V', *ELH* 40: 307–24.
51 Walsh, *Capellanus On Love*, p. 33.
52 The contrast with Diomede is certainly sharp, but Chaucer does not make Diomede in the same mode as he does Criseyde and Troilus in Books II to V, nor in the same 'private' sphere: so we cannot begin to answer questions about how Diomede would have reacted to *loss* of Criseyde *to a rival knight.*
53 Freud's essay *Mourning and Melancholia* has much of interest to the present discussion, see the Pelican Freud Library vol. 11, pp. 251–68; also the later essay, *The Ego and the Id*, vol. 11, pp. 368–9, 386–7, 394–6, 400.
54 Walsh, *Capellanus On Love*, pp. 33, 147, 157, 283 and Moi, 'Desire in language', pp. 21–30.
55 For example, I 461–2, 469, 857–8; II 1,066.
56 For example, I 873–4; II 319–33, 337–8.
57 This is part of Melvin Askew's argument in 'Courtly love'.
58 On nuclear families and gender–sex arrangements in the period see the works cited in note 52 to the Introduction.
59 For helpful introductions to Klein, see Juliet Mitchell (1986) *The Selected Melanie Klein*, Harmondsworth: Penguin, pp. 9–32 and Hanna Segal (1964) *An Introduction to the Work of Melanie Klein*, London: Heinemann.
60 *Selected Melanie Klein*, p. 181, hereafter page references in text.
61 On this, see McAlpine, *The Genre*, pp. 168–70.
62 For sensitively appreciative readings of Book III, see Elizabeth Salter '*Troilus and Criseyde*' and McAlpine, *The Genre*, pp. 128, 156–7, 159, 162.
63 Joyce Bazire and Eric College (eds) (1957) *The Chastising of God's Children*, Oxford: Blackwell, pp. 98, 113–14.
64 Herbert Moller (1960) 'The meaning of courtly love', *Journal of American Folklore* 73: 39–51, here pp. 41–3.
65 Moi, 'Desire in language', p. 26: her discussion of Love, Jealousy and Epistemology in the *De Amore* (pp. 20–30) has influenced me greatly.
66 Dorothy Dinnerstein (1976) *The Rocking of the Cradle and the Ruling of the World*, London: Souvenir Press.
67 Dinnerstein, *Rocking of the Cradle*, p. 41: the whole of chapter 4 is very relevant.
68 Here and in the sentence before last I paraphrase Dinnerstein, *Rocking of the Cradle*, p. 60.
69 Boethius, *Consolation of Philosophy*, II m. 8 and III pr. 10 (trans. in *The Works of Geoffrey Chaucer*).
70 Criseyde's generous initiative, III 1,163–86.

71 See *Consolation of Philosophy*, II m. 8 and IV pr. 6.
72 Knight, *Chaucer*, p. 54.
73 *Franklin's Tale*, 764–70.
74 On reticences in Boethius's *Consolation of Philosophy* see W. Wetherbee (1972) *Platonism and Poetry in the Twelfth Century*, Princeton: Princeton University Press. For Ockham here, see (1969) *Predestination, God's Foreknowledge and Future Contingents*, trans. M. McCord Adams and N. Kretzmann, East Norwalk CT: Appleton-Century Crofts, pp. 43–53, especially p. 50 here.
75 For example, V 360, 622, 1,216, 1,646.
76 Here V 206 and 1,212ff.
77 V 1,594; on her isolation, see Aers, *Chaucer, Langland*, pp. 134–6.
78 Dinnerstein, *Rocking of the Cradle*, p. 41.
79 Quoting V 1,698: compare V 1,324–420, 1,700 with 206–10.
80 For the last sixty-two lines and the critical traditions around them, see McAlpine, *The Genre*, pp. 177–81 and 235–46, Elizabeth Salter, '*Troilus and Criseyde*', pp. 103–6, and Knight, *Chaucer*, pp. 62–5.
81 The term 'fresshe' seems a *distinctly* upper-class one excluding the majority of people, the peasantry and artisanate: see *General Prologue*, 92 and J. S. P. Tatlock and A. G. Kennedy (eds) (1927) *Concordance to the Works of Chaucer*, Gloucester, Mass.: Smith, 1963, p. 343.
82 See Alasdair MacIntyre (1985) *After Virtue: a Study in Moral Theory*, London: Duckworth.
83 *Nun's Priest's Tale*, 152–61.
84 Moi, 'Desire in language', p. 30.
85 *Chastising of God's Children*, quoted earlier; Caroline W. Bynum (1982) *Jesus as Mother: Studies in the Spirituality of the High Middle Ages*, Berkeley and Los Angeles: California University Press, and Julian of Norwich's version (1978) *A Book of Showings to the Anchoress Julian of Norwich* 2 vols, Toronto: Pontifical Institute, vol. 2, pp. 546, 563, 580, 582–600, 605–8, 613, 615–18, 724.

CHAPTER 4 'IN ARTHURUS DAY': COMMUNITY, VIRTUE, AND INDIVIDUAL IDENTITY IN *SIR GAWAIN AND THE GREEN KNIGHT*

1 All quotations of *Sir Gawain and the Green Knight* are from Malcolm Andrew and Ronald Waldron (eds) (1978) *The Poems of the Pearl Manuscript*, London: Arnold, see epigraph. Such setting aside is not an essential aspect of romance: Susan Crane (1986) *Insular Romance*, Berkeley and Los Angeles: California University Press, and Stephen Knight, 'The social function of the Middle English romance', in David Aers (ed.) (1986) *Medieval Literature: Criticism, Ideology and History*, Brighton: Harvester. Even if it were a definition of the genre, one would need to reflect on precisely what was excluded and why.
2 The 'battery of weapons' is a quote from J. L. Bolton (1980) *The Medieval English Economy*, London: Dent, p. 213.

3 On Richard II and Cheshire see Michael J. Bennett (1983) *Community, Class and Careerism*, Cambridge: Cambridge University Press.

4 E. Miller and J. Hatcher (1978) *Medieval England*, London: Longman, pp. 173–97, here p. 174.

5 R. A. Shoaf (1984) *The Poem and the Green Girdle: Commercium in Sir Gawain and the Green Knight*, Gainesville, FL: Florida University Press, pp. 2, 4, 38–9 (similar utterances on pp. 8, 57–63). Such language here is only possible for one using it in an anti-historical, idealized, and irresponsibly metaphoric sense – 'the merchant in every man' (p. 8), 'the market of human affairs' (p. 63): economic realities are dissolved into a mythological world where all speakers are equivalent units of exchange, regardless of gender, class, and specific social formation, a convenient way of blocking out all power-relations, all exploitations and inequalities, even when allegedly referring to 'The commercial situation of fourteenth-century England' (pp. 11–14, for instance). His term 'commercium' is similarly vapid and has the same ideological function – a convenient enough one in his USA, as we are reminded by both Frank Lentricchia (1983) *Criticism and Social Change*, Chicago: Chicago University Press, and Edward Said (1982) 'Opponents, audiences, constituencies and community', *Critical Inquiry* 9.

6 On the early use of mercenaries, see J. O. Prestwich (1954) 'War and finance in the Anglo-Norman state', *Tr. Royal Hist. Soc.* 4; Miller and Hatcher, *Medieval England*, pp. 175–6.

7 Miller and Hatcher, *Medieval England*, p. 176.

8 Miller and Hatcher, *Medieval England*, p. 179.

9 Miller and Hatcher, *Medieval England*, p. 179.

10 Crane, *Insular Romance*, pp. 181, 199.

11 Quoted and translated by Crane, *Insular Romance*, p. 199, n. 57 (*La Vie du Prince Noir*, 11. 1,513–16).

12 On Bishop Despenser in 1381, see R. B. Dobson (1970) *The Peasants' Revolt of 1381*, London: Macmillan, pp. 259–61, 237–8: his disastrous 1383 'crusade' to convert the (Christian) Flemish supporters of the Avignon papacy was in keeping with this version of Christianity. On the abbot of Leicester and Henry of Lancaster, see K. Fowler (1969) *The King's Lieutenant*, St Albans: Elek, p. 187; on Pype, and for the quotation, see Rodney Hilton (1985) *Class Conflict and the Crisis of Feudalism*, London: Hambledon, pp. 68–71.

13 N. Orme (1986) *From Childhood to Chivalry*, London: Methuen, p. 56.

14 Crane, *Insular Romance*, chapter 3.

15 Figures 36, 17, 12 in Millard Meiss (1968) *French Painting in the time of Jean de Bury: The Boucicaut Master*, Oxford: Phaidon, and chapter 1.

16 Henceforth line references in the text are to the edition of *Sir Gawain* cited in note 1 above.

17 J. Bossy (1983) *Christianity in the West*, Oxford: Oxford University Press, p. 7.

18 M. James (1978) *English Politics and the Concept of Honour*, Past and Present Society, pp. 5–11.

19 A. C. Spearing (1970) *The Gawain Poet*, Cambridge: Cambridge University Press, pp. 6–12, 181–3, 200; J. Nicholls (1985) *The Matter of Courtesy*, Cambridge: Boydell & Brewer, chapters 1–4, pp. 116–18, 127–9. Nothing could be more mistaken when reflecting on this community and class than to talk about 'the empty language of social politeness', L. S. Johnson (1984) *The Voice of the Gawain-Poet*, Madison, WI: Wisconsin University Press, p. 67.
20 A. C. Spearing (1985) *From Medieval to Renaissance in English Poetry*, Cambridge: Cambridge University Press, p. 125.
21 On this episode, see Stephen Knight (1983) *Arthurian Literature and Society*, London: Macmillan, pp. 132–4; E. Vinaver (ed.) (1967) *The Works of Sir Thomas Malory* 3 vols, Oxford: Oxford University Press, pp. 1,121–4.
22 Presenting the challenge as to 'the court's renown, not its virtue' imposes a split that is alien to such communities (L. D. Benson (1965) *Art and Tradition in Sir Gawain and the Green Knight*, New Brunswick, NJ: Rutgers University Press, p. 211).
23 Lines 250–5, 275–8: see Nicholls, *Courtesy*, pp. 117–20.
24 Contradicting such readings as those in J. Burrow (1965) *Sir Gawain and the Green Knight*, London: Routledge & Kegan Paul, p. 26, who makes the analogy with 'a Morality Play'. The best guide, as usual, is Spearing, *Gawain-Poet*, p. 182.
25 James, *Honour*, pp. 1, 5–6.
26 Lines 96–9: see Fowler, *King's Lieutenant*, pp. 103–5.
27 Nothing could be more removed from the post-feudal contractualism Shoaf, *The Poem*, finds here and elsewhere.
28 For some analysis, see D. A. Pearsall, chapter 7 in Aers (ed.) *Medieval Literature*, pp. 137–40.
29 Mervyn James (1983) 'Ritual, drama and the social body in the late medieval English town', *Past and Present* 98: 3–29.
30 On the pentangle, see Burrow, *Sir Gawain*, pp. 41–51 and Spearing, *Gawain-Poet*, pp. 196–8. Both Burrow and Spearing dissolve specific *class* markers into general terms like 'social' (Burrow, p. 47) or 'civilised' (Spearing, p. 175).
31 For example, W. A. Davenport (1978) *The Art of the Gawain-Poet*, London: Athlone, p. 152.
32 See lines 813–1,125 and on hunting 1,133–77, 1,319–64, 1,412–68, 1,561–618, 1,690–730, 1,894–921. The commentary on the hunting, both literal and symbolic, is extensive: see, for example, Spearing, *Gawain-Poet*, pp. 9–10, 174, 199–202, 212–18; Burrow, *Sir Gawain*, pp. 61–70. I quote from Orme, *Childhood to Chivalry*, p. 197.
33 The role of class (access to economic resources) is crucial here, but see Don E. Wayne (1984) *Penshurst*, London: Methuen, chapter 1; F. R. H. Du Boulay (1970) *An Age of Ambition*, Walton-on-Thames: Nelson, chapter 6; L. Stone (1977) *The Family, Sex and Marriage in England*, London: Weidenfeld & Nicolson, chapter 4 and pp. 253–7; Knight, *Chaucer*, chapter 2; note 52 to the Introduction.
34 Spearing, *Gawain-Poet*, p. 174; see also p. 202.

35 On this dialectic, see Toril Moi, chapter 1 in Aers (ed.) *Medieval Literature*; Spearing, *Gawain-Poet*, pp. 201–6.
36 See lines 1,750–871: Gawain's consciousness also evoked at lines 842–9, 943–6, 1,195–203, 1,651–2, 1,760–76, 1,855–9, 2,006–8, 2,163, 2,179–96, 2,205–11, 2,233, 2,257. On this topic, see Spearing, *Gawain-Poet*, pp. 173–4, 191–219.
37 On the split in 'obligations', see Burrow, *Sir Gawain*, p. 104.
38 Burrow, *Sir Gawain*, p. 123 and Mary F. Braswell (1983) *The Medieval Sinner*, New York: Associated University Presses, p. 96.
39 James, *Honour*.
40 For these aspects, see T. N. Tentler (1977) *Sin and Confession on the Eve of the Reformation*, Princeton: Princeton University Press.
41 Lines 2,002–42. Much is made in the scholarly literature of Gawain's apparent forgetfulness of the pentangle, yet Gawain himself had never been shown as especially attentive to the pentangle. It was the poet who affirmed its special relation to Gawain (623–4) and interpreted its symbolism: why not foreground lines 611–12 as much as the religious symbolism?
42 For an example of this approach, see W. R. Barron (1980) *Trawthe and Treason: the Sin of Gawain Reconsidered*, Manchester: Manchester University Press, p. 116.
43 Spearing, *Gawain-Poet*, p. 187.
44 On this competition, James, *Honour*.
45 Spearing, *Gawain-Poet*, pp. 189–90.
46 Bennett, *Community*, and James, *Honour*.
47 Spearing, *Gawain-Poet*, pp. 226–7. See also the timely revisions to his influential book in chapter 7 of J. Burrow (1984) *Essays on Medieval Literature*, Oxford: Oxford University Press, p. 118, n. 5 and p. 126.
48 James, *Honour*, pp. 28–31.
49 Quoting Barron, *Trawthe and Treason*, pp. 128–9 – see his sources pp. 121–9; similarly, Burrow, *Sir Gawain*, 'moral theology is useful here' (pp. 134–5).
50 Spearing, *Gawain-Poet*, pp. 227–8 offers excellent commentary.
51 James, *Honour*.
52 See lines 2,400–2: *no one* invokes the liturgy and homilies on the feast of circumcision at either court – unlike the 'priestly caste' of scholars (for example, Shoaf, *The Poem*, and Johnson, *The Voice*).
53 The anti-feminism pervading courtly discourses of love and its idealizations has been sufficiently addressed in the preceding chapter, text and notes.
54 Contradictory responses illustrated by reading Barron, *Trawthe and Treason*, p. 130, Spearing, *Gawain-Poet*, p. 229, and, most odd of all, Shoaf, *The Poem*, p. 47 ('Gawain's awareness of the commerce of human affairs is vastly improved' even though 'his misogyny may be distasteful').
55 See Chaucer's *General Prologue*, 673.
56 See lines 2,445–67, comparing Gawain's earlier pride in his blood, 11.

356–7. For excellent comments on Malory's use of Morgan, see Stephen Knight, *Arthurian Literature*, p. 116.
57 Malory, *Works*, p. 1,259; on such moves and contemporary views, see James, *Honour*, pp. 10–11.
58 Spearing, *Gawain-Poet*, pp. 228–9; also Burrow, *Essays*, pp. 126–7; contrast Barron, *Trawthe and Treason*: 'We have waited anxiously for him [Gawain] to seek priestly absolution' (pp. 139–40) – the 'we', however, excludes Gawain, Sir Bertilak, Arthur, his court, the poet, and probably all not belonging to the 'priestly caste' of scholars.
59 Burrow, *Sir Gawain*, p. 153.
60 Spearing, *Gawain-Poet*, p. 230.
61 Barron, *Trawthe and Treason*, pp. 140–2.
62 See James, *Honour*, pp. 11, 8, and Knight, *Arthurian Literature*, pp. 144–7.
63 Barron, *Trawthe and Treason*, pp. 136–7.
64 The concluding prayer to Christ (11. 2,529–30) would easily be assimilated to 'fersnes' (11. 642–50) and the 'prowes of armes' in the communities described by Bennett, *Community*, and James, *Honour*.
65 Burrow, *Sir Gawain*, p. 159; repeated p. 185.
66 E. Wilson (1976) *The Gawain-Poet*, Leiden: Brill, pp. 129–30; see Burrow's self-criticism, *Essays*, p. 129.
67 See Spearing, *Medieval to Renaissance*, p. 113.
68 The final two lines in no way constitute an alternative (see note 64 above): they could comfortably be uttered by the battlers of Maldon, Roland and Oliver, Henry V slaughtering French citizens, merchants completing profitable transactions, peasant communities rising up against lawyers and lords, or armed lords and Bishop Despenser attacking such peasants.
69 See quote from Miller and Hatcher, *Medieval England*, p. 179, on p. 155.
70 Once again, James, *Honour*, is indispensable.

INDEX